D0481255

Dear Christian,

Not only can you rise to every occasion, you can overcome every challenge.

Trust your instincts, listen to your heart and you shall always be met with success.

Hope this book may have some creative ideas for your teaching role.

♡ m

The IMMORTALITY Of INFLUENCE

The IMMORTALITY of INFLUENCE

Salome Thomas-EL
with
Cecil Murphey

KENSINGTON PUBLISHING CORP.
http://www.kensingtonbooks.com

DAFINA BOOKS are published by

Kensington Publishing Corp.
850 Third Avenue
New York, NY 10022

Copyright © 2006 by Salome Thomas-EL

Scripture quotations are taken from the Holy Bible, New International
Version, NIV. Copyright © 1973, 1978, 1984 by *International Bible
Society*. Used by permission of Zondervan.
Scripture quotations are taken from the *Holy Bible, Today's New Inter-
national Version, TNIV*. Copyright © 2001 by International Bible Society.
Used by permission of Zondervan.

All rights reserved. No part of this book may be reproduced in any form
or by any means without the prior written consent of the Publisher, ex-
cepting brief quotes used in reviews.

All Kensington titles, imprints, and distributed lines are available at special quantity discounts for bulk purchases for sales promotion, premi-
ums, fund-raising, educational, or institutional use.

Special book excerpts or customized printings can also be created to fit
specific needs. For details, write or phone the office of the Kensington
Special Sales Manager: Kensington Publishing Corp., 850 Third Avenue,
New York, NY 10022, Attn. Special Sales Department. Phone: 1-800-221-
2647.

Dafina Books and the Dafina logo Reg. U.S. Pat. & TM Off.

Library of Congress Card Catalogue Number: 2005924292
ISBN 0-7582-1266-6

First Printing: May 2006
10 9 8 7 6 5 4 3 2 1

Printed in the United States of America

CONTENTS

FOREWORD

by
Will Smith

If you finish this book and are not inspired to immediately go out and effect change in your community, then you were not paying attention and should read it again. Salome Thomas-EL was called to serve and has had amazing experiences in his career as a teacher and author. He uses these experiences and his own personal struggles and triumphs to inspire a new generation to pick up the torch of service. With this book, he illustrates how as responsible adults we can and should influence those around us for the better, beginning with leading by example. He draws attention to the scores of children who are labeled early on as "lost causes," and he points out that if we allow them to go through life without any positive role models, then they will become self-fulfilling prophecies. *But*, if someone takes the time and does not give up, Thomas-EL knows from personal experience that these children can grow up and become some of the best minds of the next generation.

Influence is a powerful tool, one that we often forget that we wield. The hidden danger is that we never know exactly who we are influencing and what it is we do that influences them. Every time we interact with people, we are giving them an impression of who we are, what we believe and what we think of them. It is important that we make choices that we would want others to emulate, not only those of us that work in a very public position like Thomas-EL as a principal and myself as an entertainer, but anyone who is a parent, brother, sister, son, daughter, cousin, friend, neighbor, colleague—the list goes on.

You never know who is looking to you for inspiration, so first and foremost you must be mindful of the message that you are sending out.

In today's media-saturated society, it is hard to miss so many of the tragedies that have hit our worldwide community. Between the tsunami in Southeast Asia, Hurricane Katrina in the Gulf Coast, and the continuing AIDS epidemic in Africa, there are plenty of reminders that suffering is a universal constant. While it is important to contribute to our local communities, we should always be mindful that we are part of a global environment. Although money is often requested to aid victims both at home and abroad, time is also one of the most valuable donations we can make. Giving of one's time to any of these causes is just as meaningful as writing a check.

So read this book, be inspired by the great things that Thomas-EL has accomplished in his community, and take that inspiration and make an impact in your own. If influence can be immortal, then why not make yours worth remembering?

ACKNOWLEDGMENTS

In 2005 we lost a tremendous number of influencers who have shaped us as a nation and people

IN MEMORIUM

Constance Baker-Motley, Stan Bernstein, Johnny Carson, Shirley Chisolm, Johnnie Cochran, Ossie Davis, Arthur Fletcher, Peter Jennings, John Johnson, Pat Morita, Rosa Parks, Pope John Paul II, Richard Pryor, Chief Justice William H. Rehnquist, C. Delores Tucker, Luther Vandross, August Wilson, Georgie Woods and many, many more. Your Influence Lives On!

To the victims of hurricanes Katrina and Rita and all other natural disasters: Your courage and determination has inspired us all to remember that we are brothers and sisters in this world together! A special thank-you to the many celebrities who used their influence to make a difference in the lives of others: Oprah Winfrey, Will Smith, Jada Pinkett-Smith, Ellen DeGeneres, Tavis Smiley, Tom Joyner, Dr. Phil McGraw, Jamie Foxx, Harry Connick Jr., Branford Marsalis, Master P, Dave Matthews, Celine Dion, Kanye West and so many others. God Bless You All!

I would like to thank God (Our Creator) for loving me unconditionally. None of my work would be possible without your love and blessing. To my lovely wife, Shawnna: Thanks for persevering through the tough times with me and loving our children faithfully. A mother's love and attention are so important to children. Your constant editing of my writing and speeches has allowed me to look good and take all the credit. Keep up the good work! To my baby girls, Macawi and Nashetah: Continue to grow into intelligent and strong young ladies who will lead this nation, and take care of Daddy and Mommy when they are old and gray. To my greatest influence, my mother, Amena, who is resting in heaven: Save me a place because someday I will be worthy of your company. I am sure you are praising God every day with our beloved sister Delores who is with you. To my family: Thank you for always supporting me and keeping me focused on the mission of service. I have learned that it is not about me. It is about us! To my mother-in-law, Delores: Thanks for being a wonderful mother and grand-mom, helping us navigate this thing called parenting, and influencing us every day. To Karen and Dexter: Thanks for the countless hours of cheap, expert legal advice.

To Cecil Murphey and Deidre Knight: Thank you so much for your support and love over the years; CAA: Your representation and hard work with Disney on my behalf is appreciated. It does not get any better than you; My editor at Kensington, Karen Thomas: You have surpassed my expectations again and continue to amaze me. You are a powerful influence on your authors; Steven Zacharius and everyone at Kensington Publishing: Thanks for believing in me the second time around. I promise not to disappoint you; Ellie Deegan (The Lecture Bureau) and Nancy Eisenstein (American Program Bureau): Thanks for ensuring that people around the country get to hear my message. Derek and Quentin: Thanks for your friendship.

To Will Smith and family: Thanks for being great role models as parents and philanthropists. You make us all proud; Lonnie Downs, Jana Babatunde-Bey and everyone at Overbrook Entertainment: Thanks for your support and love; Tim Chambers: Thanks for believing in my story and inspiring me with the title for this book. You are truly a special person; Gavin and Greg O'Connor at Solaris: Thanks for giving my students a chance to tell their story to the world; Walt Disney Company: Your commitment to our project will send a message to our nation that every child matters.

Thanks to all of my former teachers; the Association of Black School Administrators (ABSA); the faculty, staff, students and alumni of Nova Southeastern University, Cheyney University, East Stroudsburg University, and Philadelphia Futures; Thank God for the staff at Bryn Mawr, Children's and Lankenau Hospitals; My pastor and teacher Sean Wise; Pastors Damon Jones, Ronald Parks, Keith Reed and Paul James; Cathy Hensford and Juanita Johnson: Thanks for your editing and proofreading; The Brothers of Diamond Lynx and Kappa Alpha Psi Fraternity Inc.; Corey and the staff at Wilkie Lexus in Haverford, Pennsylvania; My students: Thanks for allowing me to be a part of your lives. I apologize for those times when I was a little tough on you.

I would like to thank the following people for supporting the chess team, my students and me: The wonderful teachers and staff members at Reynolds Elementary School and Vaux Middle School. My brother and friend, Ishmael Al-Islam, Michael and Octavia Lewis, Elmer Smith and the entire Philadelphia Daily News/Inquirer family. The Philadelphia Tribune staff, Calvary Baptist Church, Miller Memorial Baptist Church, and Sharon Baptist Church. Alpha Kappa Alpha, Delta Sigma Theta and Zeta Phi Beta Sororities. To the best secretaries in the world: Edith Bridges, Debbie Brooks, June Ezekiel, Cheryl Henderson, Lillian Rochester and Denice Ross, I will always love you; Men of BACA, Vaux Alumni Association and all the former members of the chess team: You started the tradition and we are proud to preserve your legacy.

To Maurice Cheeks and Marc Zumoff: Thanks for your friendship and support over the years. Tony Irving: We lost you long ago but your memory lives on through our work. There will never be enough space for me to thank all the people who have touched my life. If I have not mentioned you, please forgive me. You will always be in my heart.

1

Failed Influence

When I see a life that goes in the wrong direction and it's a young person whom I've had an opportunity to influence, I ask myself, "Could I have done more?"

I don't know the answer. I don't live with guilt over my failures, but I do have to live with the knowledge that I had the opportunity to do more and I failed.

That's a heavy burden.

Of all the failures in my nearly twenty-year career in education, the one that hurts the most is the death of Willow Briggs. I was a teacher in 1994, when he entered fifth grade at Vaux Middle School. Willow was a good basketball player and the other kids admired him. Like many children in the inner-city schools, Willow came from a troubled background. In elementary school, he had been constantly reprimanded.

Willow was notorious for sucking his thumb (although none of his friends ever teased him about it), but he was amazingly mature for his age. That's an odd combination, but there were few kids like Willow (or "Fu," as most of his friends called him).

Some of his teachers predicted he would drop out as soon as he was able. Yet I saw something different about him and that's what caught my attention: *Willow could think.* He was bright and his vocabulary impressed me. When he spoke, it was obvious that he had an excellent mind.

I tried to spend time with Willow because I saw qualities in him that could make him into an outstanding leader. I knew it would be difficult because Willow had so many things piled up against him. I wanted him to understand he had great potential and could train his mind and do something significant with his life. He had charm, charisma, and the ability to outthink the smartest adults.

Through our discussions and many one-on-one basketball games, we discovered I had taught Willow's older brother. Because we connected there, he allowed me to be a positive influence in his life.

His major problem was that most of the time he used his superior ability in negative ways, and he often ended up in serious trouble. I needed to find ways to pull him out of his old habits and get him to focus on self-improvement. After thinking about it for several days, I took a chance and encouraged him to join the chess team.

I had organized students to play chess, most of whom were good students from elementary schools. Those with a good academic background easily became our best players.

"I got no time for games," Willow said when I approached him with the idea of joining the chess team.

"It's more than a game," I countered. "It's a real mental challenge. You have to be smart—really smart—to play well. I think you're smart enough that you could learn."

After I made several appeals to his bright mind, Willow agreed to try the game "and see how it goes."

That's all it took. Neither of us realized it then, but Willow would become our first outstanding chess player who hadn't been academically successful before coming to Vaux Middle School.

Willow picked chess up quickly. Perhaps to his own amazement, once he understood the game, he excelled in it. In fact, he became a celebrity at Vaux because he was so good.

Willow was a year older than most of the other students in his grade because of his problems in elementary school. The other children had known he was a poor student, but they began to recognize a distinct change in him. By playing chess, he created a new "Fu." Not only was he excellent in sports, but now he became more popular because everyone saw him as extremely smart.

I smiled whenever I saw the new "Fu" in action on the chessboard. He'd look up, smile, and go back to his game. The boy even smiled differently.

Teachers who had predicted he'd drop out were glad to hear of his achievements. One of them said to me, "I'm delighted to have been wrong."

Because he was quick at picking up chess moves and committed himself to excellence, Willow had several mentors. Not only did he become a champion at chess, but his grades improved. He was like a different boy. For the next two years, chess became his focus. Willow left the wrong crowd and made definite attitude changes. I was proud of him—as proud of him as I had been of any student I had ever worked with.

I loved to talk with Willow. Because I saw that he had so much potential, I tried to paint a picture of a bright future for him; I knew he could accomplish anything he set out to do. At first, I assumed I was the first teacher who had ever talked to him that way but I wasn't. As I learned, many other dedicated teachers had seen his potential and had tried to help him, but they got nowhere. I understood, because I knew most of his teachers and they genuinely cared about him and the other children.

Something about growing up in the inner city offers rewards for not listening to adults. Children get more respect from their peers and from some parts of the community for being defiant. I grew up on the same mean streets, so I know the hardships that boys face. Those influences can badly misdirect young people. I frequently told Willow how proud I was that he had changed.

During his three years at Vaux, Willow not only changed his behavior but also became a top student. He worked hard and even made up the year he was behind. He was able to graduate from middle school on schedule with his classmates who had moved ahead of him in elementary school.

As a seventh-grader in 1996—a kid who had played chess for less than two years—he was ranked number twenty-five in chess in the nation for his age and ability group after he played at the national championship tournament in Orlando, Florida.

Not only did Willow have the encouragement of teachers, counselors, social workers, and students, but also many people in the neighborhood volunteered to help in our programs, and they encouraged him. We made a difference in the life of Willow Briggs—we were proud of his achievements and proud of him.

At Vaux, we had kept him busy learning chess and teaching the game to younger students. We saw the best of Willow "Fu" Briggs come to the surface.

But that's only part of his story.

After Willow graduated from Vaux Middle School, he went into high school. It's unfortunate, but they had no chess program like the one he had been a part of in middle school. Willow had no community influence like the kind he had learned to rely on. Within a year, his grades went down, he skipped school frequently, and worse, he began to hang out with the wrong crowd again. Shortly after that, he got into trouble. He wasn't expelled, but it was serious enough that he could have been.

From others, I heard Willow had lost his sense of direction. I didn't see him during those months, but I often asked about him. By the time he was sixteen, the word in the neighborhood was that he often stood around on street corners—aimless and indifferent. He had reverted to the kid his elementary teachers feared he would become.

I regret only asking about him and not taking any action. Not snatching him off those corners was one of my biggest mistakes, but he was no longer one of my students. No one would fault me for my inaction. But I cared very much for Willow, and I didn't do anything about it.

I had dozens of reasons for not maintaining contact with him. I'm not sure what I could have done or said, but every time I heard a report—and it was always negative—I felt deep sadness. He had so much to offer and the stories came back that he had drifted away from all the positive influence at Vaux.

Willow started high school two years before I became the principal of Reynolds Elementary School, which is only one block from Vaux. As a principal, I felt that I would have a bigger opportunity to influence lives, could start working with them in kindergarten and those early years. In that way, I could focus more attention on helping the children in our community. I reasoned that if we didn't get the children on the right track during those formative school years, the rest of their schooling would be spent trying to catch up—and they rarely did.

One afternoon, Willow's former classmate and a fellow chess player, Shaun Snyder, came up to me while I stood outside of Reynolds immediately after school was dismissed. I always tried to be in front of the school to make sure all children walked home safely, got on the right bus, or found their parents' cars. At times, I helped stand guard when they crossed the street as they headed toward the high-rise project buildings that towered over our school.

I started to greet Shaun but something about his face made me ask, "What's wrong?"

"I hate to tell you this, Mr. EL, but it's—well, about Willow."

"What about him?"

"He was murdered last night."

"Murdered?" I repeated the word, unable to fathom what I had just heard.

As I learned from Shaun and heard later from others, Willow rarely went to school, didn't work, and began to hang out on street corners with a bad crowd. The previous afternoon, Willow and his friends stood at the corner of Seventeenth and Jefferson Streets. A neighborhood kid came up to them and said, "This is my corner and I don't want you here. I say who stays here and who doesn't. If I come back and you're still on this corner, you're dead."

In that area, rough kids claimed certain corners as their territory and they usually tried to terrorize any kids who hung around. Many times the bullies' primary interest was to protect their drug turfs and to keep police attention at a minimum. I don't think they encountered any resistance from other young people.

Willow's friends left, but not Willow. I don't think he believed the kid was serious.

Twenty minutes later that same kid came back. This time he walked up to Willow, pulled out his gun, shot, and killed him.

As the story unfolded, I don't remember what I said to Shaun. I heard the story, but my memory of the remainder of that conversation is still a blank page in my life.

Willow is dead. Those three words are what I remember.

When I heard about Willow's death, it was one of the saddest moments I've ever had. So much talent. So young. Now he was dead.

I excused myself and hurried back into the building, walked rapidly into my office, and closed the door. I kept asking myself, "Where had we failed him? Where had *I* failed him? What should we have done differently?" He wasn't the first former student to be murdered, and—sad to say—he wasn't the last. I started to cry. I still couldn't accept what I had just heard. I felt guilty because I hadn't been in touch with Willow. I kept thinking of the wasted life and what I could have done to prevent that waste. "I should have contacted him," I said to myself several times.

The tears flowed, and I tried to stop them, but I couldn't. "He shouldn't have died. He shouldn't have died," I kept saying.

I don't know how long I stayed in my office. My mind went back to the time we met, the early run-ins, the joy of watching him achieve, and the pride I had felt for him when he left for high school. By the time he came to us, many people had already written his story. At Vaux, we edited his story and changed the flow of events. Willow worked on himself and we saw drastic revisions in his life and we were sure his story would have a happy ending. For someone to tell me that the final chapter had closed on that young man's life was some of the worst news I had ever received.

We had lost another child.

Another life gone—and one that had showed so much promise.

Another funeral, and another time to say good-bye.

I have attended many funerals for my students and former students, but I didn't go to Willow's. I couldn't say good-bye. At times, I regret not having gone, but I could not force myself to go.

Many sleepless nights followed his death. "What did we do wrong? What more should I have done?" I couldn't get away from those haunting self-accusations.

His death took place almost a decade ago and I still can't forget him. Even today, I miss Willow "Fu" Briggs.

His murder was similar to what happened to nineteen other students at Vaux during my time there. But none of them ever touched me as deeply as the loss of Willow Briggs. That young man still lives inside me, inspires me, and influences me to touch many others so they don't end up like him.

Did I fail Willow?

When I look at the facts and evaluate everything we did, my mind says no, but my heart says yes. Perhaps I should have contacted him, made more of an effort to see him, found ways to keep him involved in chess and school activities. I know that to dwell on what I "should have done" isn't productive. I can never get beyond the sense that I personally failed to reach him. And this ongoing grief is more than just one boy named Willow. It's Willow and nineteen other Vaux students who have been murdered in the inner city.

None of those deaths should have happened.

But they did, and they still do.

And when they do, it means our influence has failed.

I've often thought that if some of us had started a program at his high school—if I had gone there and offered to help them get a chess program going—he might be alive today. After his death, we initiated programs at several other high schools. That's one good thing that resulted from the loss of Willow. After his death—and because of his death—we went to other inner-city schools and helped them begin chess programs to influence and change kids. We wanted to give the Willows of the inner city opportunity and hope.

Even now, I believe that if Willow's high school had implemented a chess program or something to challenge his mind and stimulate him to achieve, he would still be alive. Maybe instead of being shot that afternoon, he might have been at chess practice, involved in a chess tournament, or in a room somewhere reading about chess.

Willow's death, more than any other, has made me focus on the influence we have on our young people and how everything *we* do affects everything *they* do.

I've tried to find ways to help students stay off the streets. Since then, not only have we focused on programs to help students while they're in school, but even after they go on to college, we try to continue to enlarge the sphere of positive influence. For example, many of our students went on to George Washington Carver High School for Engineering and Science. We started a chess program there with my former students, Demetrius Carroll, Earl Jenkins, Nathan Durant, and Ralph Johnson. We also had students who played in similar programs at Benjamin Franklin Learning Center High School, another magnet school[1] in the inner city.

After Willow died, I realized how important it was for me to influence people who could pass it on and positively affect others. For instance, I thought of my relationship with the teachers in our school. If I improved my relationship with them, they could improve the relationship with their students.

Today, I am more conscious of how powerful our relationships are with students. Prior to Willow's death, there were times when I assumed that if I stayed at Vaux in a supportive role—as a teacher—that would be enough to help the Willows in the community. I was wrong. I needed to move on and become a leader. What I did was right. It was good; it simply wasn't enough.

Perhaps I've been too hard on myself, and some have told me so. But I also know that the death of a boy I cared about changed my life. When I have discouraging days (and I have many of them), I start to think of the other things I could do with my life. "I don't need to beat up on myself like this," I say. But when I have calmed down, I know I can't push the memory of Willow out of my heart. I believe God put that burden on me so I don't forget—so I can't forget.

1. A magnet school is a public school that provides a general education, but it also specializes in particular subjects such as the arts or computer science. These schools draw students from inside and outside their geographic area.

*   *   *

One of the things I struggled with was that I had left Vaux; Reynolds Elementary School was only one block away, but it might have been five miles. Whether I liked it or not, moving to Reynolds meant that those former students would have to make an extra trip to see me. They had been accustomed to coming to Vaux, not only to see me but also to talk with teachers who had been there thirty or forty years. Many teachers who went to teach at Vaux never left until they retired. The students appreciated that dedication and felt close to them. They knew those teachers cared. They said they came to visit so often to say hello or to play chess, but I think they also came to get additional doses of influence. One of those sources—and I was only one of them—had moved a block away.

My transfer to Reynolds meant those former students would have to take an extra step. Most of our young people wouldn't do that. If I had called them, they would have come immediately to see me. Most of them didn't take the initiative or reach out for support.

They hadn't learned early in life that even when we get knocked down, we can still get back up. They hadn't figured out that facing setbacks are growing pains, part of maturing, and learning to become successful. I like to tell students, "What knocks you down makes you stronger and prepares you for the next obstacle."

I currently work with the CEO of schools in Philadelphia, the After School Activities Partnership (ASAP), and several other wonderful organizations that were developed to help change how students are educated outside normal school hours. It is the best way we know to help keep them alive and moving ahead to attain healthy goals.

One of my major goals is to start chess programs in every Philadelphia school. Even some of the most skeptical have admitted that such programs help to save the lives of young people. If we had instituted similar programs ten years ago, Willow might still be alive.

Yes, Willow is dead. I didn't save him, but I can help to save others. I now use his story as a testimony for how he came from failure and used chess to become a success.

His death *has* brought about a number of changes. For example, we've started a program for children of incarcerated and deceased parents. We encourage college students and graduates to return to the inner city and volunteer with enrichment programs. Also, the America's Foundation for Chess, headquartered in Seattle, Washington, has begun implementing a national chess curriculum in second- and third-grade classrooms around the country. When we have accomplished this challenge—and we are committed to this cause—more than 9 million elementary school kids in our country per year will learn the benefits of good decision making, problem solving, and conflict resolution.

Will we succeed? That's not the question. The question is: Don't we have to try? What will we do to help our inner-city, suburban, and rural kids become successful? If we implement and sustain these programs, I'll feel that Willow's death will have had a purpose.

As I look at my students, I often think, "These children are alive. They have a chance to stay alive and to make a difference in the world." Because of Willow's death, we've saved many children. Through his death, God has taught me that I have an awesome responsibility to care for other children. I can also have a tremendous and powerful influence on our young people, and as long as they are alive, I have the opportunity to challenge them to change.

I don't think every day of Willow and other kids we've lost, but I think of them often. Some days I've felt as if I can't handle it anymore. "I'm so tired," I say, or I pray, "God, please remove me from this responsibility. I can't do it anymore."

That's when an image of Willow comes into my mind. I remember the many photos of Willow. Or I see him the first week of school when he still sucked his thumb. In some ways, he was just a baby. I often think about his many chess battles with players who were much older. I can close my eyes even now and see him bent over that chessboard, his eyes taking in the whole board, trying to figure out the next two or three moves. Then he'd become aware of me, look up, and grin. "This is easy, Mr. EL," he'd say before he again concentrated on the board.

"This is easy, Mr. EL." I always remember those words and that child's face. The memory reminds me that he had overcome many odds, and we at the school had helped him make significant progress. We pulled back too soon—and the reality is that we had to pull back because he went on to high school. Besides, there are always other children who need attention, affirmation, and encouragement.

Every year we get students who can't read or who read far below grade level, *but they can improve*. Smart is not something they are; it is something they can become. They can't pull themselves up without help—our help.

Yes, I think of Willow often, but I decided to learn from that young man's death. I've looked at my influence on the children and I've considered the influences that have affected my own life. As I think of the powerful, lasting impression of certain individuals in my life, it makes me even more committed to be as strong an influence in the lives of children as I can.

I want to be able to prevent more deaths by learning from the failure to rescue Willow. In this instance, I've used the failure as motivation. When I saw the success of the chess program and the triumph of Willow and others, I felt a deep sense of satisfaction. I didn't realize that I needed to find ways to continue to build on that success, a system of sustainability, so those students could continue to feel successful.

I learned that I need to find a way to continuously be a part of students' lives. I want to make such a powerful impact that they'll hear my voice when they make decisions. I've had powerful voices in my life. Sometimes I can hear those strong female influences in my life as a child, like my mother or Marsha Pincus, who did so much for me when I was in high school. Or I can hear Dr. Deidre Farmbry and Michael Robinson, from my high school days and early career as an educator, saying, "Believe in the unthinkable and impossible for yourself and your students."

Those who helped me have also influenced thousands of children. Not only do we need more teachers and parents like them, but each of us needs to learn how much more we can do. Because I have responded to their influence, I hope that, through me, students can also hear those other, powerful voices, and say, "I can make it."

I saw the same things in Willow those teachers saw in me. He was not only smart but extremely creative. He read below grade level when he first came to Vaux School. He was like nearly 50 percent of the children in our nation's elementary and middle schools. Within two years, that young man went from a near-nonreader—the boy some predicted wouldn't even make it through middle school—to finish as one of the top twenty-five chess players in his division in national chess tournaments. I vividly remember his teachers, many of whom were new to Vaux School, working hard with Willow. They were a big factor in his success there.

"I'll make you famous," was one of the first things I told Willow. If he would commit to playing chess and helping to improve the image of the school and community, I promised to make him a star. My words came true. Willow was the first student to be featured in a major newspaper article on our chess team. His face appeared on the cover of the *Philadelphia Inquirer.*

To this day, I remember the headline on the front page of the local section that appeared in 1996: A SCHOOL MOVES BACK TO CHESS. Below that was a photo of Willow staring at a chessboard. He became the poster boy for our program.

With Willow, we developed a great chess program. Years earlier, the school had won seven consecutive state and national chess championships. We were on the way to winning others.

At Vaux, the children became accustomed to playing chess *every day* after school, and it became part of their culture. The students never had to ask, "Is there chess practice?" It was a way of life. Sometimes on Saturdays, students played chess at school, in my home, or at the local community recreation center.

For the first weeks after his graduation from Vaux, Willow came back regularly and played chess against some of the younger kids. I wish I had been there to encourage him. Maybe I should have told him how important he was to those younger kids. With no chess program, it's easy to see why he lost focus. He didn't commit a crime or cause problems. He was simply a boy who was in the wrong place at the wrong time.

Willow's life and death motivated me then and continue to motivate me more than a decade later. I don't want to miss any opportunity to help. I failed—or at least I feel I did—and I don't want it to happen again.

I am determined to let other people know about the importance of their words, their personalities, and their opportunities to impact the young. I want them to understand the privilege of working with people who care about them; and I urge them to take advantage of those opportunities.

My compulsion—my mission—is to work with teachers and leaders whenever and wherever I can. Increasingly, I realize how important it is to recognize the influencers, to honor and reward them. They are the ones out there fighting the biggest battles. They struggle and some days they feel inadequate and wonder if they've accomplished anything. Too often they don't realize how important they are or how they have changed the lives of young people. I know because I missed that opportunity myself.

One of the most common problems I've encountered is that although most givers understand how to give joyfully and sacrificially, they don't allow themselves to receive appreciation and honor from others. Because I want to push parents, teachers, and other influential leaders, I often say, "Accept this recognition. Allow me to build you up and recharge your engine because you're working hard and giving generously."

The true essence of leadership is service, and many leaders understand that. The best leaders don't look for rewards and recognition; they need them anyway. We all need to be appreciated, and no one ever gets enough recognition.

I'm always touched when young people let me know that I've made a difference to them. Like other givers, I'm learning to say, "Thank you," without embarrassment.

Our children don't realize the power of *their influence* on people like me. By their words of appreciation, they unconsciously challenge us to do more. Their responses have helped me move beyond the loss of Willow and other students.

I know that all of us in leadership roles have faced failures. We have known at least one Willow—maybe not someone murdered, but certainly someone of outstanding ability who was lost to the world. It's hard on us when we see the potential and then it is lost.

When that happens, we feel we've failed. Perhaps we have. But the one thing our failure can do is challenge us to be more open, approachable, and sensitive to those others who could so easily be lost—and will be lost without our influence.

2

Commitment to Personal Influence

During my early years as a teacher at Vaux, I overheard someone mention that there had been a fire at the home of one of my students, Lovisha Love-Diggs. That afternoon I visited the house and saw that it was badly damaged.

The family had many needs, but the most immediate was to have a place to stay for a few days. Lovisha had several younger brothers and a sister. After we talked, I felt I had to do something. They didn't have much money. I didn't either, but their need was more important than my bank balance. I dropped them off at a nearby motel and they were able to get a room at an extremely low rate. I had enough money to help pay for a one-week stay and some food.

During my childhood, when our family was in great need, people in the community had come to our aid. I had been influenced by the compassion of others, so it seemed like helping the Love-Diggs family was the obvious thing to do. I would have reached out to any family in our community, so to me, it wasn't a big thing.

The family, however, saw my actions differently; they never forgot what happened that day. Even today, years later, whenever I see Loveisha's parents, they remind me of my help in their time of need.

The first time her mother mentioned how much I had helped them, I had honestly forgotten about it. I felt embarrassed and said, "It was such a small thing."

"You don't understand, Mr. EL. To you, it may have been a small thing. To us, it was big—very big—and we won't ever forget."

Afterward, I thought, "She's right. Her perception is what counts." I'm grateful for that, but I'm more grateful for the influence it had on Lovisha. After she graduated from Vaux, she was able to enroll in one of Philadelphia's top magnet schools, Bodine High School, and from there she went to West Chester University. Lovisha now works as a counselor for the homeless and for those who live in shelters. I never imagined she would take on the responsibility of serving others and giving back. I'm proud of her.

After they moved back to their home, I asked Lovisha why she hadn't told me about the fire. "I overheard two of your classmates talking about it or I wouldn't have known," I said.

She hung her head. "I didn't think you would help—you or anyone. I mean, you have your own problems."

I understood. Most children don't want others to know they need help. Most adults probably don't either. What I didn't say was that I almost missed an opportunity to help a needy family because I hadn't influenced her enough personally to allow her to share problems that affected her life inside and outside the school. She hadn't felt comfortable enough to tell me.

That incident helped me realize that I must learn to allow others to get to know me on a personal level. I was a teacher, but I was also someone who cared about the students and their needs. I didn't have to become their best friend, but I did have to let them realize I would be available to them when they had needs.

Shortly after I was married, I took my wife, Shawnna, to Lovisha's church, Miller Memorial Baptist. While we were there, Shawnna met Lovisha's brothers and sisters, her mother, and her grandparents. Of course, they told the story all over again for Shawnna.

Again, I was embarrassed and wanted to say, "It happened a long time ago. It wasn't that big a deal." They were still grateful and I didn't want to take away anything from their appreciation.

As I listened to them tell the story to my wife, I learned another important lesson. I came to understand the power of personal influence. It's not that we intentionally do things just to influence or change others—that's manipulation—but the right kind of influence happens when we help others. *Our actions flow out of who we are.* We demonstrate to others things we often can't put into words.

Although we're often unaware, one small act can change a life. For Lovisha and her family, I assumed I was just another teacher at her school. But when the opportunity came and I acted upon it, my actions became significant and I exerted a strong influence on their lives.

In a similar example, my coauthor, Cecil Murphey, told me a story about his time as a seminary student. He rode a motorcycle to school every day. He was extremely conservative and closed to opinions that didn't agree with him. One day Cec had a fairly serious accident on the motorcycle that kept him in bed for a week.

His wife notified the seminary. The first person to visit was a professor, Hal Lyon—whom he considered one of the most liberal members of the staff. Dr. Lyon came to my friend's apartment, talked to him, and prayed with him. When he finished, the teacher had tears in his eyes.

"He and I never agreed on theology," Cec said, "but he opened me up. I was able to listen and to appreciate people who disagreed with me."

The two men also became friends in the process.

That's the power of personal influence at work. I've had many experiences in my life with teachers and coaches who have influenced me—directly or indirectly. That includes individuals who start organizations to help youth, who influence people in a personal way with their work.

I don't mean to refer simply to areas like teaching and coaching. I want to truly communicate the power of our personal influence. For example, my pastor at Calvary Baptist Church in North Philadelphia, Sean Wise, has had a powerful effect on me. Sometimes he and I talk and that's helpful. But his influence is even more evident and powerful when he stands at the pulpit. He gives illustrations from his personal life. Because he makes himself vulnerable to us, his illustrations and messages stay with us. We see him as a person who not only speaks to us but who also lives the Christian life, or as we often say, "He not only talks the talk, but he walks the walk."

No one is perfect, and sometimes I think it's important that we let others see how imperfect we are. Of course, they'll see that anyway, but we need to let others know we're aware of our own imperfections. That helps them to open up to us. When we show our failures and imperfections, we're influencing people. It is a way to say, "I make mistakes just like you do. We can move beyond mistakes and we can learn from them. Failing at something doesn't make us failures."

People are more likely to listen to us when they know they've made a human connection with us. That connection comes through stories about our life or personal influences, whether verbal or nonverbal.

Some experts estimate that 85 percent of communication is

nonverbal. Nonverbal communication includes body language and facial expressions. If that figure is close to correct, it's important not only that we speak about our beliefs and principles but also that we live them. If we live authentically, we can communicate with people in such a way that we influence their attitudes and behavior.

In the fall of 1997, I turned down a substantial promotion and raise. I never imagined the tremendous influence my decision would have on the students and community surrounding the school. I had been a teacher at Vaux since 1989 and no one was going to tell me to leave my kids. I walked into the office of Principal Harold Adams. He told me he had received a phone call informing him that I had been transferred to another school and promoted to assistant principal.

"There must be a mistake," I told him. "I haven't applied to another school for any position." I looked right at him and said, "I don't want to leave Vaux. I want to be here for these young people."

Mr. Adams knew, perhaps better than I did, that at times he and I were the only positive male role models that those young people encountered. What better place to encounter positive male role models than in school?

"The superintendent's office called and the decision has been made," he said. "You are being transferred."

As I walked out of the office, I said to myself, "Mr. Adams doesn't understand. I'm not leaving these young people. The superintendent doesn't understand that I'm not leaving these young people. Maybe later I'll agree to a transfer, but right now the children need me."

I was angry enough to take on the school district or the entire city in order to stay at Vaux. Later in the day, I received a call from the superintendent's office and I repeated, "At this point, I have made a positive impact, and I know I can influence the lives of many of these young people."

"You have been transferred," the assistant to the superintendent told me when I phoned.

"I'm not leaving," I said. "I can't go. I need to be here for these young people."

"We respect your wishes, but you are being transferred. You'll receive an official letter of notification."

That Saturday I received the official letter telling me to which school I had been assigned and was to report on Monday. I wasn't trying to project myself as some kind of hero and I knew I had faults—many of them—but I had grown up in the inner city. I remembered how tough it had been to grow up without a father. I had a few positive male role models (see Chapter 11), though I wish I had had more of them.

I didn't report to the new school. Instead, on Monday morning, I walked into Vaux Middle School just as I had done for the past eight years.

The word had gotten around—as it always does in those situations. Some teachers and children assumed I would leave, but I was committed to stay. Before I left school Friday afternoon, I had told everyone I would see them on Monday. Until I walked into the building Monday morning, they hadn't believed me.

"I'm glad you chose to stay." I don't remember how many other teachers and children said that, but it felt so good to know that they were happy I had not gone. I actually thought some had wanted me to leave until I saw their faces.

It didn't take any serious thinking to make my decision not to leave. I didn't regret it then or even now, almost ten years later. I made the right choice. Life is always filled with choices, and we can choose to stay in many different situations and exert personal influence, or we can leave. I refused to desert the young people.

I've tried to impress on students at my school to make their decisions and to stick with them. "Stay in school. Graduate from high school and go to college." I want them to make good choices, and I want to be there to encourage them after they make those crucial decisions.

Of course, I have had disappointments. I can name a number of former students who didn't go on to college and a few who dropped out before finishing high school. Each time I think of what life will be like for them I am saddened. Then I remind myself of people like Otis Bullock, who not only graduated from college, but went on to Temple University Law School. He graduated, passed the bar exam, and has started to practice law in the inner city. Those are the encouraging ones.

I think of Blair Biggs, who graduated from Lincoln University in Pennsylvania as an honor student, and Samirah Lawson, one of my first female chess players, who graduated from Morgan State University in Maryland. I laugh when I think of the many pranks that Quan Carr played on the other students at Vaux and on me, but he stayed the course and graduated from Virginia State University. Both Rodney Veney and Shawn Murphy graduated from Cheyney University in Pennsylvania. Rodney, who has completed his master's degree, was a young man whom many people thought would never graduate from high school.

Rodney grew up in a tough neighborhood like all of his friends and graduated from Reynolds and Vaux. He constantly seemed to move along with the wrong crowd. But Rodney had something inside him. Even though he didn't know it, he was waiting for the adults to say, "You can achieve."

Several teachers at Reynolds and at Vaux saw the potential in him. "You can make it," they said in many different ways.

"Because you've grown up in the projects doesn't mean you can't make it."

They let him know that where he came from didn't have to determine where he was going. The teachers at Ben Franklin High School encouraged Shawn and Rodney to go on to college.

Shawn is now working as a behavioral counselor in an inner-city middle school and planning to attend graduate school.

Rodney and Shawn, along with many of my other students in Philadelphia, hear these words from me quite often: "When other people tell you that you're going to the state pen, you tell them, 'No, I'm choosing to go to Penn State.' That's what you say to people and you say it to yourself. After a while you'll see it begin to become a solid principle right in your own life. You begin to influence yourself by saying, 'I'm going to college, and I'm going to get educated.' "

There are others whose lives have encouraged me and helped me to believe in the profound power of personal influence. One of our top chess players, Demetrius Carroll, chose to attend Kutztown University. He had been offered a scholarship to every state university in Pennsylvania. Some other chess players such as Nathan Durant and Earl Jenkins made the same choice to enter Kutztown. Those young men have been together since sixth grade and were members of the Vaux national champion chess team. Now they're roommates in college and will soon graduate.

I want to tell you about Demetrius Carroll. His father didn't live with him, his mother moved to South Carolina, and he was raised by an older sister and an aunt. Before he came to Vaux, he already knew how to play chess, but he had been kicked off the team because of his behavior. Mr. Jackson, who oversaw the chess program at the Robert Morris School, said Demetrius wouldn't listen to him. Mr. Leroy Harvey, who is my fraternity brother in Kappa Alpha Psi and a good friend, saw great potential in Demetrius. He recognized the boy's many discipline problems and agreed he should be removed from the team. Like many young boys who grow up in homes where there are no men, Demetrius didn't know how to respond to discipline from a man.

Mr. Harvey asked me if I would take an interest in Demetrius when he came to Vaux. He cared about his student and asked me to care as well. Without the slightest hesitation, I agreed.

When Demetrius came to Vaux, he changed. Somehow, the positive influences from Mr. Harvey and others had taken effect. Demetrius not only played chess, but became one of the best chess players ever to live in his community.

My fondest memories of Demetrius are from the chess tournament at Parsippany, New Jersey, in 1997. He and his family had recently moved and his clothes were in storage, but he decided to go to the tournament anyway. Despite the circumstances, he was absolutely determined to do his best. We had to buy him clothes to wear. I smiled as I watched him. As he dressed, his tie had to be straight, and his suit had to be neat and clean (even though it would be wrinkled by the end of the day). His commitment and determination paid off. At Parsippany, he defeated an expert-level player, something that had not happened in thirty-five years at that tournament. To see Demetrius overcome some very large obstacles and be inducted into the National Honor Society was uplifting.

To watch Demetrius win at the U.S. Amateur East Chess Championship was truly an exciting moment. The U.S. Amateur East is the largest team-versus-team event in the world, even larger than the Olympics, with more than 220 teams. I was proud of Demetrius and his teammates, who beat players from Bucknell University—and a team of four men whose combined age was more than two hundred years. This was beyond everyone's belief.

Afterward, several tournament officials told me, "We want to honor that young man. We're going to treat him and your entire team to dinner in the hotel restaurant."

"Sir, are you sure you want to let my children in your hotel restaurant?" I asked. This was the Parsippany Hilton. "These are inner-city kids and they don't know what it's like to eat in a place like that. If you want to do something for them, give me a few dollars and I'll take them to McDonald's."

"No, we want them to have a special dinner so we can honor them."

"Sir, you don't want to let my children—"

"No, this was a great achievement and has never been done before in thirty-five years. We want to treat all of the children to dinner."

I didn't argue again. Just before we ate, I took the children to the side and I said, "Listen, we're going to go in this big restaurant and we're going to eat." I tried to explain that this was big-time. "So if you see something on the menu and can't pronounce it, don't order it."

We went in, sat down, and received menus. Of course, they ordered filet mignon and crab bisque ("fill-it mig-non" and "bis-kay" to the kids). They couldn't pronounce the words but they ordered them anyway.

I shook my head and laughed.

In retrospect, I'm glad they had that opportunity. This was new for them. That evening, they began to realize that there are young people who eat in expensive places every day, or at least every week. They saw other children who were exposed to nice restaurants and excellent environments. That also told them, "You have eaten here once; you can do it again."

I realized it was important for our children to have that experience. It's no accident that most of those young people present at that dinner are in college now.

More recently, Demetrius was nominated for the National Collegiate Honor Society. At the time he was going through a most difficult period in college—his Aunt Francine had died. She had raised him as her son. It was a tough time for Demetrius but that young man had already overcome so much.

That's the power of self-discipline and personal influence.

Denise Pickard, who became famous for defeating Arnold Schwarzenegger in a chess match, is now in college. She followed her chess buddies Demetrius, Earl, and Nathan to Kutztown University in Pennsylvania. Anthony Harper, another student who played chess for us, has become a phenomenal basketball player, and he still plays chess. He's in college in West Virginia. I learned recently that he had been offered scholarships to about fifteen four-year colleges across the country. Thomas Allen, who played the 1999 Nationals in Ohio without losing a single game, is in college in Pittsburgh, Pennsylvania. Latoria Spann, who knew the French Defense better than any boy to ever touch a chess piece at Vaux, is in college in Philadelphia studying nursing.

Those were all children who started playing chess and were exposed to environments where they could see the benefits of getting educated. I saw how important personal influence was. Those students have accomplished many great things and I am proud of every one of them.

When I was offered additional money and authority to leave Vaux Middle School, it didn't take me a second to turn down that money. The transfer had nothing to do with money. I refused because some of those young people depended on me. The children didn't know, but this worked both ways: I also needed them.

This isn't a job where I simply spread my arms and do all the giving. I have also received—more than I can possibly explain. I draw a lot of my inspiration from the passion of my students and their families. When I talk to their parents and see the earnestness in their eyes and hear the concern in their hearts, I am proud they allow me to influence their children. They believe their children can become successful—or at least they want them to try.

Part of my concern is that people sacrifice their relationships—that is, they don't recognize the power of their personal imprint. They don't spend enough time with their spouses or their children. I'm guilty myself and I'm committed to making changes. Some of us are so busy doing things in the community or putting our energies into our work that we have nothing left for the most important people in our lives. I almost lost my family because of my inability to see how much they needed me. On many occasions, my wife and children would be home while I was at the school or some community event. The life of the spouse of an educator can be lonely. Our work requires so much time spent away from home. Several times Shawnna told me that I was ruining our relationship by spending so much of my time at school and chess tournaments with the students.

When I took the chess team to Parsippany, New Jersey, I made that trip without my wife's blessing. Officials had scheduled the tournament on Valentine's Day and my wife had eagerly looked forward to spending the day with me.

I begged her to allow me to take the students on the trip and celebrate with her at a later date. Shawnna didn't argue because she wanted to support my work in the community. But I knew—even then—that she preferred to have me home to be with her. I failed her. She asks so little of me.

The students played successfully, and it was one of our great triumphs. However, by the time I returned to Philadelphia, I had admitted to myself that I was wrong. Almost as soon as I walked inside our house, I said, "I'm sorry. I was wrong. I shouldn't have gone. I could have sent someone else."

Shawnna forgave me. She understood my passion for the children and my dedication to the community. I'm grateful, but this was a matter of priority. I had failed. Shawnna is my wife, the person I love most in the world. She also needed to know that I had a personal commitment *to her*—a commitment that came first. By going to Parsippany on Valentine's Day, I had placed my career and personal interest before my family.

"I won't make that mistake again," I promised. "You're too important to me."

3

The Influence of Parents

As a single parent, my wonderful mother raised eight children. For her, the children always came first, and we never doubted that fact. That was her philosophy and that's how she lived. She never had a driver's license or owned a car. I never heard her talk about buying new clothes or anything else for herself. It was always, "What do my children need?"

That's what good parents do: They make sacrifices for their children. I write this chapter because I hope that others, especially young people, will understand their most important job when they become adults: to be good parents. That won't be easy. They have to learn to put their families first. When they provide that kind of commitment, they can also exert the most positive parental influence. Another factor—and one they often don't realize—is how much their attitudes affect their children's behavior.

Too few people realize the extreme power of parental influence. More than anyone else, parents have the opportunity to provide a strong, healthy effect on their own children. It's important that we *want* to raise our children in a family setting. Our children shouldn't be born and raised in settings where they're separated from their parents. How many children will have to be left to be raised by relatives, neighbors, or friends before we decide to do something to save our children?

As an educator in the inner city, I've seen too many instances of parents who leave their children temporarily—or so they say—and they never come back to claim them. I can't imagine what life would have been like for me if my mother had left me in someone else's care and hadn't visited me for weeks or months. Even worse, I can't conceive of leaving my children with someone else. It's unthinkable to me to place myself in a situation where I might never see my two children again.

This abandonment of our children is at an epidemic level, and must stop. In some instances, it's not physical desertion, but emotional. Sometimes one or both parents are present, yet neither one shows any significant interest in the children and their education. That's a different kind of desertion.

Every child needs two parents, and I wish that could always be the case. Without question, it's tough raising children in single-parent homes. In my role as an educator, mentor, and parent, I often see the results of our fatherless society. Because I grew up in a single-parent home myself, I know what children go through. I've suffered greatly from the lack of a positive father figure. If not for the grace of God and the strength and determination of my mother, Amena, I might have been in trouble as a younger man or could be homeless today.

Many of the children I work with grow up in environments that do nothing to help them grow or live productive lives. Some have parents who seem barely able to tolerate them or who would rather do something else than give them attention and guidance. The children don't get to choose the environments in which they're raised. I probably can't do much to help their home situations, but I'd like to influence them to become positive role models when they take on the responsibility of parenthood themselves.

I commend all young people who have overcome the challenges of being raised in single-parent homes or who have been raised in homes where they don't feel loved and wanted—and there are many. I admire those single parents who sacrifice so much to raise their children. That's an awesome job and a tremendous responsibility.

Although many women and men do an outstanding job as single parents, there are definite disadvantages to being forced to raise children alone. The research is conclusive that children who grow up in homes with both parents:

- Are less likely to be single parents themselves.
- Are more likely to get educated.
- Have a greater chance to get married and stay married.
- Will more likely live longer.
- Have a greater opportunity to be more successful financially.
- Are less likely to commit suicide.
- Are less likely to need to fight addictions, especially alcoholism.

For such positive outcomes to occur, there must be a focus and a goal to raise our children in wholesome family environments. For those of us who are parents—or who will become parents—it is imperative that we find a way to foster that positive environment for every child.

I don't want to imply that there aren't traditional families who are dysfunctional. Most of us probably know of two-parent families that are chaotic, abusive, and destructive. I refer to good, wholesome two-parent homes where the parents are members of and attend church; they take their children with them instead of sending them alone or with neighbors. Any number of research projects have shown that children who go to church or some other religious institution with their parents have a higher chance of success in life. Those statistics are especially significant for blacks, because many of our children will grow up in single-parent homes or in two-parent homes prone to violent behavior.

If we can influence children *now,* even if they grow up with only one parent or live in dysfunctional situations, they can overcome the negatives, marry, raise healthy families, and become successful. It can happen. *It does happen, but it doesn't happen often enough.* We must believe that a healthy home situation can be a reality for every person, young and old. The most important goal should be to break the cycle of poverty.

In addition to demonstrating the success of families who attend church, the research also shows that these parents are more likely to remain married. Religion and faith are important, and this is especially true when we raise a family.

Many adults commonly drift from the church during their teen years and the early stages of their marriage. After the birth of their children, they often remember how important the religious environment was for them. "I wasn't sure I believed all of that anymore," one man in my church said, "but I knew that my early religious instruction kept me on the straight road. I wanted that for my children."

He and his wife returned to church and took their children with them. He said, "Becoming a parent motivated me to straighten out my life. I decided I wanted to give my children the best education I could. Can there be any better education than getting them into the church where they can learn right from wrong and how to care about other people?" Today, he's a strong believer and an active elder.

Our faith is—or can be—a strong part of how we influence our own children. How disheartening it is to realize that so many young people who grow up in single-parent homes or with dysfunctional families have no template for a successful home environment. They tend to believe that their abnormal situation is normal, and they perpetuate the cycle of violence and poverty. We can't allow that to continue to happen. It is long overdue for us to help them understand and to say, "Yes, you are growing up in poverty but you can still live a healthy, successful life. And we want to help you."

I often tell my female students, "When you get older and are ready to date (they moan when I say they are too young to date) and a young man approaches you for your phone number and a date, you tell him, 'I'll give you my phone number. But while I'm writing my number down, I need you to solve a quadratic equation and factor a polynomial.' (Our girls learned to solve algebra problems as elementary students.) 'And if you *can't* do it, why don't you call me after you've graduated from college?'"

I usually finish my take on their future mates with advice I borrowed from my good friend Dr. Lee Jones, Dean of the College of Graduate Education at the University of Wisconsin at Whitewater. "If the young man who seeks your acquaintance is not *on* his way, then he is *in* your way!"

I also tell them, "If you're going to be seriously involved with someone, you need to look at that person and ask yourself, 'Is he going to be a good husband? Is he going to be a good father?' Raise your expectations. Don't settle for whoever comes along. Hold out for the best."

That portion of my course is usually given to them when they reach high school, but I can't wait until ninth grade to stress the importance of education and examples of good parenting.

In middle school, I point to myself and ask, "What is my most important job?"

"To be a good principal" is usually the first response.

I shake my head and wait.

It may take three or four answers, but they finally get it. "Yes! That's right. My most important job is to be a good father to my children."

I don't stop there. I also say, "We can't ignore the importance of our relationships with our families and how we influence our children. Our relationships with our church, our pastor, and people in the community affect how we influence our children."

In his autobiographical novel *The Kite Runner*, Khaled Hosseini beautifully expresses the realization of a parent's imprint. Amir and his father (whom he calls Baba) left Afghanistan a quarter of a century earlier when Amir was barely in his teens and moved to California. When Baba dies of cancer, members of the Muslim community come to the mosque to pay their respects. They tell Amir how much they appreciated his father and how deeply he influenced their lives.

> I smiled politely, thanked them for their wishes, listened to whatever they had to say about Baba.
> "... helped me build the house in Taimani ..."
> "... bless him ..."
> "... no one else to turn to and he lent me ..."
> "... like a brother to me ..."
> Listening to them, I realized how much of who I was, what I was, had been defined by Baba and the marks he had left on people's lives. My whole life, I had been "Baba's son." Now he was gone. Baba couldn't show me the way anymore; I'd have to find it on my own.[2]

An effective parent-child relationship is grounded in the awareness of the outside influences that our children receive. Consider some of those powerful pressures such as television,

2. Khaled Hosseini, *The Kite Runner* (New York: Riverhead Books, 2003), p. 152.

music, videos, movies, and the Internet—all those media can send good messages, but they can also send harmful messages to our young people. Let's ask ourselves, "How can we move back to the way things were twenty years ago when the primary motivators for our children were family, the church, and school?"

There is no simple, easy answer, but we can get back to soundly proven family values. Pulling our children into the safety of the family must be the cornerstone of our parental influence.

I frequently tell my students as well as my own daughter: "You want a good picture of yourself? The best way to do that is to look at your friends. Simply look into their eyes. Listen to the way they talk. Look at the type of friends you have and the people you want to be around. Think about the things they do and you'll understand the type of person you are."

My point is this: *Good people have good friends*. If the family is healthy, they'll help you attract the right kind of friends. That's another one of the things good parents do—guide their children's choice of friends.

When we examine the matter of parental impact, we must ensure that we give our children wise advice and encourage them to have the right kind of friends. I say the same thing to parents that I say to the children in our school: "You want a good picture of yourself? Look at your friends. Are the colleagues you bring to your home the type of people you want your children to see as role models? Are your friends the kind of people you want your children to be around, to follow, and to imitate? If you bring the wrong kind of friends around, you are saying to your children, 'Who you associate with doesn't matter.'"

It does matter. We become like the people we're around the most. An excellent example is to look at smoking in the home. Even first-grade children know that smoking isn't healthy. If their parents smoke, even though they know the dangers, children will have a tendency to smoke as well. By the time they're in middle school, their friends influence them. If their friends smoke—no matter how much they've been taught verbally that smoking is an addictive habit—they will likely become smokers. Friends matter. Friends shape our behavior. The role models our friends have at home not only shape their behavior, but affect us as well, since the influence of these role models filters through our friends and reaches us.

I've struggled to convince my daughter that she watches too much television. By being aware of her TV habits, I've been forced to scrutinize my own bad habit of watching so much television. Although most of what I watch is either news or sports, I'm still her role model. If I'm going to have a positive influence on her TV habits, I need to demonstrate the right behavior as well as talk about it.

If parents lovingly guide their children's selection of friends, they can save disappointment and heartaches later. If they are healthy role models and their friends are also good role models, they will strongly impact their children's outcome in life.

As parents, we need to teach these lessons early. Think of it this way: *Every teacher is not a parent, but every parent is a teacher.* The parent is the first teacher every child encounters. The first classroom a child will ever sit in is the mother's womb. We must understand the power of early environments. Children require advice *and examples* from parents on how to relate to others. They learn from observing the way adults behave when parents don't know they're being watched. Children learn from us how to interact properly with other males and females. As parents, we will teach our children, whether or not we're aware. Our examples teach them about male-female interaction. They'll learn about our values and attitudes from our actions, even more so than from our words. We set the pattern for them. This places a strong responsibility on us and forces us to realize the significance of our role as parent-teachers.

Children can learn so much from their fathers. Specifically, they observe the way men treat and respect the women in their lives. This is perhaps one of the most important lessons that fathers teach, though we don't seem to emphasize its impact. If the boys see disrespect, that's the pattern the boys will follow. If the girls see it, that's the pattern of behavior they will expect. As Henry Ward Beecher said more than a century ago, "The best way to love your children is to love their mother."

We need to teach young people that violence is *always* wrong. Think about how O. J. Simpson's life would be different had he mastered that lesson early on as a young man. The same is true if we examine the life of the boxer Mike Tyson or the professional basketball player Kobe Bryant. In their court cases, both men denied they had sexually abused women, but they never disputed they had been violent with women. All three men, who were fathers and husbands, might have led different personal lives if they had learned early on that violence is never an option.

We can start turning our children against violence by teaching them about fairness. Life isn't always equitable, but they should learn always to be fair even if others don't treat them the same way.

When I began to write this book, my older daughter, Macawi, was four years old. Almost from the time she was born, I began to talk to her about being fair, showing respect, and being humble. One time I tried to explain about being humble. We talked about a situation and I asked, "Is it all about you?"

"No, it's not all about me, it's about you, Daddy."

"No, it's not about me either," I said.

She tried to figure out the right answer, but she still didn't have it. I wanted her to learn about the importance of improving the world, about making a difference in the lives of others, and about encouraging and empowering others. We live in such a "me-centered society" and it poisons our kids. We need to reverse that and change the world we live in. We must help our children learn to give themselves to a life of service. People who do only for themselves just make it in life; those who do for others get ahead!

"Do something for somebody every day for which you do not get paid." Those are the words of Albert Schweitzer.

"The more I help others to succeed, the more I succeed," said Ray Kroc, the founder of McDonald's.

Those are two of my favorite quotations because they underscore the essence of service.

We have to "be there for our children." I hear that expression often, but I'm not sure most parents understand the true meaning of these words. In order to "be there" for our children, we need *to be there*. Being physically present and preoccupied with work or other problems isn't being there for them. Being present means to be available—listening, teaching, role-modeling, or having time for them to simply come and sit in our laps. That's being there. *It's never too early to talk to our children, but sometimes it can be too late.*

When I speak about the power of parents, I often tell my audiences how my father didn't live with us, contributed very little to our support, and never visited any of the schools where I was a student. He never came to any of my basketball games and he never attended the plays in which I was involved. My dad didn't come to my high school or college graduation.

I held out hope that he would attend my wedding. I even selected an outfit and shoes for him, but he did not attend. He had disappointed me most of my life because of his absence, but I hoped—and I prayed—that he would at least come to my wedding. It really hurt me when he didn't attend and he never explained.

My dad's absence left a big void in my life—a void I still feel.

Even today, as a parent myself, I still wish he could have been there. He's dead, so that's not possible, but I realize I needed my father more than I ever thought I did.

I'm not alone. Thousands of other kids have missed out as I did by not having a father present. My mother was always there for those events and I'm grateful, but she couldn't completely compensate for his absence.

As young people, we want our fathers to be present in our lives and to be involved in what we do. I make a special plea for fathers because so many of us men are absent. Our children need to see positive male role models early in life. Not being there is not something we can make up for later.

If you're a parent, my message to you is this: Be there. Spend time with your children. Time is so important and you'll have only a few years to make your imprint on them. *If you are not there to teach them, someone else will.* That someone else may lead your children in the wrong direction.

Besides being there for them and teaching them, as parents we need to listen to our children. I'm amazed at how few parents stop to listen when their children are asking for their attention.

In her autobiography, *My Life So Far,* Jane Fonda tells about a time her father was reading a book. She sat down beside him with her own book. For more than an hour, not a word passed between them. At one point, she began to laugh at something she had just read. He paid no attention to her. No matter what she did, she could get no response from her father.

Throughout her life story, Jane Fonda bemoans the fact that her father was rarely around. Even when he was physically present, he was emotionally absent. Her father, Henry Fonda, was considered one of the great stage and film stars of the last century. Maybe he was a great actor, but his children didn't think he was a great father.

As I read the book, the point became even more powerful

that parents need to listen to their children. We not only need to hear what they say to us, but need to listen to the way they talk to their siblings and their friends. We need to respond and let them know that we hear their concerns and appreciate them.

My advice: Allow your children to talk and express how they feel about events in their lives and the people with whom they're in contact. Let them talk to you about their feelings toward others. As you listen, you can begin to understand the types of interactions they have with peers and adults. As soon as they are able to talk—even when their communication is limited to mostly gestures—you need to listen. *If we don't listen to our children when they're young, they won't listen to us when they're older.*

Even though you're a parent, think of this from the perspective of your children. If they have to grab you and beg you to listen to them, what message are you giving them? Aren't you saying they're not important—that they don't deserve your time and your interest?

The worst thing children can say about a parent is, "My mom (or dad) doesn't care." Those words may not always be verbalized, and they may not be true, but the thought comes from their perception based on their parent's behavior. However, to listen—to truly listen—can make a vast difference. The attention you give your children tells them they are important to you. You show your love by your presence and attention. You do make a difference—a big difference—in the quality of your children's lives.

By contrast, we read of terrible tragedies involving violence perpetrated by children. Two immediate examples are the Columbine High School shooting in Colorado, and one later in Red Wing, Minnesota. In the latter episode, a young man killed ten people. We learned later that in both situations, the shooters had talked to their friends about their problems and their plans to deal with them, but they had never discussed their pain with their parents. According to the news media, the parents were shocked; they didn't have a clue about the angst and anger their sons felt.

I'm not trying to judge the parents and I don't think they were terrible people. In fact, they were probably typical parents who worked hard and dealt with family issues every day—people like you and me. But if they had listened—and if thousands of other parents had listened—similar tragedies could have been prevented. We assume those tragedies happen only in the inner city, but Columbine wasn't a poor community and it certainly wasn't the inner city.

It's easy to say that these problems are "out there" and forget that violent incidents can *and do happen* in middle-class and even upper-class neighborhoods. Regardless of their income or location, parents struggle everywhere.

Similar tragic events happen all over our nation and the issues affect everyone. Just by simply listening—daily—to our children, we can make a difference in their lives and in their futures.

One of the best things we can do as parents is to use our influence to help our children learn how to express anger without violence. Anger is not bad and children need to recognize that it's a normal emotion. They also need to grasp that they don't have to retaliate or act out of their anger. They learn it best if they observe their parents model healthy, nonviolent behavior—and thus guide and show them how to cope with anger and avoid violence. Our children need to see that they can talk it out, walk it out, or channel that anger in a positive direction. Children can use that emotion to drive them to work harder in school or at home, or simply to avoid similar stressful situations.

We could prevent many cases of spousal abuse if we helped

young men early in life to learn that violence isn't the answer when they're angry. Aggressive behavior happens because it's the only pattern they know: Anger for them means violence with their words, their fists, or sometimes with weapons. Why? The most obvious reason is because that's the example they've witnessed in their own lives.

We can save more young lives if parents make it a point to provide an environment where our children can feel comfortable in talking to us.

Let's look at this from another perspective. An abundance of research shows that young people in poor communities live in homes that have fewer than one book per home. By contrast, children in more affluent, middle-class and upper-class communities live in homes with a minimum of two hundred books.

I remember growing up and seeing my mother's home filled with books. It seemed as if almost every weekend we were at garage sales to buy books or used furniture sales looking for more bookcases. Although my mother had never had access to any of that research about the number of books in a home, she knew the importance of reading. She recognized that the pursuit of knowledge and striving for excellence were the roads she wanted each of her children to travel.

Because she created a home filled with books—all books that she read—my mother not only had a powerful impact on me, but also made me realize the importance of reading and education. Having those encyclopedias and other books in our house spoke as much to me as her words.

I want to carry on my mother's legacy. I read to both my five- and two-year-old daughters. They know some of the stories so well they finish the sentences for me.

My five-year-old knows the titles of all the books in her

room and there are quite a few. She knows the characters very well. If I try to skip a paragraph, she says, "No, no, Daddy, you missed some." I love that.

I want that kind of experience for every child in America. I want to see every student in our country reading at grade level or above. At least 90 percent of our prison population never read at grade level when in school. For children to learn to read well, we need to teach them early in life how to read and to comprehend what they read.

That's the influence my mother had on me. Because of her example and influence, I grew up with a love for reading. She never told me I needed to read as much as she showed by her example and encouragement. She took me to various lectures, museums, and other places of culture. She frequently talked to me about books. When I was a boy, she'd tell me an exciting story and then say, "Now go read about it and learn more on your own . . ."

Yes, I learned to love to read because of the influence of my mother. She passed away in 2002. When she died, she left me the greatest gift in the world: I received her entire book collection, and I'll always treasure it. I still read and reread those timeless classics. I will make sure those books are passed on to my own children, to the other children in our family, and someday to their children. That's what should happen with knowledge and the love of reading.

It should be a family tradition—the passing on of books and a love for reading. What greater, more powerful gift could a parent give? The family needs to be engaged in literacy and to encourage others to pursue education and a love of learning. Reading should be a family habit.

My mother's influence wasn't only in reading. She was constantly active in the community. Although she never liked politics, she became involved because she knew that was one way she could make a difference in our community. She became active on a local committee, and before long, she became the block organizer in our neighborhood. We lived in the projects and then in low-income public housing—all inside the inner city of Philadelphia—and she had to work hard to support eight children. My mother had every excuse to avoid personal involvement.

She exposed me to various communities and cultures. Even more, while I was still in elementary school, my mother took me with her to visit events on college campuses. Mom wanted me to experience diverse situations and cultures because she knew that if I learned the values and history of others, I would naturally become more aware of my own culture.

Part of the exposure was to teach me never to look down on anyone as being inferior or of lesser importance. By her life— her influence—she also taught me that learning to love others would make me a better person and allow me to realize the contribution I could make to the larger world.

She was a single parent, but that didn't slow her down. In fact, she helped me appreciate the strengths of women. By observing the mothers in our neighborhood, and their influence in the community, I grasped what women go through trying to raise children, provide an income, get an education, and maintain an active role in the community.

My mother's hands were full. I wasn't the only child. In fact, I'm a twin and one of the last-born in our family of eight children. Mom did everything she could to give all of us the best education possible.

When we were children, she always took us to church, and not just on Sunday. We were there on Saturday for various church events. We were there for Bible study. Anytime our church needed volunteers, Mom had us there. We didn't resent it because she helped us see that it was a privilege to serve.

After I became an adult, I recognized my responsibility to be involved in the church and the community. Whatever or wherever the community, I was to be involved and supportive. That was the expectation and influence of my mom.

My mother supported my teachers and the school. Whenever I came home and complained about a teacher, she would give me the same stern look. For some reason I was sure she would defend me and stand with me against my mean teachers.

"What did you do to upset the teacher?"

"Nothing."

"And she got mad at you? For no reason? What did you do before she became upset?"

"Nothing."

"Tell me what happened."

It took a few minutes, but eventually she would find out why the teacher was upset. She would also show me that usually it had been my fault. If I had caused the problem, she would give me no sympathy. If she had felt a teacher had mistreated me, she would stand up for me.

As a principal, I wish there were more parents like my mother.

Often I think about that when I have parents who come into my school after their children go home and complain, "The principal disciplined me and he also gave me a detention."

More than a few parents never ask the children what they did wrong. They rarely call us on the phone and ask, "What did my child do to deserve this?" Instead, they march to the school, filled with anger, and demand to see me or the teacher responsible. "Why did you discipline my child?"

Many times I've had parents say to me, "I don't like your discipline program."

"If your program was working," I respond, "I wouldn't have to use mine."

Sometimes those parents yell at me. I've had a number of them walk out angry and a few have threatened me. Not all of them act that way and some of those parents listen. When they want to know what happened and not just to vent anger, things change. They're the parents who care about their children—really care—and want them to get the best possible education.

I want people to understand that parenting is important. *Almost any man can father a child; almost any woman can bear a child. It requires much more to be a good parent.*

Think of it this way: The message that parents give to their children is the message those children take to the rest of the world. If parents express violent anger, feel frustrated, and see little good in the world, their children don't have much chance to develop a different view.

I don't want to bash parents. I have known many wonderful, caring, wise, and teachable parents in all the schools where I've worked. The chess and math programs would never have succeeded if it hadn't been for strong parental involvement and support. My Second Chance Program was for kids who got into trouble and was an opportunity for them to change their attitudes. When their parents worked with me, those kids changed.

We have a wonderful parent-supported reading program called the 100 Book Challenge. My former boss, Gaeton Zorzi, and his wife designed and initiated the program. Thousands of schools across the nation now subscribe to this wonderful, challenging program. We involve every child in our program, even those in preschool and kindergarten. The goal is to have every child read at grade level. All of them don't make it, but most of them do. The teachers push the 100 Book Challenge, but it succeeds best when the parents work with us. When parents properly support effective reading programs, their children will be successful.

Bill Cosby and several other celebrities received a lot of criticism when they spoke out about parents falling down on the job and not taking responsibility for their children. I understood what they were saying but I also think we need to commend those parents who struggle financially, and yet they somehow find a way to provide a home and do an excellent job of raising their children. They see failure and struggle daily just as I do, but they continue to fight for their children.

Cosby later said he wished he had said that many parents are doing a great job. I hope he was serious, because I am serious when I say I've worked with many wonderful mothers and fathers. Sometimes we educators see so much bleakness, failure, and death, we spend a lot of time crying out. It's easy for us to overlook those faithful, wonderful parents.

Being a parent is tough, but no one ever said it would be easy. I firmly believe that parenting is the best job in the world. Senator Hillary Clinton convinced many people that the entire village is the answer when it comes to raising a child. I beg to differ on some aspect of that philosophy. When our child has that 101-degree temperature at midnight, the village isn't there to offer medicine and a cold bath. When our child goes out on that first date and doesn't come home on time, the entire village doesn't pace around the house or call every possible cell phone number available. It's Mom and Dad who worry and pray alone at night. In a growing number of families, it's Grandmom and Granddad.

Our second daughter was born February 29, 2004. We named her *Nashetah*, a Native American word that means *second-born warrior.*

She's a fighter. Scheduled for delivery on June 2, she was born at twenty-six and a half weeks and weighed only one pound thirteen ounces. Nashetah fought through every day. She's healthy now, and I'm grateful to God for her and for the medical staff at Lankenau Hospital near Philadelphia, who helped us through many very rough times.

As I watched my wife go through that process of constant care for our infant daughter, I gained deep respect for her and for the women around the world and their selfless giving and love. Prior to the baby's birth, Shawnna herself was hospitalized for almost a month, and after she was born, our daughter stayed in the hospital for 84 days. Shawnna was there every one of those 84 days and spent most of her nights there. She had to teach me how to plan and cook meals for our older daughter and myself. Shawnna had her priorities in the correct order—our newborn daughter came first.

I understand the daily struggles of parenting so I know how tough it is to be a parent. I also know that we can never forget that we are the first teachers for our children. We can't pass that responsibility on to anyone else. We cannot allow MTV, BET, or HBO to teach our young people. God designed that job description for us and we're the only ones who can fill it.

If every one of us could look twenty years into the future and think of what we'd like our children to become, it would affect the way we teach our children now. We are marking them for life—and the more positive our influence and our teaching, the greater the opportunities and possibilities they'll have later. Our choices today will affect future generations.

I traveled to South Bend, Indiana, in February 2005, to participate in a live television interview with the LeSea Broadcasting Christian television station. While there, I also visited several schools and talked with young people about my students and my work in Philadelphia. I gave away a few copies of my first book, *I Choose to Stay*, to students who had enough courage to stand and ask or answer questions. I always do that when I visit schools because I believe it is important that we reward students for taking risks. So many times they don't take leadership roles because they feel uncomfortable speaking in front of their peers.

One particular young man stood up and I asked, "Do you have a question?"

"No, I don't have a question." He said he had heard me talk about my mother and how powerful her influence had been on me and how I wanted each of them to be dedicated to their parents. "I wanted to thank you for saying those positive comments about your mom."

"Thank you," I said. "My mom passed away a couple of years ago, but her influence still lives on."

"My mom really made a lot of sacrifices for me also," he said.

I told the young man his mom must be very proud of him and that she was doing a great job. I asked him to come to the front. I gave him a copy of my book. I noticed that there were tears in his eyes. When I looked at his teacher, she was crying also.

"Did I do or say something wrong?" I asked the teacher after we dismissed.

"That young man recently lost his mother. It touched him for you to mention his mom. He misses his mother a lot. I'm glad I brought him to this program today because it was important for him to be able to hear you say that about your own mother."

I was able to talk to the boy and let him know that as an adult I still struggle over the loss of my mother, so I could imagine what he was going through. I told him to understand that his mother had planted seeds in him and her legacy and influence lives through him. His immediate response was, "When are you going to visit my church here in Indiana?"

"Maybe someday soon," I said. "If they invite me, I'll come."

It was so encouraging for me to see a young person who understood the commitment that his parent had made. Although she's not on the earth with him, I told him, "She's here in spirit and she's looking down and watching and she wants to see you go to college and get educated and give back to the community."

That is the true immortality of influence.

4

The Influence of Husbands, Children, and Siblings

Those of us who are husbands should be aware of the tremendous influence we have on our wives and children. It's essential that we provide emotional support for our wives. I have had countless conversations with men who have expressed how uncomfortable they feel because their wives make more money, have more education, or are more successful in their careers.

As long as they resent their wives' achievements, they will never be able to fully support them. When men see the success of their wives as a part of the success of the family, they will encourage, love, and support them.

Our priority must be to love our wives—not just with our hearts—but with a commitment to help, to stand beside them, and to be present whenever we're needed.

As husbands, if we are going to improve our relationships with our spouses, we must also learn to respect and love other men. That may sound contradictory, but if we men are constantly competitive with each other and feel the need to prove we're stronger, faster, or tougher, that affects the way we treat the women in our lives. I don't mean only our wives, but all women, including our mothers, sisters, and daughters. We also must teach our children to love others—not just by laying down rules but by living the right way as an example to them. We need to face the fact that raising children isn't only a mother's role. Especially, we should teach our boys how to treat girls and women with respect. Our boys need to learn that early.

After working nearly two decades with children in the public schools, I've realized that most boys won't ask for guidance when it comes to learning how they should treat women. We have to go to them and show them how. Part of our responsibility is not only to offer guidance but also to provide ourselves as excellent role models. We can no longer allow the criminals on the street or violent athletes and entertainers to teach our boys how to be men.

As fathers and husbands, part of our adult and parental responsibility is to enlighten them and to help them understand that they must love themselves and respect others. As we show them respect, we can help them grasp what it is and how it works.

We also must teach our daughters to refuse to allow themselves to be treated with disrespect. They can influence the males in their lives in positive ways. In our school, I urge girls to report boys who treat them badly. We want to eliminate that type of negative behavior.

In recent years, a controversy has arisen about women and their lack of success in science and mathematics. There's been an ongoing debate at Harvard University about women in the sciences. Controversial statements made by the president of the university ignited the debate. Many women have already proven they can be just as successful, if not more successful, than men. We men should support, nurture, and lovingly encourage women—all women. That's why we've always encouraged girls to be involved in our chess program. Several of our girls have gone on to become more successful than most of our boys.

When I think about men supporting women, immediately my mind races to the story of one family I spent time with when I visited South Bend, Indiana. My purpose in going there was to tape a show for the Christian television station at LeSea Broadcasting. Kelly Morgan, the cohost, asked me to appear on her TV program, *The Harvest Show*. My coauthor, Cec Murphey, had taped a program with them for one of his own books and mentioned my name to Kelly as someone he thought she would like to interview. Kelly contacted me, and a few weeks later, I flew to South Bend to do an interview. Then I planned to go back immediately to Philadelphia.

Cec had told me, "When you meet this woman, you're going to see she's a powerful Christian mother, wife, committed community member, and dedicated to serving her church."

When we met, Kelly amazed me by her dedication to her profession, career, family, and faith. She was also smart, lovely, and extremely articulate. After the show, she and I talked for a long time. When she told me her story, I realized how really successful she was. Kelly, an African-American, was born and raised in Brooklyn, New York. Her adult life started early as a young single mom and her story brought back memories of my own mother, who grew up in New York City.

I knew I wanted to hear more of her story, so I joined Kelly, her husband, John, and their two young children for a late lunch. My own views on life as a husband and father were about to change tremendously. I always thought I had been supportive. I still had lessons to learn.

As we started to eat, I watched the warmth of the family as

they interacted with one another, especially with John. I could readily see the influence that man had on his family.

As I watched, I wondered if I could be as supportive as he was. Kelly was the star, and to many, he was "just" her husband. That fact didn't seem to faze John. Everything he did showed me how confident he was as a man and how strongly he supported her career.

Earlier in the day when I visited the schools in South Bend, John took the time from his job to make sure I was comfortable and properly introduced in each building. Like Kelly, he was from New York, but he didn't want me to leave the state of Indiana without knowing that the people there cared about others.

John and Kelly met in New York City after John had graduated from Morgan State University in Maryland, and held a good job. Kelly had been a promising music student at an early age, and had mastered the piano and violin. Her life and career had been interrupted when she became pregnant as a teenager.

When they met, Kelly was a single mom on welfare. John saw so much potential in Kelly that he often talked to her about following her dreams of a career in music. Kelly shrugged off his suggestions.

They fell in love and married, but John wasn't ready to let his wife give up on her dreams. "You are going to go to college. You can do it," he said. He refused to listen to her reasons why she couldn't be successful. That went on for weeks.

One day John picked her up at home and drove her to an office where she applied for a college scholarship. She applied for admission to several colleges and was accepted at Nassau Community College in Garden City. She went to school and John stood behind her. "You can do it," he said whenever she showed any doubts. Kelly became a top student at Nassau, where she majored in communication and maintained a 4.0 grade-point average, the highest in her graduating class, which meant she was a top candidate for valedictorian.

Three weeks before her graduation, however, Kelly still hadn't received any information from the college about the valedictorian speech.

John, an educated man himself, was familiar with graduation protocol and knew that his wife should have been on the list of potential speakers because of her 4.0 GPA. Both of them were well aware that the top student addresses the students and families at the commencement exercise.

"I just dismissed it," Kelly told me. "It was not a big deal. Besides, I'd been through so many disappointments in life, not being chosen valedictorian didn't seem like a big thing."

She didn't realize that it *was* a big deal for John. Until then she hadn't really grasped how proud he was of her achievements.

"We are definitely not going to forget this," he told his wife. "If you are the valedictorian, you are the one who should give that address. Those young people in the audience need to see *you*. The women in attendance have to see that other women can achieve success at high levels and especially in academia."

He also pointed out that Kelly would be the first African-American to graduate from that school as the valedictorian.

"The first in the history of the school," she said as she interrupted the story. The glow in her eyes made me realize that the honor meant more to her than she had admitted. Why not? She had worked hard and had proven her ability.

They contacted the school. One professor responded to their inquiry with, "We made a big mistake, but it is too late to correct it now. We have already reviewed the final speeches and are ready to make a decision on our valedictorian address." Another faculty member offered her money as compensation for the error.

Kelly understood the school's position and error but it hurt her most that not one of the students preparing for the speech was from a minority group and none was graduating with a 4.0 grade-point average. She would have been the only one in the group. Kelly was so happy to be graduating and overcoming so many obstacles that she was satisfied just to finish school.

"No! We won't settle for that," John said. That was a real husband and father in action. "I am proud of my wife and the mother of my children," he told the school officials. "I want her to receive any honor that she is due. She earned the right to be valedictorian."

Some administrator said, "We forgot to notify her and somehow we erred and asked someone else."

"That makes no sense," John countered.

He received a number of we-are-sorry-and-you-are-right-but-it-is-too-late responses.

"That is not good enough," John said. "She earned this honor, and she should have it."

He told me that he contacted other people at the school, the NAACP, and other organizations to prevent this terrible injustice from taking place. They never challenged the grades of other students. The point that John kept making was that his wife had the highest GPA in the class. "She should be the valedictorian. You are sending the wrong message—you're saying that it doesn't matter how well she does or how well any other minority student does—only Caucasians are eligible."

They denied any ethnic preference.

"She will be the first—the very first—African-American valedictorian in the history of this university."

I don't know all the details, but the people in the administration finally saw the light. They admitted it would be a travesty if Kelly was not the valedictorian. One of the professors told Kelly, "If you write a speech and submit it within twenty-four hours, we shall consider it—along with the others."

That wasn't quite what they wanted, but they complied. Kelly wrote the speech. She received the official word that she would be eligible to give the valedictorian address.

As I sat at the lunch table and listened, I thought, "What a powerful, spiritual man Kelly has for a husband. This man is not only proud of his wife, but willing to fight for justice for her."

By contrast, I thought of several male friends who were honest enough to tell me they resent the success of their wives. Many are openly honest in expressing how they feel their manhood is threatened.

"I just don't think I'm important in the family when Mom is more successful."

That way of thinking is wrong. The amount of income doesn't determine the value of a person. John Morgan remains an inspiration to me. He stood beside his wife, and he has been an outstanding role model for their children.

As I listened to their story, I became aware that I still needed to do more to be supportive of my own family. Whenever my wife talks about wanting to go to medical or law school, I've learned not to dismiss it as idle chatter or conversation. I want and need to encourage her to do anything that she wants to do.

Before I finished lunch with the Morgan family, I learned that Kelly had majored in communications and music, and in 2003, she graduated from Hofstra University in New York, *summa cum laude* (with highest honors). The battle from welfare mom to college graduate was not one without many, many struggles. It took her almost eight years to finish her degree after leaving Nassau Community College. But she did it.

Kelly's life and testimony are an important message to single moms, teen parents, and all the other women who must deal with life's daily trials and tribulations.

"Persistence overcomes resistance," is something I like to

say. I wish every woman had a John Morgan in her life to support her.

I've learned a lot from observing my brothers and sisters. They've worked hard for most of their lives, and they've had their own trials and hardships and have been able to overcome them. As a young child, I watched my older siblings tackle their problems. Their examples showed me that we all have misfortune and hardship, but we can also bounce back.

When we can see people—parents, siblings, friends—who fall down and get back up, we recognize that the blessing is in having the ability to get back up. Just get up and try one more time. I learned from my brothers and sisters the truth of the words of Friedrich Nietzsche, "What does not destroy me, makes me stronger." Our one-parent family of eight children faced many hardships. Because my siblings were older, they had a more difficult time than I did, but they were great teachers in my life. I had six older brothers and sisters to depend on but the oldest ones didn't. They didn't realize it but they were teachers in a way. They taught and talked to me about life and learning from the mistakes of others.

My brothers and sisters have been supportive of me in my career as an educator, mentor, father figure, and author. They often visit my school and they look upon my success as success for the family. For example, my brother George, my first chess coach, helps with our chess program as a volunteer, and he has never asked for money to do that. He learned from our mother that we give whatever we have to give and encourage others any way we can.

I hope the young people I teach will grasp that fact. As they are supported and encouraged, the day will come when they need to volunteer without expectation of reward. It's a way to give back for the blessings they have received.

I hope George doesn't mind my mentioning that many of my students defeat him in chess. That dates back to Demetrius from my early days at Vaux all the way to Kyle Tribble, one of our newest and strongest chess talents at Reynolds Elementary School. But whether he wins or loses, George is there. He supports the others and he cares.

5

Influence Through Discipline

Discipline is a form of love.

I'm amazed that many people don't understand that fact. If we love our children, we set parameters for them. They *need* limits and guidelines and they need those limits from the significant adults in their lives. They *want* limits—even if they don't admit it. Part of being able to know they are loved is that children know what they can do and what they can't do.

I have a friend who told his children, "Whenever your friends want you to do something you don't want to do or to go where you don't want to go, you tell them your father doesn't want you to, and I'll back you up." He was trying to help them realize that he couldn't be with them all the time or make each decision for them. He also wanted to give them an easy way to say no to their friends.

He said his children were ridiculed a few times, but they held their ground. Eventually, their friends respected them. One boy said to my friend's son, "I wish my dad cared enough to tell me not to do something wrong."

Our children know they need our guidance, even if they don't acknowledge it.

The Book of Hebrews quotes from Proverbs and offers a further explanation:

> "My son, do not make light of the Lord's discipline, and do not lose heart when he rebukes you; because the Lord disciplines those he loves and he chastens everyone he accepts as his child. Endure hardship as discipline; God is treating you as his children. For what children are not disciplined by their father? If you are not disciplined—then you are not legitimate children at all. Moreover, we have all had parents who discipline us and we respected them for it. . . . Our parents disciplined us for a little while as they thought best; but God disciplines us for our good, that we may share in his holiness. No discipline seems pleasant at the time, but painful. Later on, however, it produces a harvest of righteousness and peace for those who have been trained by it."[3]

That's the principle we want to inject: At times, we have to make decisions that may appear harsh, but if we stand for what we believe is right, our children benefit. As the quotation above says, "Later on . . . it produces . . . peace for those who have been trained by it."

"If you love your children," I often say to parents, "you have to discipline them. If you discipline your children, that means you love them." When I refer to discipline, I don't mean beating them or verbally abusing them—and the parents understand what I mean. With discipline we must set limits, but we have to set them lovingly.

More than two thousand new cases of abuse are reported *every day*. We can't allow that to go on. We must find effective ways to love and discipline our children and to stop the violence of abuse. We cannot continue to ignore our children and allow them to be hurt.

---

3. Hebrews 12:5–11, Today's New International Version.

Children need to hear the word *love*—and they need to hear it often. They *must* hear positive and affectionate words. Too often the only time they hear the word *love* is when it's associated with some type of sexual activity. As young as possible, children have to understand that their parents genuinely love them and want the best possible life for them.

Some parents hold back because they don't want to spoil their children. Or they're afraid they'll lose their children's love. Children may sometimes angrily say, "I hate you," because that's how they feel at the moment. Those words don't mean they'll hate you forever or even in five minutes.

One parent told me that her son said, "I hate you," and she said, "That's all right, because I love you enough for both of us."

"I do love you," he said, "but sometimes I don't."

That's how children are. We don't base our parenting plans on the fear of displeasing them; we base our discipline on what they need and what is best for them. When we have true parental love for our children, we say to them, "I love you, I want to help you, and I won't allow you to be anything but your best."

The example below is not the traditional father-son relationship, but I must say it is very close. My former student, Shawn Murphy, was and has always remained an inspiration to me. Maybe I especially remember him because he started at Vaux Middle School during my first year as a teacher. He was also one of the first students who showed me I was called to be there. We talked several times the first week I arrived at Vaux. I learned that he lived in a small house with almost twenty other people. He didn't complain; it was just the way it was for him.

From the first moment, Shawn impressed me with his extensive vocabulary and quick thinking. He was a fine basketball player—and basketball is my favorite sport. Actually, I don't want to remind Shawn how impressed I was with his athletic ability when he was younger because we still do battle on the basketball court, although I am almost twice his age. I don't want to give him any emotional advantages.

Despite his success in sports, in middle school he had been identified as an at-risk student and placed in a special program. Those were the children I enjoyed teaching. At-risk means at risk of failing school. It was an alternative program, or what we later called the Second Chance Program, an alternative learning center where we took students who had gotten into trouble. The Second Chance Program developed at Vaux because our principal, Harold Adams, used a similar program at his previous school and it had been quite effective. I worked with a group of teachers and parents to design and implement the curriculum. I was also one of the first teachers to work in the program at Vaux.

Above, I mentioned the sophistication of Shawn's vocabulary. I met him when he was about twelve years old and he threw around words such as *controversial* and *conspiracy*. He not only used those words, but knew what they meant. He was well read in sports, too. He knew every statistic for all the major sports—at twelve years of age. I was more than twice his age, an avid sports fan, and I didn't know half those statistics.

I found it hard to believe that he was only a young boy—and an at-risk student—who used an adult vocabulary and could pull vast sports information out of his head without effort. As far as the school was concerned, however, Shawn was one of those kids the system considered below average, a boy who couldn't keep up with his peers, and who had behavior problems. Those factors thrust him into the at-risk category.

About that time, my mother and I started a Saturday morning school just for students like Shawn. Our goal was to teach those children who hadn't absorbed the required skills and information during the week. After school and on Saturdays I taught classes, mainly basic math and writing, but also a little algebra. My mother taught some world history with a strong emphasis on the history of Africans and African-Americans. At the time, those subjects were not a part of our school's curriculum.

My mother always baked macaroni and cheese along with sweet potato pies for the children. I used to laughingly tell my mother, "Your good cooking is the only way I can keep the attendance strong. I know I'm not the attraction."

I clearly remember Lovisha and Shawn, and several others like Chanel, Roger, Lasheena, and Rodney, all waiting for me to stop teaching so they could eat some of my mom's good collard greens.

My mother never argued with me.

We started the Saturday Academy for those students the school labeled as low functioning so they could catch up on their studies. Of course, some of the gifted students enrolled because they wanted to learn more and they yearned for a sense of family that they found at our Saturday school.

I didn't care about the labels the system gave them, because I believed I could teach any kid at any age to do high-level mathematics. Some of those who came had been discipline problems—big-time discipline problems—and were accustomed to being suspended frequently. I realized that part of their problem in school was that they hadn't achieved success in the classroom.

We wanted to change that. One teacher, who had grown up in a similar community, warned me about taking on those problem children. I told her, "If I can show them that they can achieve—that they can stand alongside the best students in the classroom—I think we can eliminate most of the problems."

It wasn't easy and some of them passively fought me, but most of those children proved themselves capable of being good students and shedding the at-risk label.

I'll never forget that on his first day in my class, Shawn said he wasn't able to achieve in school because "there's a conspiracy against me."

He was too young to understand what a conspiracy was, and I knew it was something he had learned from listening to adults. But the fact that he had memorized the word and used it correctly told me that he didn't belong among the underachievers. "If you can use a big word like *conspiracy* in a sentence," I told him, "you can achieve anything."

He didn't show any excitement, but I sensed he wanted to learn. "Would you like to join my Saturday morning class?" I asked.

"Yeah, that sounds cool," he said without much outward enthusiasm.

Shawn came to my Saturday morning class and my after-school program. He learned quickly and never missed a session—something new for him. Shawn believed me when I told him he could achieve. The more he achieved, the more he seemed to want to learn. Within a few weeks, he started to spend a lot of time at my house. Later, I took him to meet the motivational speaker, entrepreneur, and TV personality Tony Brown, when he visited Philadelphia.

Mr. Brown spoke a few words to Shawn personally: "Do your best in school." Even though he spoke only a few words, they impacted Shawn. Tony Brown is a hero and role model for many people, young and old, in every community. He is an example of the success they can achieve with hard work.

Shawn did his best. He learned math so well that when he reached high school they assigned the former so-called "low-level" student to tutor his peers in algebra.

The others who attended on Saturdays also learned. Even the worst discipline problems became good students. The Saturday Academy may have been small in numbers, but many parents and teachers considered it important enough to put so much time and effort into giving those kids extra help.

Yes, it was small, but it was a beginning. The following year Harold Adams expanded the Second Chance Program.

Chess became one of the more challenging tools I used to motivate the at-risk students. "You have to be real smart to play chess," one boy said.

"You're right and you're smart enough to learn."

By helping the students focus on being smart, when they learned to play, they began to believe they were smart. That's how many of them traveled on the road to achievement. Once they realized they could master the basics of chess, they were open to mastering other things in the school curriculum.

Shawn didn't join the chess team and didn't play much chess. When I invited him, he'd shake his head. "They're too good for me." After he graduated from college, he came back to our school to volunteer with the students, and he realized he needed to learn to play chess well if he was going to be of maximum help to the students.

He started working at our school as a therapeutic support specialist so he could help assist students with behavior difficulties. So many times I've shaken my head in amazement at that fact. Shawn had been one of those kids with behavior difficulties, and ten years later, he came back to influence and change kids who were just as he had been. Long before he graduated from college, Shawn realized that his mission was to return to the inner city and make a difference. After I moved from Vaux Middle School to Reynolds, Shawn also came to visit and became a mentor to many of the students.

There's more to this story about Shawn Murphy. He made outstanding academic progress, but financial support in college was a constant problem. He could count on something from home, but not much. He was like most young people in the inner city who had to rely on grants and scholarships in college.

We stayed in touch and I did what I could for him. He called me regularly from college and I always felt uplifted after his calls. I especially remember the time he called during his third year of college. He didn't say much, and there was a sadness in his voice.

"What's wrong?" I asked.

"I'm not going to be able to register for classes. They're telling me that my financial aid hasn't come through yet and they're not going to allow me to register if I don't have the money."

He wasn't just sad. His voice cracked and I realized he sounded as if he had been crying. Shawn had worked so hard for so long and now it seemed as if his dream had been stolen from him.

"There's got to be some way out of this. What can I do?"

"I don't know," he said. "I've asked but they won't let me register."

"What would it take for you to be able to register?"

"They want at least a thousand dollars as a commitment and they want it today. It's the last day of registration." He was trying hard not to break down. "Mr. EL, I don't know what to do. My family can help a little but I need more. They don't have the kind of money it will take to keep me here—you know that."

"Where are you now?"

"I'm on campus." He was at Cheyney University, thirty miles outside of Philadelphia. It's part of our State University System and one of America's oldest historically black colleges.

"I'll be there in a couple of hours," I said. I told my wife I'd be gone for the rest of the day. I jumped into my car and drove to the bank. I had some money there but not much. I visited Shawn's grandmother and she was the sweetest lady I've ever met. She wanted to do whatever she could to keep Shawn in school. She didn't have much money, but she gave me what she had.

After visiting several other friends and relatives, I raised enough money to help Shawn. I drove to Cheyney University, met Shawn, and handed him the cash.

"Thank you, Mr. EL," he said and his eyes lit up. "I can't think of anyone else in the world who would have done something like this."

"This is a team effort," I said. "Many people have contributed to your education—some of them you don't know. This is how we support you."

"I appreciate what you've done, and I love you."

When he said he loved me, those words melted me. I didn't cry then—I didn't want Shawn to see me like that. I had learned from the wrong people that crying was a sign of weakness. Later, I learned to see the truth. Shawn also said something that touched me as much: "You're like a father to me and I appreciate you."

He was right. I was doing for him what a caring father would have done. I wasn't trying to replace his father because his father loved him and was quite proud of Shawn. I just wanted to be there whenever he needed me. I thanked Shawn for giving me a chance to help him, to be there for him, and I told him I loved him and was proud of him for working hard. He had earned the right to be helped. He had disciplined himself. He had fought against the odds and the statistics that predicted he wouldn't make it out of the inner city.

As I drove back from Cheyney University, I shed tears of gratitude for that young man and to God for changing Shawn into such a fine person. He was a kid who wanted so badly to rise above poverty and the problems that cause so many to fail. Even though I was just one of many, I was grateful to have been able to help.

What about the Shawns who don't have someone to call on? There are many of them.

I didn't worry about the money. I knew that someday Shawn

would pay me back (and he did). I looked at loaning him the money as an investment in the future of one of our young people. It was simply something I was supposed to do—it was one of those times I felt God nudged me to forget about the small amount left in my checking account and help that young man. Shawn had already overcome many problems and had worked hard to succeed. He deserved every bit of help I could offer.

When I started teaching the Second Chance Program at Vaux School, I developed my own curriculum within the program. We focused on reading a great deal but we placed a large emphasis on higher-level mathematics. I made that change after I discovered that many of those troubled students were advanced and possessed true higher-order thinking skills. I had taken over the program assuming they were all slow or unable to learn at a normal pace. Many of those kids were bright but extremely undisciplined. They didn't know how to apply their thinking skills, so I developed a way to help them.

In school, we normally begin teaching mathematics in the base-ten system. After a few weeks, that was no problem for those kids, so I took them into the base-two, or binary, system. From there, we progressed to adding, subtracting, and multiplying variables. It wasn't long before they could solve multi-step equations. They had the minds to grasp that information in elementary and middle school. They didn't slow down, and eventually they were able to do math beyond the level of some of their teachers. They heard those words directly from the teachers themselves—including me.

Of course, there were exceptions, but most of those students were able to solve algebraic problems in elementary and middle school. Those who had been the worst discipline problems showed me that once they learned to think with a self-controlled mind, they could achieve. We taught them to play chess and they proved extremely proficient.

Try to imagine this situation. A student who has been called dumb or had a history of behavior problems, enters the at-risk program. There is a stigma to that, because everyone knows what kind of kids go into Second Chance. Then something happens. Within weeks, that boy who was called "dumb" or "stupid" is able to walk around the school and say to the other children, "I'm a chess player."

It was never to brag or boast. They were proud of their hard work. Once students said, "I'm a chess player," they had to prove it, and they did. To call themselves chess players was big time at Vaux and at Reynolds. When the other students realized those once-troubled students were now chess players, they immediately gave them respect. The most exciting aspect of the transformation was that the other kids viewed them as intellectuals. That meant more to the chess players than anything else.

Working with those students in the Second Chance Program allowed me to do more than help them get good grades, earn respect, or move beyond their behavior problems. More important, many of those students changed the way they felt *about themselves*. As they achieved success in chess or other areas, their self-esteem increased. Each bit of success added to their self-confidence, and they began to realize they weren't unteachable or destined for failure.

The most difficult thing to teach those bright children wasn't chess or the binary system of numbers, but discipline. They had to learn that chess was a serious game and a great builder of character. Chess was a great method to teach discipline, especially for those kids with behavior problems, because the game forced them to think ahead, to anticipate what the other player might do. They couldn't make hasty, emotional decisions, and the game demanded patience. More than anything else, the students learned that they could choose their behavior but they couldn't choose the consequences.

As they improved their skills in chess, their classroom performance increased. They themselves seemed the most surprised by the change. They were able to leave the alternative programs and work in a regular classroom, and they were successful at fitting in.

They had learned discipline. They became likable children and good students—and most of them positively impacted other students. Their sense of self-esteem multiplied even more. When they sat in traditional classrooms and realized that not every child could solve algebraic equations, they began to appreciate themselves and their abilities even more.

"Mr. EL, I *am* smart."

I've heard students once labeled at-risk say those words many, many times after finding that they could be successful. It was as if they had finally figured out something we teachers had seen much earlier. I couldn't have told them they were smart because they probably wouldn't have believed me. They had to learn to *feel* smart. The best teachers know that smart is not something children are; it is something they become. Children aren't born smart. Children learn from their experiences in the home, school, and community. Self-control and discipline helped my students arrive at that profound understanding of themselves.

It wasn't just the chess players themselves. Teachers and other children would say to them, "You really are smart." Those affirmations encouraged them even more.

Along with all those responses, the children slowly began to realize they could be successful in areas beyond chess. They were able to think about becoming successful in life. They could make it out of the ghetto. They could become anything they chose to be.

Some of them have excelled—not enough, but some. Of those, a few have also returned to the community and poured their love and commitment into helping other boys and girls become successful.

I'm glad Harold Adams titled the program Second Chance, because that's exactly what it was—a second opportunity for those kids to move out of the at-risk classification and become leaders and examples.

Shawn was one of those kids who benefited. In other chapters, I tell you about additional successful students. I highlight Shawn here because his rapid progress encouraged me to pour myself into the program. When I started with the Second Chance Program, I didn't know if I could pull it off. Shawn was one of the first to prove that the program worked.

Although he lived in a tough situation, I also saw that he wasn't afraid of discipline and he respected those who wouldn't allow him to get away with negative behavior. I never received a disrespectful response or heard a resentful reply from him. And several times, I had to really come down hard on him.

Children want discipline and guidance. They want to be loved. All children need someone to be crazy about them.

One day, perhaps three months after he had started in our Saturday morning classes, Shawn stared right into my eyes and said, "I'm going to change. I'm going to make a difference. I'm going to be the first person in my family to graduate from college."

I believed him.

Shawn graduated from Cheyney in 2001, and that was one of the most exciting days of his grandmother's life. His family was proud that he returned to the inner city to give back to the community. He coaches at our local community center in the Francisville section of Philadelphia, and he mentors young people. He has become recognized as a specialist in social service and behavior modification.

Shawn visits schools regularly to speak about his life and how important it is for students to respect themselves and their teachers. He also pushes the children to plan to go to college. "You can be successful. You can go to college. You can do great things and you can come back and help this community," he says. "You can be me because I was once you."

After Shawn tells them about his difficult childhood and successful turnaround, many of them believe they can do it, too.

Influence through discipline is a major factor in the education and edification of children. Discipline—when properly applied—is a form of love. Parents need to be willing to discipline their children early in life. I often say to parents, "The message you give to your children is the message they will take to the world." If your children feel loved, they will reach out to others with the same kind of love, compassion, and concern.

Our children must learn early—the earlier the better—that they have freedom to make choices but they don't have freedom from the consequences. Too often they want to choose their actions, but they don't want to face the results of those choices.

Accepting consequences is what self-control and discipline teach. Success in life isn't only about getting what we want, but it's also about caring for other people. As I point out later, part of discipline is also learning to give back. Through discipline we learn to make sacrifices.

It doesn't matter what we focus on—it could be a diet or learning to play the violin. The positive results come through effort—directed effort—that is, through discipline.

As I've thought about the chess program, I think the reason it appeals to children is that it demands self-control. For some of those students, it's the first time they've learned exactly what that term means. Chess gives them structure and it removes chaos. The room must be quiet and even the observers have to be respectful and disciplined. They don't consciously reason that way, but on an unconscious level, I'm convinced they truly want parameters, structure, and order. They yearn for it even if they don't say so.

The most valuable lesson they learn from chess, or from anything that requires discipline, is that the most difficult things in their early lives prepare them for the obstacles they will face later on. They may not always realize it at the time, but those who demand the highest standards and thus make life difficult for them today are trying to make life a little easier when they become adults. Those children who choose to give in to their wants, desires, and easy paths are truly setting themselves up for failure. I think of the spoiled children who come into our schools. Some have never learned the word *no* and it's painful for them to realize they can't do whatever they want whenever they want. But once they learn, they're always happier than they were before. They realize someone loved them enough to set limits for them.

Some parents see so much pain and violence around them, they want to protect their children. In their desire to help, they withhold discipline or try to bribe their children. What they don't grasp is that they actually make it harder on the children. They're not protecting them. In fact, by withholding firm discipline, they are not preparing their children for the real world.

I read an article about Mike Tyson, the former heavyweight champion. During his career, he earned 400 million dollars. The article said he had filed for bankruptcy. He never learned how to handle money—that is, he didn't learn self-control. He also surrounded himself with the wrong people. He never had the opportunity to receive the influence of the right kind of discipline. He has now paid the price. The Mike Tysons of the world don't understand that when they receive blessings through their talents and abilities, they need the self-discipline to make those gifts valuable and lasting. I feel sad about Tyson. I wish he had put money into a homeless shelter, a school system that needed it, or a community center. He had a marvelous opportunity to develop and make something of himself that would provide a legacy for those who came after him.

He didn't have that kind of self-control. He spent the money freely and partied with it. He spent it on material things and then he lost all of it. It's like the parable of the prodigal son in the Bible. (See Luke 15:11–32.) In the story, the younger son demanded his inheritance, went away, and wasted every cent. While he had money, he had friends. When he no longer had wealth, no one knew him.

This is a sad story, but it is a familiar one for those who refuse the influence of discipline.

6

Healthy Influence

During my high school days, I attended a seminar where a renowned educator was scheduled to give the keynote address. He had acquired prominence in this field and had taught many teachers. In addition, he had written three best-selling books on education reform.

As he hobbled onto the platform, he looked ancient. Although I expected to see some change in his physical appearance through the natural course of aging, this dramatic change shocked me. In addition, his voice was raspy and even with a lapel mike it was difficult to hear him. He came in with a cigarette in his mouth and smoked almost nonstop during his fifty-minute lecture. From time to time, he paused and coughed before he could continue.

A woman sitting next to me whispered, "I used to love to listen to him talk. Now it's painful to listen." She also made a comment that he used to speak with excitement in his voice. "Now it's embarrassing to sit and listen to him." It was sad for me to watch what appeared to be a pitiful old man trying to talk about encouraging and invigorating students.

"What a waste of time," I thought. The information he was

disseminating was sound enough, but I found it painful to listen to him. Just before he finished his torturous lecture, I skimmed through the biographical sketch about him.

He was only fifty-six years old.

Did he have something important to say to us? Yes, he did. Was he able to communicate it? No. He had a great opportunity but he negated his influence by his bad physical condition, which was obviously brought about by unhealthy habits. What should have been one of the most inspiring moments of my life was reduced to a time of distress and disappointment. Sadly, his legacy was tarnished.

It probably seems strange to link health and influence, but they truly belong together. Moreover, to impressionable young people, influence can be greatly compromised by what appears to be a lack of care or concern for self. What the speaker intended to do was motivate us about education; what he actually did was communicate the importance of maintaining a healthy lifestyle.

Of course, there are issues that come with the natural course of aging. There may be little we can do about those things. However, we should not hasten our demise. A few years ago, I became more conscious of my health. By that, I mean not just physical fitness, but also mental fitness. I was becoming concerned about my nutrition, as well as my strength and agility. I wanted a more holistic approach to self-preservation.

It took me a long time before I realized that if I'm not physically strong, I won't be able to help as many people, including myself. When I was in my teens and early twenties, nutrition and fitness didn't mean much because I was young and healthy. As I got older, however, I realized the importance of good health and physical stamina—not from a sense of vanity but that of influence. How could I have a lasting impact on other people if I didn't take care of myself? If I'm lying in a hospital bed after having triple-bypass surgery because I'm not eating right or not exercising, I can't do the things that I want with my life or accomplish my goals.

Former President Bill Clinton battled heart disease. It pains me to think about what would have happened to our country had he become ill during his presidency. He did so much to bring our nation together and to improve opportunities for women and other minorities. If his health had been better—if he had taken better care of himself—he could have had even more influence after he left office. He himself admitted he had not eaten properly or exercised regularly. I'm thankful he survived his heart problem, and I hope all of our leaders realize how their health and lifestyles affect the people they serve.

To decide to take better care of ourselves isn't an easy choice. Too many of us face a physical crisis before we wake up to the fact that *we* are responsible for our health. I'm fortunate in that I didn't have to have a physical problem to get me motivated. But once I realized how out of shape I was and how much I needed more physical stamina and mental acuity, I made changes. Immediately, I decided to exercise on a regular basis. "It has to be a way of life," I said to myself. "This can't be something that I decide to do only when it's convenient."

We don't have to become fanatics—the kind who go to the gym every day and subject themselves to rigid programs at the expense of spending time with their families. I know a few people like that. They have robust, muscular bodies, but they don't really live. They base their whole lives on their exercise programs. That's not what I mean. We must have a proper balance. *We take care of our bodies and do those things needed to live better; we don't live to do those things.* Our bodies (and our minds) need exercise and movement. Lying on a couch and munching potato chips is not really living.

Instead, people of influence should be those who ask themselves, "What did I do to improve myself *today*? Am I eating properly? Am I lowering my cholesterol and my fats? Am I making sure I'm eating a good number of healthy calories? Am I drinking plenty of water?"

The people who have been most successful in their careers and who have had the strongest influence on me have been those who have been conscious of their health. They have been models of fitness for me. Their success in this area communicates discipline and self-control in a visual way. That speaks loudly without the utterance of a word. I know that mental and physical improvement gets me in better shape—and keeps me in better shape—to focus on my job each day.

Fitness makes us better teachers, preachers, counselors, social workers, writers, nurses, doctors, attorneys, or any other profession. Children in a classroom respond better to a vigorous, mobile teacher who covers the entire classroom with his or her energy than to a sluggish authoritarian who constantly dictates from behind a desk. A preacher who is vibrant, and filled with clarity and expressiveness, holds the rapt attention of his or her congregants. A fit health-care worker inspires patients to submit to a better lifestyle or dedicate themselves to swifter rehabilitation.

I am a Christian, but obviously this advice would hold true if I were a Jew or a Muslim. In several places, the Bible points out that my body is a temple, as in Romans 12:1 and 1 Corinthians 3:16–17; 6:19–20. I believe that my body belongs to God and I serve God by taking care of my body. This means I must practice being a good steward of this physical house by actively regarding what I eat and do to maintain good physical health. I don't worship my body. I worship God by caring for my body.

My coauthor, Cec Murphey, who is in excellent physical condition and runs every day, cites these words that changed his life: "So whether you eat or drink or whatever you do, do it all for the glory of God."[4]

---

4. 1 Corinthians 10:31, New International Version.

The way we take care of ourselves sends messages to those around us. If we have a positive attitude toward taking care of ourselves, we send out a positive message—call it vibes or sensations—that can affect others.

If we're positive, it makes everything around us appear to be more positive and benevolent. We're also more excited as we go about our daily routine. We know we're taking care of ourselves and that we're showing God that we love Him enough that we're making sacrifices to ensure that our bodies are able to serve Him and His children.

When I went to college in 1982, I was thin. I weighed about 150 pounds and was almost six feet tall. I realized how small I really was when I tried out for the football team. I didn't make the team at East Stroudsburg University in Pennsylvania, of course. It was more than my size—I needed to be stronger and healthier.

In the early part of my freshman year of college, I first heard the statement that college students put on fifteen pounds their first year—"the freshman fifteen." There were some who eventually became believers of that statement; initially, however, we laughed about it. There is solid research that proves it's a fact. Because of poor diet and lack of exercise, many students put the weight on *and* they put it on quickly. They're not aware of it, but they're setting themselves up for serious health problems in the decades ahead.

Researchers say students have become more sedentary; that is, they sit more. They go to the cafeteria for buffet breakfast, lunch, and dinner and end up eating more than usual; they're not moving as much; and many don't get enough sleep. Computer games have replaced the old Frisbee toss that kept many of us active between classes.

Sleep deprivation trips up many students—as it does many adults. Thousands of young people fight sleep by trying to overcome their dependence on it. Some still try to ignore their own needs by overcommitting themselves to more work or additional extracurricular activities. They don't realize that the body repairs itself from daily wear during those nocturnal hours. Depriving ourselves of needed sleep means the repair work doesn't get finished. *If we deprive ourselves of sleep long enough, we suffer physical consequences.* This situation may well be tied to the mismanagement or misappropriation of time. When we don't accomplish all we should during the course of a day, we attempt to borrow from our time of slumber. Writing down a daily schedule may give us a better idea of how we should plan and prioritize our daily activities. Or we may need to admit that we can't condense thirty hours of activities into a twenty-four-hour day.

Most experts say that adults need at least seven hours of sleep a night. Too many people go into sleep-deprivation mode by pushing themselves and depending on artificial stimulants such as caffeine products. The worst thing about sleep deprivation is that we're not at our best when we're not physically rested. We tend to be more irritable. We lose our concentration. We've also learned through research that sleep-deprived people have more accidents. If we see ourselves as others do—impatient, tired, and unfocused—how effective is our influence on them?

Even when we're exercising, sleep is an important component because we need to be well rested to gain the maximum benefit. Our bodies prepare for more stress when we sleep. We want to be the best, not just in our battles in the gym but also in our battles at work, in the church, and in the community. If we're committed to serving others and to becoming positive influences, we will get sufficient sleep, eat nutritiously, and get plenty of exercise.

If we truly want to influence others, we'll work toward being as healthy as we can be. When we're healthy, we're alert, active, and energetic enough to fight and win our daily battles.

*   *   *

As I wrote above, I was a small guy in college and decided to work out regularly to become stronger and more physically fit. Steroids were not an option for me. Old-fashioned hard work was what I chose. I remained fairly well self-disciplined with my physical regimen during college and after I graduated. I did make some improvements; however, some days I didn't exercise. I had great excuses for not hitting the gym. Every day I didn't get physically active seemed to make it easier to miss it again the next day.

Once I hit my thirties, I realized that I was no longer the guy who was concerned about his lack of weight and was confronted by the fact that I had a different battle: I had to fight gaining too much weight. The combination of a slipping level of self-discipline, married life, good eating, and getting older was catching up with me. We have to realize that, as we age, our bodies burn calories at a different, slower rate. Realizing this may help us ward off problems before they get to what seems insurmountable levels.

Several things prompted me to get into a disciplined program. My own body was a big factor. I always have to start with myself because it would be hypocritical to determine a course for others without proper self-examination. Looking around, I also saw that many of my students were overweight, unhealthy, and without energy. I point this out because I had gained weight and muscle and was a grown man, and yet some twelve-year-old students in our inner-city school weighed more than I did. That was a serious issue.

It is one thing to gain weight as we age; it is quite another to be an obese child because of overeating or lack of exercise. I kept thinking that we had to do something to help them. I knew that just telling them to diet or to add information about exercise during the normal school day wouldn't work. They wouldn't know how to begin a program, they wouldn't always have the support, and they possibly wouldn't have the right food at home.

We had to help them by taking a different approach. We started a summer program where students were enriched in literacy and mathematics. We also took them to visit museums and other cultural events. As part of that program, we took walks—at least a mile—every day. We also went to the gymnasium for a 45-minute workout in which there were varying degrees of participation. The teachers involved modeled commitment to the regimen. I wish I could say it made a lasting difference on the students (I am not sure I can), but it helped, and it was developing an awareness. During our trips, I'd say a few words about nutrition and wellness. If I couldn't reap a harvest, at least I could plant a few seeds.

We frequently talked to the students about nutrition in the summer program and throughout the school year. We brought in nutritious foods for the students to taste so that they'd know what they were. Many students wouldn't try a healthful food because it was new to them, and they would say something such as, "I don't like Brussels sprouts." They meant they had never tasted them. We wanted to change their lifestyles and their eating habits.

I became quite concerned when, in 2003, the Centers for Disease Control and Prevention (CDC) raised the alarm over the large number of children and teens who had been diagnosed with adult onset (or Type II) diabetes—something that had been unheard of a decade earlier. That meant children—our children—were being diagnosed with serious problems that had always been adult physical ailments. Those same children are encountering the serious side effects of people thirty to forty years older, such as kidney problems and heart disease.

Here's something else that's disturbing. A lead story in *USA*

Today bore this headline: YOUR APPEARANCE, GOOD OR BAD, CAN AFFECT THE SIZE OF YOUR PAYCHECK.[5]

The big surprise to me was that it appeared in the Money section—the business part of the paper. I would have expected the editors to put the article in the section called Life.

Here's one part of the article:

> Another area where employees feel an impact is their weight. A study done in part by New York University sociologist Dalton Conley found that an increase in a woman's body mass results in a decrease in her family income and her job prestige. . . .
>
> As health care costs climb and national attention turns to the problem of obesity in the USA, overweight workers are feeling pressure to slim down. The latest data from the National Center for Health Statistics show that 30% of U.S. adults age 20 and older (more than 60 million people) are obese.

The article points out that the Borgata Hotel Casino & Spa prohibits bartenders and cocktail waitresses from gaining more than 7 percent of their body weight from the time they begin weigh-ins. "That means a 125-pound woman couldn't gain more than 8.75 pounds.

"Those who do gain more receive a 90-day unpaid suspension, and after that may be fired. . . ." [6]

The article makes other interesting points. It cited lawsuits filed on behalf of overweight people, ". . . but in many cases courts have determined that being obese is not a disability protected by the law."[7]

The article goes on to say:

5. *USA Today*, July 20, 2005, pp. 1B–2B.
6. Ibid., p. 2B.
7. Ibid.

Richard Chaifetz, president of ComPsych, a Chicago-based employee assistance provider, says overweight employees may not be as productive.

More than 20% of very overweight employees have low morale, almost twice that of employees of healthy weights, according to a June survey by ComPsych. The survey was based on a poll of more than 1,000 client organizations.[8]

One final comment from the same article: Harrah's Entertainment faced a lawsuit for requiring women to wear makeup. They rescinded the ruling, but spokesman David Stow said, "Our main goal is to ensure all our employees have a professional and well-groomed appearance when they come into contact with the public."[9]

Doesn't that say a great deal about health and appearance in our world?

If we were going to help, we had to change our students' lifestyles. I knew that the way I lived would influence them, even if unconsciously. If I wanted them to learn to eat right, I had to set the example and eat right myself. Immediately, my eating habits improved.

Shortly after I became the principal at Reynolds School, I banned junk food. I would not allow students to bring junk food such as potato chips or candy bars to school. Many of our children came to school with nothing but fattening, empty-calorie foods for breakfast. It wasn't unusual to see students come to school with grocery bags stuffed with sweets and potato chips.

It's unfortunate, but many of the urban corner stores frequented by our young people sell processed, prepackaged, high-calorie, nutrition-free "food." Those stores are accessible to

8. Ibid.
9. Ibid.

children who don't have the opportunity to leave the community or purchase healthy snacks, such as apples or a bunch of grapes. Students were filling their stomachs with cookies, candies, and chips of different flavors. Something radical had to be done. All of our students were eligible for the government's free breakfast and lunch program and we urged them to eat at school.

The teachers supported my ban. I didn't know how parents would feel but I was prepared to take a stand. After I explained to them what we were doing and why, the parents understood and approved of our actions. Some of the kids who had previously brought junk food to school told me they hadn't known it was unhealthy. They appreciated that the teachers cared about their health.

If students wanted to bring in fruit, juice, milk, or healthy snacks, we had no problem with that. "No Doritos and sodas," I said, and they knew we meant it.

We didn't allow them to drink anything at school except water, juice, and milk. That was something on which we would not waver. In addition, we wouldn't allow them to drink anything with sugar in the morning. We might not be able to change their lives entirely, but we had to start someplace. We tried to teach and to influence them the best we could during the hours they were in our care.

Before I left Vaux Middle School, our family center received a grant to build a small fitness center inside the large gymnasium at the school, but it was to be more than simply another school gym. Teachers and members of the community designed and planned for its use. Some of the parents still use it today.

That's the place where I decided to work out regularly. I could have gone to another gym, one that was more convenient, but I wanted the children to know I was in the fight with them, that I believed in exercise, and that I was trying to keep my body in shape. Some days I didn't feel like working out, but I did it anyway. I was doing that for myself but also for the children. I realized that the best way to demonstrate the importance of exercise and good health to the students was to embrace them myself.

One day, I said to a group of young students who were standing around outside the school building, "I'm going in to the gym to play for a while. Anyone want to work out?"

A half-dozen followed me. After that day, others joined us. Before long, most of the children knew that if my car was parked outside the gym, I was inside the fitness center working out or shooting baskets. Many of our students now work out regularly.

Occasionally when I go to the gym by myself, I don't see anyone around. I begin working out and before long I hear someone tap at the window. Or my cell phone rings and a small voice says, "Come open the door, Mr. EL. I want to come inside and work out."

Whenever I allow students to come inside, l phone their parents to be sure they have permission. I do that because of one experience. One time I allowed a boy to participate. His family didn't have a phone, but he assured me he had his parents' permission.

Later that day, his grandmother got to a phone, called me, and gave me an earful. Somehow she found out he had been in the gym with me but never did any of his chores at home before he left. I apologized.

That was the last time I allowed any student to work out in the gym without permission. (I've never had a parent refuse permission, but my calling to ask is another important lesson to teach the kids—get permission and keep your parents involved in your life.)

How could I refuse young people who want to improve themselves? That was my plan all along. Instead of talking to them constantly about fitness, I decided to influence them into wanting to become fit by being an example. I believed that would be a stronger incentive. I never realized it would require so much work on my part—being faithful and self-disciplined—but I've benefited tremendously. I'm in better shape at the age of forty than I was at thirty.

Because I'm in shape, I now have a voice to help them. Some of them want to lose weight, but they can't afford the Atkins program, South Beach Diet, or NutriSystem so they decide to go on the Thomas-EL plan. My plan is easy—it includes lots of movement—as much movement as possible. I encourage them to do plenty of walking. I urge them not to ride in cars on short trips. "Walk to the store with your friends," I say. "Walk to school. Drink plenty of water. Eat less junk food."

Some of my former students who are now in high school or college still come in and do some light work with dumbbells and a few other resistance exercises to increase their lean muscle mass. They also serve as examples to the younger ones.

The program is working—though not fast enough. Still, I'm delighted about every child who comes. Some students have been able to lose weight. They are usually the ones who wanted to compete in high school athletics, so they got into shape.

We also learned—as we assumed all along—that those who exercised regularly became better students. Exercise teaches them self-discipline and it impacts their studies.

I think of Rodney Murray, who was a large and overweight fourth-grader when I met him during my first year at Reynolds. He was also a student with a high number of suspensions, probably ten a year, because of fights and arguments. While a student at Reynolds, he had a strong interest in sports but he could never compete at a high level because of his weight. Rodney decided he wanted to work out, get into a good exercise program, move more, and eat better.

By the time he entered eighth grade, he had reduced those suspensions to one or two per year. He had changed. Rodney learned chess and became good at it. He defeated my brother

George several times, so he was quite happy with his game. He lost at least twenty pounds and became an active basketball player. He lifted weights with us, too. I marveled at the change in him. His father was incarcerated and his grandmother was raising him. He could so easily have been another inner-city dropout.

Rodney goes to church and is actively involved. He received an award at his eighth-grade graduation for his service to the school and community. He made a big turnaround and we all applauded him.

In the spring of 2004, he wanted to enroll at Dobbins High School, and he told me he wanted to play basketball and football. He applied, but he wasn't accepted—it's not an easy school to get into. Dobbins is a vocational-technical high school where students are able to learn a trade and prepare for college. They offer training in a variety of subjects such as computers and business.

Rodney, almost in tears at the end of the school year, told me how disappointed he was about not getting accepted at Dobbins. I knew that young man's heart and we weren't going to drop it. "I'll see what I can do," I told him.

I called Charles Whiting, the principal, and he was out, but I left him a message. An hour later he called back. He said he had received the message about Rodney Murray. He had the boy's records in front of him and said, "He had a high number of suspensions in the past, but I noticed this year he's reduced them. He had only two this past year."

We talked several minutes and I did everything I could to help him realize that Rodney could be an asset.

"I'm interested in admitting Rodney," Charles said, "but you'll have to bring him in so the three of us can meet together."

I called Rodney at home. "The principal wants to meet with you if you're willing to come in and talk with him."

"I'm willing to go," he said, "but you'll go with me, won't you?"

"Yes, I'll go with you, and this is what you need to do. Get a decent outfit. You don't have to get dressed up but I want you to wear something clean and presentable." I had expected Rodney to wear jeans and a T-shirt. "At least wear a shirt that has a collar—a polo shirt or something like that."

"Okay, Mr. EL," he said.

Two days later, I went to pick him up for the interview. Rodney had put on a dress shirt that was clean and neatly pressed. I smiled when I looked at his feet. He had on a pair of shoes that exactly matched the shoes that I wore.

"Nice shoes, too," I said.

He laughed. "They ought to be. You gave them to me."

I had forgotten that. Whenever I buy new shoes, I always bring in some of my older ones for the young men who might need them for church or other functions. I'm not the only one— many of the teachers at our school donate clothing to the students.

Rodney reminded me that when he graduated from eighth grade, he had needed a pair of good shoes, so he grabbed a pair out of my office that I had put out for students who wanted them. He was wearing those same shoes and had taken good care of them.

I shook my head as I thought of the transformation of that boy. Three years earlier, he wouldn't have cared how he looked and would probably have come out in a T-shirt and sneakers. I was proud of the change in him. He was now exercising regularly and really cared about his appearance.

I want to make it clear that I was only one person of influence in Rodney's life. He had great teachers who influenced him, encouraged him, and took time with him. I particularly know of the powerful influence of Mr. Mordecai, who struggled to get Rodney to be more responsible for his actions. I smile when I think about Mrs. Hensford, Mrs. Gay, Ms. Debrow, and Ms. Krovetz. Those teachers often fought with Rodney, but they also talked with him, and even spent their own money to help him.

When we walked into Charles Whiting's office, I wish I had a photograph of the surprised look on that man's face. It was probably one of the first times a student had walked into his office to meet him dressed as nicely as Rodney.

After I introduced him, Charles Whiting stared right at Rodney and asked, "Do you want to come here to Dobbins?"

"Yes."

"Why do you want to come here?"

"I want more for my life. I've had a lot of adults who have had an impact on me and I want to help other people," he said.

Earlier, Rodney's grandmother had told him that this would be one of the most important moments in his life. "If he accepts you," she'd said, "your future will be different."

Rodney wanted to go on to college, which was one of the reasons he wanted to attend Dobbins. Although it's a trade school, many of their graduates go on to college.

"Son, I'd be a fool not to let you be a part of my school the way you've presented yourself. You have an excellent attitude."

As Rodney and I walked back to my car, I said, "I'm going to be honest with you. We've done a lot of things together, we've fought, we've cried, and had a lot of differences, but today you've made me proud of you and what you've done with yourself. I'm proud of you because that principal was impressed. And not only did it make you look good, but you made me look good."

As Rodney and I drove along, I thought about the power of influence. I started by wanting Rodney to improve his behavior and academics. We pushed him to get in shape, to lose weight, and to be healthy. He had done all that. I thought of his teachers and everyone who had tried to help him. Our efforts had paid off. But not well enough.

Rodney has since had some setbacks and problems, but I still think he can make it. He wasn't prepared for the challenges at Dobbins. I hadn't prepared him properly for a magnet high school and I accept responsibility for that. Rodney recently called me and expressed his sadness about ruining his opportunity there. "Learn from that experience," I told him, "and use it to improve your focus."

I want to see great things happen in his life—and so do all the other teachers who have worked with him in the past. We will continue to support him in the future.

Not every child turns out well. Some fall by the wayside, but enough stay on track so we know we can make a difference. I think of a number of the boys and girls who had gone through our schools during my years at Reynolds and Vaux. Some of them have changed. Some have become hardworking, successful people. The influence won't end there, because influence is immortal. Because they have been motivated, they will motivate others, who can help change more lives, and the influence continues.

When we have those bad days in our schools—and we have many of them—I find it encouraging and comforting to think of former students I mention in this book. Their success keeps us going. They prove to us, to themselves, and to the world that our influence *is* immortal.

7

The Influence of Grooming

By now, most people know something about the broken window theory. In 1982, James Q. Wilson and George Kelling developed the theory to explain how neighborhoods deteriorate. They studied urban decay to find out why some neighborhoods escaped the ravages of the inner city while others right next door—with the same demographics and economic makeup—would become a hellhole that the police despised entering.

The researchers conducted a test. They parked a Jaguar in the South Bronx in New York. They hid and watched to see what would happen. They left the car parked there for four days. No one touched the car.

On the fifth day, the researchers broke one side window. Within four hours, the car had been stripped, turned upside down, and torched. From there, the two men went on to develop what has become popularized as the broken window theory.

To summarize, the theory works this way: A window gets broken at an apartment building, but no one repairs it. Before long, something else on the outside of the apartment gets broken and that isn't taken care of. Graffiti starts to appear. More and more damage accumulates. Evidence of decay appears, such as more broken windows, accumulated trash, and deteriorated building exteriors. People who live and work in the area feel more vulnerable and begin to withdraw. They do nothing to stop the physical signs of deterioration. They become less willing to intervene to maintain public order, such as attempting to break up groups of rowdy teens who loiter or fight on street corners. Tenants move out and crime moves in.

The broken window theory applies to many areas of life. In the 1980s, the New York Transit Authority decided to clean up the subways in the city, and they worked on this same theory. They began by getting rid of graffiti, even though critics insisted they should focus on more pressing issues.

Graffiti, said the new Transit Authority Director David Gunn, was symptomatic of the collapse of the system. He started with seven trains that connect Manhattan with Queens. The projects went on from 1984 until 1990. Each night crews cleaned the graffiti off the cars. If a car came in with graffiti, workers cleaned it before sending it back into service.

Kids made a three-day job out of painting a car. The first night, they sneaked into the train yards in Harlem and painted the car white. The second night they returned when the paint was dry and outlined their drawings. The third night they added color.

The Transit Authority allowed the young people to paint the cars, but they cleaned them before the trains went back on the track. The graffiti artists finally stopped painting.

To begin the second stage of reform, authorities began to arrest people who didn't put tokens into the turnstiles. They estimated that 170,000 people a day used public transportation without paying.

The point of the successful project was that the broken window is the tip-off. If the window remains broken, worse things follow. If people repair the window immediately, there tends to be no deterioration in the community.[10] If neglected, things continually get worse.

Although I never related my work experiences to the concept of the broken window theory, I believe this principle applies to schools and offices, too.

This concept applies to the matter of grooming and personal appearance. The way we appear to others tells them a great deal about us—or at least it leaves a strong impression. What they see may not be who we really are, but if we put them off by their first impression of us, how will they find out who we are?

If I have a teacher apply for a job and he has dirty fingernails, unpressed pants, and looks as if he has no interest in personal hygiene, why would I want him in our school?

If teachers are careless about their appearance, they are tacitly giving students permission to be careless. If the boss wears casual clothes, soon everyone wears casual clothing. It's not just the clothing that I want to emphasize, but the attitude that goes along with the clothes.

Casual is casual. The more casual those in leadership positions become, the more they signal to those they serve that it's all right to look informal and to be careless in their attitude. Our attitude affects the quality of our work.

Let's look at it another way. Behaviorists tell us—more than we want to hear—that everything we do and say reflects who we are. Even though we're unaware, the words and gestures we use, the clothes we wear, our hairstyles, the cars we drive, and the colors we choose—all of them tell others about who we are.

It's not important for children to have expensive clothes, but the way they wear them and the manner in which they present themselves tells the world about who they are.

---

10. For a fuller discussion, see Malcolm Gladwell, *The Tipping Point: How Little Things Can Make a Big Difference* (Little, Brown, 2000), pp. 141–146).

Cecil Murphey, who was a pastor for fourteen years, told me that when he went to his second church, the secretary chewed gum constantly and wore clothing that could have been washed and ironed more often. She couldn't understand that she was the first person people saw when they visited the office. Her appearance left an impression—and a wrong one.

He fired her within a short time. After that, a number of members of the congregation admitted, "We were embarrassed by the way she looked."

He shook his head because the secretary had been hired by his predecessor and had worked there for four years before he arrived.

How we appear to others *is* important. As the saying goes, we never get a second chance to make a first impression. Not only is it important for us as adults to be well groomed, but the way we appear also influences others so they know how to dress. If we come across as indifferent about our clothes, we influence others to say, "It doesn't matter."

Physical appearance is important in the professional environment, even though we live in a casually attired culture. Research and experience teach us that those who maintain a professional appearance are more likely to be promoted. They simply *look* professional. If they look professional, there's a strong chance they *are* professional.

We live in a world where women now show more of their bodies, and this isn't a rant or a diatribe on morality. I object to clothes that expose too much cleavage, private parts, the midriff, and undergarments because they're not professional looking. I also believe that women at work should show themselves in the best, most professional way. Much of the media, dominated by men, portray women in a negative way on a daily basis.

Women present a more positive presence when they wear skirts, dresses, suits, or pantsuits that cover their body and don't expose too much. Certain parts of the body should be viewed by us, our spouses, or our significant others only. The over-exposure of the body isn't professional, it's not positive, and it's one reason many people—men and women—don't survive in professional leadership positions.

Think of it from the employee's perspective. They find it difficult to respect leaders who do not command respect with their appearance. Here's a simple principle: *If they don't look like leaders, they can't lead, no matter how much ability they have.* That's more covert than overt, but it's a lesson I hope men and women will heed.

One of the things I try to impress on our students, especially the older ones who graduate from high school and plan to prepare for college interviews, is "Always look your best." Colleges want young people who are going to bring something positive to their school. They don't want to take away from students' creativity, but they want them to understand that they send a message by the way they dress.

This is also important information for teachers and principals in schools. We know from extensive research that administrators and teachers who dress more professionally have fewer discipline problems. For example, the *Journal of Family and Consumer Sciences Education* studied the perception of teaching effectiveness as it is defined by the way teachers dress. They found that when teachers wear traditional business attire, their students view them as being professional, responsible, and competent. Traditional business attire indicates a more professional image for both males and females.

They went on to say that how the teacher's image is projected to the students, parents, and general public affects how professional the teacher is viewed as being.

As a matter of principle and common sense, I believe that all administrators should be dressed professionally every day, everywhere. As is the principal, so is the school. No principal should feel that he or she is above the staff or students in matters relating to perception and appearance. Arrogance is the Achilles' heel of the administrator. An excellent principal is an excellent teacher. If we are to send the correct nonverbal messages, we must be clean in our behavior, speech, and dress. Our clothing and shoes should be kept in good condition.

We must bear in mind that not only are our children and parents learning, but so are our coworkers, no matter what our occupation. As I stated in the last chapter, we should be in good physical condition. We are models for those we serve and this is a stressful business. If we don't take care of ourselves, how can we serve the good of others?

Students are less likely to approach principals and teachers disrespectfully if they're dressed professionally. It's simply a matter of perception.

When we visit hospitals, we have no trouble determining who are the doctors or nurses. When we come to a school, we should be able to recognize the professionals as well. That is done through our appearance and the way we dress.

I want children to see me and to think, "That's how I should look." I want to be their role model—and I am, whether I like it or not. Children respond to the models they see each day. We are their examples and they learn more from watching us than they do from listening to us. We need to understand that the nonverbal messages we transmit are important and powerful. Those messages come through appearance.

Several years ago, USA Today published a major story on school administrators who had problems with the attire that a few teachers felt was appropriate for school. Some of the items included in the controversy were flip-flops, tattoos, low-rise jeans, short miniskirts, and bellybutton rings. Numerous administrators expressed shock and amazement at what they saw. In response to that article, many administrators have implemented dress codes in their schools. A large number of schools have attempted to help new teachers make the transition from the way they dressed as college students so that they can look like and be professional role models. I have had similar discussions with many of the teachers I have worked with. Few have been opposed to stricter dress codes for adults. We all believe in freedom of expression, but we also need to recognize that students look to teachers for leadership and guidance on how to dress.

There's a major move to increase standardization of what educators wear in the schools nationwide. Many educators are convinced that our students are influenced by the way we, their leaders, dress. Their first models of professionalism come from the adults, parents and teachers, who are the most prominent in their daily lives.

If we come to work dressed as professionals, not only will we be respected as professionals, but I also believe the public's perception of our value will increase. I firmly believe there is a strong correlation between our attitudes toward professional dress and our struggle to receive adequate compensation.

If we are not taken seriously, it is because we don't treat our profession as if it's important enough for us to dress appropriately. Professional dress is an important issue in the entire service industry. When we represent an industry or profession, we need to dress so that we appropriately reflect our organization. We're not only representing ourselves, but also standing with thousands of people in the same profession. Whether we like it or not, we are symbols of our individual professions—or what they should be. If we want to be respected, we need to look like people who deserve respect.

I frequently challenge students in high school and college to modify the way they dress. Perhaps not every day, but they should at least be prepared to appear in a professional outfit when it's appropriate.

"If you go to meet Bill Gates, you can't wear a pair of jeans and a T-shirt," I tell them. "Bill Gates may have on that type of outfit but that man is worth billions of dollars. If you're meeting with him to ask for his support or funding of a project, you have to impress him and to look like a person who deserves respect. Before he hears a word from your mouth, he will see what you're wearing. Most people are going to look at you, and when they hear your message, they also want to look at the package of the presentation—that's you."

I tell my children often that being different is a luxury that most people can't afford. "Your lives are like fine diamonds, but first you have to be sanded and rubbed firmly. You'll get hurt in the process. You may fall down, but you need to get back up by yourself. You have to get smoothed around all the sharp edges before you become that expensive diamond."

I want the young people I influence to be flexible enough to travel comfortably on different paths before they discover their own way. They must be willing to do whatever it takes to become successful. "With flexibility comes longevity," is the way I say it. Of course, I don't refer to making shady deals or committing illegal acts, but I mean a willingness to bend and to be molded, to have a teachable spirit, and to become their very best.

In the corporate world, casual office dress has become quite popular, but recently I've read that some companies have started to mandate professional dress because they've seen that the casual appearance has led to less productivity. They've found that employees have higher self-esteem when they dress neat and clean, and look professional.

This issue of proper dress warrants that I talk about school uniforms. This has become a national issue. Many schools, especially the charter schools, have gone to mandatory uniform dress. For many inner cities, it's mandatory that students wear uniforms. I believe strongly in them and believe they do four positive things. Wearing student uniforms:

1. Decreases gang activity and substance abuse.
2. Reduces behavioral problems.
3. Increases attendance.
4. Increases academic achievement.

Some experts disagree with my thoughts on uniforms but few of them have ever been administrators or teachers in a school. "Poll the educators in your community," I tell those experts, "and ask *them* about their views on uniforms." Principals around the country cite reductions in negative behavior such as teasing about name-brand clothing. They have also cited less fighting after requiring uniforms.

There is definitely a reduction in the number of students who appear in school inappropriately dressed. I spoke with a principal in a suburban school district who found a student journal detailing every outfit the writer had worn for the entire month. The student was deeply concerned because she was afraid she would have to wear the same outfit twice in the same thirty-day period. That is the type of data that researchers probably don't receive but we educators battle with every day.

Because I believe in uniforms, I decided to require them when I arrived at Reynolds in 1999. In addition to the four things mentioned above, I also pointed out to parents, "If we have intruders in our building, we immediately recognize them because they don't wear our uniform."

Parents have become overwhelmingly supportive. Although a few parents continue to send their children to school without a uniform, most of the children wear the uniform every day.

I saw a television news story about an adult male who went into a high school and fondled several female students. He was able to blend in with the students because he appeared to be young. The school security personnel saw the man on one of their video cameras but he was able to escape. After the event, the officials said they couldn't understand how that man was able to blend in with the students so easily. I knew why. No one wore uniforms. He looked like many of the others who walked the hallways, and the girls he touched probably assumed he was another student.

We realized quite early after we required school uniforms that there was another major benefit to this change of dress. When we took field trips, such as to the zoo, all children were required to wear uniforms. No matter how well we trained them, a few students would always get lost. When they wore uniforms, it made it easy to identify them. Instead of spending a lot of energy trying to remember what the lost students wore to school, we only had to show security personnel one child in a uniform.

I often say to people who argue against uniforms, "Why do you think they are worn in the military? Why do police officers wear uniforms? Or firefighters? Why do Boy Scouts and Girl Scouts have uniforms?"

Uniforms send a strong message of unity and discipline.

One final point: I believe uniforms can inspire pride among students. When they wear uniforms, even though they sometimes complain, our young people feel they *belong* to a community. They also realize that their behavior in public is a reflection of the school.

We can influence our children and colleagues to achieve at the highest levels. However, they must first visualize us as a picture of success.

8

The Influence of Exposure

In February 2003, I arranged a visit to the state of Vermont for fifteen students and four chaperones. The impetus behind the trip was actually an elderly white gentleman from Philadelphia who, in 2002, read about our school and our chess team in the newspaper. As a result, he sent me a letter that read, "My son's a principal in Vermont. His name is Michael Freed-Thall and he started a chess program in his school. They have not yet achieved the status of your school's team, but I think it would be good for you two men to meet."

He mentioned that Michael had grown up in North Philadelphia. Of course, the demographics had changed since Michael left. At the time he was growing up, that section of the city was an integrated neighborhood with a mixture of white and black residents; now it's predominantly black.

"After reading and hearing about your students," he said, "I think it would be a wonderful way to establish a strong relationship. Is it okay for me to give your number to my son?"

I called him and said, "Okay, fine. Yes, have him call me."

I discovered that Michael's school, Folsom Educational Center, was located in South Hero, Vermont, a small city near Burlington.

In many ways, Vermont seemed so far away from Reynolds. He called and we chatted for a few minutes. When I inquired about his school and city, he said, "It's cold here all the time, and we don't have many minorities. Our students would definitely benefit from developing a relationship with your students."

I also thought it would be an excellent idea for our all-minority urban school to correspond with students from an all-white suburban one. As one of the first steps toward building a relationship, Michael and I developed a pen-pal system between our schools. Before long, students from various classes started to write to each other. A fifth-grade class became highly enthusiastic about the idea and so did two seventh-grade classes.

Michael and I talked by phone regularly. One time he said casually, "Why don't we have some of our kids meet?"

I was both surprised and excited by the prospect of such an endeavor. We began to discuss all the logistical problems involved, but we especially emphasized the tremendous opportunities for exchange and exposure. Excitedly, I said, "Why don't I bring some of our kids to Vermont?" Our chess players were accustomed to flying to chess matches in various cities across the country so it would not be a problem for the students on the chess team.

Michael, in his careful and reasonable tone, cautioned, "Vermont isn't a diverse state and our city isn't either."

"I understand, but our students need to get out of their comfort zone," I immediately countered. "If they're going to change the world, they need to get out and *see* the world."

I must interject here the wonderful complementary relationship between Michael and me. Though we both must exercise our leadership and interpersonal skills by virtue of our jobs, his style is quiet, organized, and focused. Mine is gregarious, daring, and ambitious. Michael worked very hard to keep me organized and on task. However, where the children are involved, we are both active advocates for progress.

At Reynolds, I began to discuss the trip to Vermont with the students. Initially, most of them were worried or afraid, but the more we discussed the trip, the more eager they became to visit a different city. I worked with parents, teachers, and members of the community to make the trip a reality. Among those who had been the most active in writing letters to the children in Vermont, we chose fifteen students based on their grades, attendance, and behavior. We decided we didn't want our group to consist of only chess players. Of the fifteen students chosen, about half of them played chess.

We worked out schedules and travel arrangements before we decided to go in February, even though that is generally an extremely cold month in Pennsylvania and even worse in Vermont. The plan was for us to leave Philadelphia on a Sunday and return on Wednesday night of the same week.

Because the students had developed relationships with one another through the mail, we wanted them to visit and discover how different or alike they were once they met in person. The anticipation of students from Reynolds grew as they shared the letters they received, which were quite honest, and even humorous. They discovered differences in their sports interests. Soccer stood out among the Vermont students, while basketball was the dominant sport of choice for students from Philadelphia. Music likewise presented some different tastes. However, students from both cultures had common factors such as blended families, pets, and strong opinions about school. Those likenesses were very comforting for our students, and made them feel more relaxed about meeting their newfound friends.

The more we planned our visit, the more we discovered about that small northeastern state. In addition to establishing new relationships, we discovered that Vermont was the first state to abolish slavery in its state constitution. Our students needed to know that there had been people from other communities and cultures who fought for their ancestors' freedom.

The trip took a great deal of preparation. The Vermont families offered to open up their homes to us, but we opted for staying in a hotel so that the children wouldn't experience too much culture shock at first. Also, I did not want my students to eat all the food in the cabinets of our new friends—and a few of them would have done that because students from Reynolds can eat!

Having our students in one place allowed us to immediately attend to any unforeseen problems. We had to be sure there would be responsible chaperones in place all the time.

Another part of the intense groundwork consisted of helping the parents and children select the right kind of clothes to pack. We had to make sure our students had gloves, hats, and warm clothes. Of course, some students arrived without those items, but we were prepared and purchased extras. But more important, we observed that the students shared clothes with each other. That kind of friendly exchange impressed me more than anything.

The big day finally arrived. On February 16, 2003, we were ready to "seek out new life and new civilizations," as they used to say on *Star Trek*. Parents, friends, and well-wishers traveled with us to the Thirtieth Street Train Station in Philadelphia to see us off. It was inspiring to see the support they gave to this ambitious project. We boarded the train, settled in, and headed north for Vermont. The train ride was a wonderful experience. For most of the students, it was their first opportunity to travel via Amtrak.

It took approximately twelve hours to get to Vermont. On board, we read, played chess, watched DVD movies, ate, and slept. The most rewarding aspect of the trip for me was to have the opportunity to talk to the children and their parents in an informal setting. I finally had the time and opportunity to get to know them better on a personal level. The children observed the various landscape changes, which were frosted with snow.

When we arrived in Vermont at ten o'clock that evening, the

temperature was thirty degrees below zero—and that didn't include the wind-chill factor. The cold darkness engulfed us like an ice chest. It seemed as if we had pulled into Siberia instead of Vermont. Just before our students walked off the Amtrak train at the station, the conductor told them, "Please make sure you have on a hat and gloves. Don't touch anything metal with your bare hands, because if you do, your hand will be stuck there forever."

Those words scared our kids, and I assured them the conductor meant exactly what he said. As we got off the train, the severe cold shocked them—we officially knew we weren't in Philadelphia anymore.

Michael Freed-Thall was there to greet us. I kidded him by saying, "Is this the best weather you've got?" Inside I was saying, "Maybe I should have considered a June trip." We later heard that we had escaped the biggest snowstorm of the season in Philadelphia.

The next morning, we had a continental breakfast at the hotel, and then the South Hero students arrived by bus and all the students paired off with one another. We boarded our school bus and headed for the Folsom School, which is located on an island consisting of the two small towns of South Hero and Grand Isle.

The people on the island welcomed us with marvelous hospitality, initiated by an assembly program that featured their school's orchestra. Mr. Freed-Thall officially welcomed us and I said a few words in response to the welcome.

After that, our students were released to share classes with their students. In social studies, they created Venn diagrams and discussed differences and likenesses; in mathematics, they completed grade-appropriate work and played math games. After we ate lunch together, students either played chess or helped to create murals. One of our fourth-graders, Kyle Tribble, won first place in the chess tournament hosted by the Folsom

School. That was special because we had seventh-graders competing and several eighth-grade students represented Folsom. The local newspaper published a story highlighting the trip and the connection between our students.

Later in the afternoon, the Philadelphia young ladies wowed the Vermonters with their dazzling jump-rope skills, causing even the young men to try their hand at it; while the females from Vermont gave our young men something to think about on the basketball court.

On Tuesday, our students had the opportunity to visit Lake Champlain, a 600-square-mile body of water that separates Vermont and New York State, named for Samuel de Champlain, the first white man to have seen the lake. He was also the founder of Quebec, Canada. Because of the severe cold, the ice was three feet thick and solid. There were shelters constructed on the lake for Vermont ice fishers. On seeing that, we knew the frozen lake could support a great amount of weight. But no matter what we told our young people or how much we urged them, we couldn't get the Philadelphia students to walk out on the lake.

"I'm not ready to go out on that lake yet," was the common response.

They even watched fishermen drive trucks on the lake, but they still wouldn't go out there. Because we understood their fear, we didn't push them. The trip alone was a big enough cultural leap. Afterward, back in Philadelphia, they excitedly told everyone about seeing trucks drive on the ice.

The trip was a two-way cultural jolt. Our children mingled with people who hadn't been exposed to many African-Americans. Most of them had never seen more than half a dozen black kids in their entire lives.

Before long, our children realized that the Vermont students weren't that different from the people they knew and went to school with: They all liked hip-hop music and wore baggy clothes.

The kids were beginning to recognize many connections between the groups.

It was also a rich and wonderful experience for our children to visit the homes of the Vermont students and teachers. We went out to dinner several times at nice restaurants, one of which printed a special menu commemorating our visit. We were able to see what types of things the Vermont students did in their free time, especially eating at Pizza Putt, where they could play miniature golf.

One experience during the trip that resonated with our students occurred the afternoon we visited the Rokeby Museum in Ferrisburgh. Frederick Douglass and Harriet Tubman had both stayed in that home, which is now a museum. The Rokeby House (as it was called then) was one of the last stops on the Underground Railroad before slaves made it to freedom in Canada. Montreal is only a two-hour drive from Burlington, Vermont, which translates to under a day's walk. Although they close the museum during the winter, they opened it for a few hours just for the benefit of our children. We wanted them to get a feel for the history the Rokeby Museum represented. They read displayed letters written by slave owners in Virginia and other Southern states asking the Robinsons, the Quaker family who owned that home back then, to send their slaves back. Most of the owners promised they would eventually free them. The Robinson family refused every request and told the Southern "owners" their former slaves were already free. They would do nothing to return them. Moreover, when they stayed at the Rokeby House, they were treated as equals with everyone else, being able to work and earn the same wages. There was detailed information about one particular slave who had walked from North Carolina to Vermont.

Some of our students cried as they read those letters. As they toured the home and grasped a little of the history, they understood that their ancestors had been bought and sold into slavery as if they were possessions. They read of slaves who had fled north where they could be free. Many slaves died on the way or were captured, but many of them made it. The students grew in appreciation of the courage and determination of their forebears who were determined to be liberated from the oppressive state of enslavement. They also gained a sense of admiration about the role of white abolitionists. Our children actually stood in the very house where some of the runaway slaves came, slept, and rested before they made the last part of their journey and reached Canada. The children marveled when they saw the secret bedroom where the Robinsons hid slaves.

Sipping fresh hot chocolate, we sat down and discussed the social and cultural implications of such a place. After that, we put on snowshoes provided by the Vermont children and walked about two hundred yards to the site where an integrated school once stood.

It was no surprise to me that most of those fifteen students who went to Vermont were later accepted at Philadelphia's top magnet high schools. They had undergone a life-changing cultural experience.

Positive influence brings positive results!

Exposure is important for our young people. Culture is important. That is to say, an awareness and love of the richness of their own culture, and a healthy appreciation for the components of other traditions. To actually experience, both directly and indirectly, the intersections at which cultures meet for either good or bad, and to see the change produced in both ways of life as a result, is to open eyes that can never be shut again to our dependency on one another. For them to be introduced to such magnificent experiences in Vermont broadened their perception of the world. Not only did history come alive for them, but the two cultures of children together helped them appreciate how different groups in the past had worked in concert for what was a victory over the shameful practice of slavery in America. What a powerful tool for these future leaders of America as they considered the triumph over racial conflicts!

One profound experience that must be mentioned here is an activity that the students participated in at Saint Michael's College in Vermont. Kyle Dodson, Director of Diversity, arranged an activity where students were divided into three heterogeneous groups and given supplies such as scissors, tape, and cardboard. They were directed to "build communities" on designated areas on the floor.

In observing the groups, we, as adults, were quick to notice that the groups were having varying degrees of success. One group was successful in completing the project. We concluded that they were more resourceful and focused. The two other groups did not seem to proceed as well.

At the end of the activity, the students themselves discussed the ease or difficulty of their endeavor. They noticed what we had not: Some groups had more supplies than others. Kyle Dobson had deliberately designed it that way. Not surprisingly, the unit with the most achieved the greatest success. The others had to borrow or do without. As a result, they were impatient and frustrated.

The point of the whole project was that there are groups and communities who have more than others, sometimes by design. However, we are all expected to achieve the same goals. Until there is equity in all areas, there is little likelihood that equality can come about. When the groups were asked for materials and they gave them, they were actually creating a healthy economic and social balance. That was a marvelous eye-opening experience for the children from both communities.

Through all the activities that went on, our students saw what life was like beyond Philadelphia's inner city. For the non chess players, it was the first time they had been that far away from home. As I stated earlier, I'm not sure any of them had ever traveled on a train before.

They were children, of course, so it wasn't a perfect trip. They complained about the long train ride. I reminded them, "Our ancestors didn't have trains in the early days. That meant slaves had to walk to Vermont from the South. It took them *weeks* to walk that far. Some of them were hunted down by men on horseback, beaten, and taken back to the South. Don't complain about a twelve-hour train ride," I said.

They didn't complain again.

As we prepared for our return to Philadelphia on Wednesday morning, February 19, 2003, we were informed that the East Coast had been bombarded with snow. Cities like Boston, New York, and of course, Philadelphia were hit with some of the heaviest snowfall in almost ten years. Some areas received as much as thirty inches of snow. Our train was delayed several hours, and the trip was a slow one, but we returned home safely. Our families greeted the weary-but-persistent travelers with smiles.

Before we left Vermont, we talked of returning the favor and hospitality to our friends.

In April 2004, it was time to return the favor and host the Vermont students and their families. A group of twelve students and ten adults from Vermont visited with us for four days.

During their stay in Philadelphia, the Vermonters wanted to visit the National Constitution Center at Independence Mall in Philadelphia, the Philadelphia Art Museum, and the Ben Franklin Institute. They spent time with our students at Reynolds Elementary School also. They had a chance to see much of life through the eyes of our children. They had a wonderful time and built even more rapport with our young people.

When the Vermont students first arrived by train at Thirtieth

Street Station on a rainy day, it was obvious they were apprehensive. We had a welcoming committee consisting of students and teachers, and one of our school's community partners, Elmer Smith, a columnist for the *Philadelphia Daily News*, wrote about the event.

Some of the Vermont students had never been in an urban area. They didn't know what to expect because they had heard stories about Philadelphia and the crime in the inner city. They rode by bus to Reynolds at the corner of Twenty-Fourth and Jefferson, an area that was as different from South Hero as maple syrup is from a soft pretzel. We, too, had an assembly of greeters that featured our school band, singers, and other participants. Students visited art and music classes and played computerized math games. Students and groups started to gel. By the end of the first day, all fear had vanished. As far as I could tell, all the children began to bond.

In a reversal of what we did, they came in on Wednesday and left early Sunday morning. One of the student comments from the first trip was that they did not spend enough time together.

This trip provided more social interaction among both adults and children. We went to the Franklin Institute to see a science film, and we also saw a special film that highlighted the history of Philadelphia. At the Spaghetti Warehouse, our students were able to thank the senior Mr. Freed-Thall (Michael's dad) for his noble vision and passion for children. His letter and my subsequent phone call to him two years earlier had brought families from two different parts of the country together. On a beautiful and sunny day, we saw the Philadelphia Phillies play at their new Citizens Bank Ballpark and we ran up the "Rocky Steps"[11] to the Philadelphia Museum of Art. Surprisingly, some of our

---

11. The now-famous steps actor Sylvester Stallone ran up and down in the film *Rocky*.

Reynolds students saw a completely different view of Philadelphia than they had seen before. For the first time, they had been exposed to a different side of life in the very city in which they lived.

The eighth-grade students of Reynolds were engaged in an art-and-writing project through the Philadelphia Arts in Education Partnership. Throughout the year, they worked on art and writing from the drawings and watercolors of African-American Dox Thrash to the paintings and sculptures of Edgar Degas.

The concluding activity was a display of their art projects and the public reading of their poetry at the Philadelphia Museum of Art, the oldest art museum in the country. Our Vermont friends were treated to a nice reception, and they were a very gracious audience to our students as they performed.

The culminating excursion was seeing William Shakespeare's *Comedy of Errors*. In many Philadelphia schools, we had received copies of a study guide for the play. The study guide allowed us to discuss the twisted, humorous plot of mistaken identity, acculturation, and presumption. By having them engage in the discussion, we were assured the students understood the message of the play. That also afforded us an opportunity at our home school to explore in greater depth an aspect of literature that we ordinarily would have only skimmed.

I must admit, at Reynolds we emphasize the literature of African-Americans. We make no apology for that. For too long, we have not had the opportunity to study the great literary contributions of talented African-American writers. Our school district has made a tremendous effort to correct that neglect. Our district is the first in the nation to mandate that all high school students take a course in African-American history. In our community, Shakespeare, although brilliant, takes a backseat to Langston Hughes.

On the other hand, Shakespeare wrote many plays that explored cultural themes, including the daring tragedy of *Othello*. The acting troupe that presented *Comedy of Errors* to us adapted it in a very modern way, without compromising its meaning. It was a big hit with the students. I suppose many of them identified with family misfortunes, sibling displacement, and humor. From the laughter and comments we heard, it appeared that they all enjoyed it.

After leaving the theater, it began to dawn on the children and adults that their wonderful time in Philadelphia had come to an end. The drive back to the hotel was filled with emotion, mostly sadness.

When the children said their good-byes Saturday night, many of them cried. Since then, our children have received letters, phone calls, and e-mails from Vermont. The adults told me that during the whole ride back to Vermont, the only thing the kids talked about was the experience of being with the Reynolds children and how much they liked the visit.

"If our children hadn't received the invitation to meet your students, they would never have known that life in the inner city is more than what we see on television," one teacher wrote. "Our children wouldn't have known that many inner-city kids come from good homes with parents who embrace and support education. We saw so much respect and love. This has been a powerful experience for all of us."

One Vermont family adopted one of our families and we promised to follow up with a teacher exchange. That will be a challenge for sure.

The experience with the Vermont students was one of those unique opportunities to influence, and I doubt that most of us realized the significance of the relationship that began when Michael's father contacted me. Until our students had been exposed to the broader world, they had no idea what lay beyond Philadelphia or that people had different lifestyles than they did. They had seen movies and videos, but that's not the same as visiting in person. It was a marvelous example of how culture influences people.

We could have taken our own children to visit museums and let them see various art projects, the theater, and the opera, and that would have been fine. When they grew up, they'd take their own children to visit museums and operas and the theater. However, we needed to expand those cultural trips to include visits to other communities and cities. If we're truly going to break the cycle of poverty, we must give our young people viable avenues out of the inner city. It is our duty to provide them with living examples of diversity and family so they can realize what must be done to change our society.

They need positive influences to inspire and motivate them. This way, they are more likely to form healthy opinions about themselves and others based on true experiences, rather than stereotypical generalizations from a distance about individuals or groups.

The Vermont experience is an example of what happens when we give young people a chance. Strong relationships developed, and love and friendship flowed between two cultures and communities. The participating students became sisters and brothers—white and black students from two different states and two totally contrasting environments—and from that they found unity and friendship.

That's what we want to visualize happening more often. We should see similar experiences in other urban areas for children. They cannot occur just once and with one group of children. The opportunities must be diverse and available to as many children as possible. We know we're not alone in this mission.

This cultural exchange wasn't something new that began with Reynolds or Folsom. Other schools have done the same thing. Similar exchanges have occurred in the Midwest. Rural school students were brought together with inner-city school children from the Kansas City area. Unfortunately, not enough educators and parents have that vision.

Our approach was slightly different because we connected students from a different part of the country whose culture and race were different. We must be more vigorous in our efforts to present our young people to the broader world. That means not only to expose the students in the inner city to the North but also to expose students from the Northwest to those from the South. It is crucial that we begin to break down all the barriers. I'd like to see black students from the Deep South meet with our black students from the North. I'd like to see white students from the East and white students from the West or Latinos from the Southwest meeting with those in the North. Why not Asians from one coast meeting with those from the other coast of the United States?

When we bring young people together from different environments, they will begin to realize that they're more alike than they are different. The implications for political awareness are limitless. They will be the next generation of leaders in our country and we want them to see the magnitude of the world and yet the minuteness of our thinking. We want them to form friendships and partnerships with people of diverse backgrounds so they will understand and develop a burning desire to change our country that will eventually change the world. That should be the mission.

This especially applies to young people who grow up in poor, inner-city communities, because they're often exposed only to poverty and gangs. They need hope. They need to see the world and to know that their lives can be different from their parents' and neighbors' lives. We want them to understand that where they live is not the entire world; it's only a small piece of a very diverse planet.

When I consider my students who have been successful, I realize that one of the major factors was their exposure to other environments. Our chess players, as I've mentioned elsewhere, saw what fine restaurants and nice hotels were like and they met people who didn't worry if their parents would be able to pay the rent or the electric or grocery bill. Without any further intervention, those children started to dream of their own success. They saw examples of success living before them, so they knew it was possible.

Because I grew up poor, we couldn't travel, but my mother exposed me to as much culture and diversity as she could. She always spoke about various places around the world; I read about the big cities and other countries. My mother frequently taught me about Native American, African, European, and Asian cultures and other religions. When it was time for me to leave the inner city for college, I was ready.

Perhaps it's the realization of how much I missed that pushes me to expose our children to so much more. I want them to travel. I want them to get as diverse an education as possible.

When I've taken students to chess tournaments, they always come back richer for having had the experience. At one point, I thought I was going to have the financial support to take the Vaux students to Africa to play chess against some of the top players on that continent. On that trip we not only planned to teach other young people how to play chess, but also hoped to meet Nelson Mandela. We couldn't raise the funds, however, and it's one of the big disappointments of my career.

The most exciting example I can present when speaking about culture is to point to our chess players. People can't imagine how it transformed some of our young people when they went to Columbus, Ohio, or to Phoenix, Arizona.

I remember so well when I took the chess team to Orlando, Florida, in 1996. It was our first national championship trip. I can see, as if it were yesterday, the awe on the faces of our students as they stared at the plane they would board. It was the first time any of them had ever flown. I understood that. I had graduated from college before I ever flew on an airplane.

The chess players not only flew to Orlando, but stayed in a large, high-rise hotel, visited Disney World, and met children from all over the country. Their world expanded and their appreciation of life increased.

Disney World was a highlight for them and a poignant experience. There's a story connected with that trip that I want to share. I hadn't traveled to Disney World before, and I had no idea how expensive it was to visit such attractions. When we arrived at the park and saw the entrance price, I didn't know what to do. I couldn't afford to pay for the admission of all of our students. Our children didn't have any money. We hadn't charged them anything to go on the trip, because we raised all the money from people within the community. Most children from our community can only dream of going to Disney World.

I walked up to the woman at the first ticket booth. "Is there any way we can get a discount?" I asked. "I've brought a group of kids from Philadelphia, and we don't have enough money for everyone's admission. These kids have never been outside of Philadelphia; it would mean so much to them to visit Disney World."

"Sir, there is nothing we can do."

"Surely there must be something."

"We could contact your school district to see if they could arrange payment."

I told her what school we were from in Philadelphia. I knew I would probably get reprimanded upon my return for asking the Disney office to call my district, but I was a desperate man.

Then, embarrassed and ashamed of not being able to get them into the theme park, I walked away. I sat on a bench with the kids all around me. They could read the dejection on my face. They tried to be encouraging, but I knew every child wanted to go into the park. I prayed silently, *God, there must be a way for these kids to get inside. Please, Lord, don't let these kids go home disappointed.*

No peace came and no miracle from heaven materialized. After perhaps twenty minutes, and with the children becoming restless, I walked back to the same ticket window and said, "Is there a time—maybe later in the day—when the ticket prices are reduced?"

"All your children will be admitted," she said and smiled. "The admission fees for all of your children have already been taken care of. We thought you had left the park."

At first I stared at her. The answer had come and it took a few seconds to sink in. "Thank you! Thank you!" I kept saying. I raced back to our kids and repeated the good news. Their dejected faces registered such utter joy, I felt like crying while they yelled joyously.

I never learned who took care of our fees. It may well have been some official at Disney or an administrator in our district office who knew how special this trip was for our children. They truly deserved it. It may even have been the woman herself when she realized how badly our kids wanted to go inside. I know only that God answered the prayer of a man who desperately wanted something special for a group of truly deserving inner-city children.

Although there was no direct person to thank or show gratitude to, that apparent random act of kindness showed the children that their plight moved the heart of a person or group of people. The *influence* of such a benevolent gesture probably lingered in the hearts of the children long after the excitement of the rides and attractions faded. I see it now as I watch one after another of those children graduate from college.

Even now, my soul sends out a sincere thank-you to our benefactor who had compassion and love for others. As John O'Donohue once said, "Compassion is the ability to step outside our own perspective, limitations and ego, and become more attentive in a vulnerable, encouraging, critical, and creative way with the hidden world of another person."[12]

12. John O'Donahue, *Eternal Echoes: Celtic Reflections on Our Yearning to Belong* (Harper, 2000).

9

Influence in the Workplace

Many people in the workplace never understand the power of their influence over coworkers. Without being aware, they impact those who work beside them, under them, and over them. They are also influenced by those around them.

Let's examine the various kinds of influence within the workplace.

1. Those who work above us. Some people will draw from your ability to submit to their leadership. It's something I often see in schools when I observe new teachers becoming integrated into our system. It's intimidating for a new teacher to come into an established school, especially those in tough neighborhoods. Not only do they face new and difficult situations, but they come in as strangers among those who have been teaching for years, as well as working with children who have already become part of the learning community.

After they join us, they meet teachers who have been there for twenty-five or thirty years—the ones who have dedicated themselves to faithfully serving the children and the community. Smart, new teachers open themselves to the older, more mature teachers. Those mentor-teachers not only care about the children, but also reach out to help new members of the staff.

The mentoring relationship is usually quite informal. It's not as if the more experienced teacher walks up and says, "Okay, you've been assigned to me. Please visit me when you have a problem and I'll show you what to do." As I've observed, the experienced teachers seem naturally to gravitate toward the un-seasoned teacher. The new recruits also move toward teachers they sense care and will help.

I think about my own career after I started to teach at Vaux Middle School. A few weeks after I began my first year, a teacher named Mrs. Bobbie Dixon called me into her office and immediately I thought I was in trouble. She was a lead teacher who also served in an acting administrative position.

"What did I do wrong?" I asked before she could say any-thing.

She laughed. "No, you didn't do anything wrong."

Once I had relaxed, she said, "I've noticed how you interact with the students. I see a positive relationship forming between you and the students."

"It seemed like the natural thing to do," I said. "I didn't con-sider that it was anything unusual. I'm just being myself. I was raised in this community."

"We have to fight with some individuals to get them to in-teract with the students," she said. "You seem to do that natu-rally and I see that you're out there every day. I hope you never lose that enthusiasm and compassion."

That was the reason she called me into her office: She wanted me to know that she appreciated what I did for the stu-dents.

I thanked her, and before I left, Mrs. Dixon said, "You can go far in the school system but I hope you never lose the ability to interact with young people. I hope you'll always understand that our job is about them. It's about the children."

I've never forgotten those words. She also talked to me about how hard it was to attract men into the profession. I was already committed to staying in education in the inner city, but her encouragement meant a great deal to me.

As I walked away, I thought, "She isn't my mother, sister, neighbor, or wife, but she's someone who's been here for quite some time. She knows the situation and what works and what doesn't." Later, I realized Mrs. Dixon knew something else—the importance of influence. The influence of coworkers to support one another and encourage new ones who have joined the team—inexperienced teachers like me. She had been my informal mentor.

I see many of our teachers who function that way. When first-year teachers start their careers with us, several of the experienced teachers make it a point to say casually, "If you like, I'll be happy to explain about the culture of our school." In one form or another, they say to the inexperienced person, "Don't underestimate our young people because you see that they come from humble beginnings or they live in a poor community. This community is the home of many other students who have gone on to graduate from college, law school, and medical school. Some have been national chess champions and National Honor Society members.

"A number of our former students have become successful in the corporate world, as well as city and state government. We are proud of those who have decided to dedicate their lives to teaching and other service professions like nursing, social work, and counseling. We want them to begin with high expectations. What we do isn't anything close to babysitting. This is teaching and influencing the children to become the best that they can be."

Because they carry the scars of frequent battles, and have survived the test of time, many of those experienced teachers are as effective with other teachers as they are with their students.

2. Those who work below us. When people come into our places of employment, those of us who have been on the job for extended periods of time need to understand the importance of the messages we send to them. After they come into the job, the first things they learn about the culture and environment may well be what they hear from us.

We need to be able to support and nurture relationships with others and we can do that by reaching downward as they reach upward to us. One of the first things I did after making a commitment to educating children was to enroll in graduate school. I wanted to be an example for those young people to lift their vision beyond the inner city. It was my goal to learn everything I could and to find every possible resource to help them. I believed that my example to excel could positively challenge the students to continue with their schooling. I was a kid who came from the projects—like them—and if I stayed at it, they could, too.

I wanted to return to graduate school immediately, but I couldn't afford it. During my first year as a high school teacher, I spoke to one of the English department heads, because she had inquired about my plans for the future. I said I had finished undergraduate school in debt with student loans so I couldn't think about going into debt to get a master's degree.

Thelma Arnold, head of the English Department at Strawberry Mansion High School, stared right into my eyes, and said, "People go into debt all the time. When they decide to buy a new car, they obligate themselves for twenty, thirty, even fifty thousand dollars and don't think twice about it. But we complain about going into debt to pay for an education. The car may last a decade, but the education stays with us for the remainder of our lives. We must begin to invest in ourselves."

After I left, I kept hearing her words inside my head: "The car may last a decade, but the education stays with us for the remainder of our lives."

I've never forgotten those words. They changed my attitude and my philosophy. The next day, I enrolled in graduate school and eventually received my master's degree. At the time of this writing, I've almost finished my doctoral program. The education process has been a struggle for me as a teacher, husband, father, and mentor to young people. The time commitment is unbelievable, but it's worth the effort.

One thing keeps me going. Before my mother passed away in 2002, I promised her that I would receive the doctorate before I left this earth. I also have set out to develop myself as a professional. I attend all the conferences and workshops for educators that I can—even those that are required only for teachers. As a leader, I want to lead by example.

Why is this important? First, I want the teachers in my school to understand that I appreciate their commitment and dedication. Second, if it's important enough for them to be there, I should be there. I need to learn what they're learning. I want my relationship with them to reflect their relationships with their students. I also want to treat teachers as the ultimate professionals.

3. *Those Who Work Beside Us.* A common warning I hear from the educators who care the most for their students is, "Don't go to the teachers' lounge." That's because those who want to improve the culture of the school know that the teachers' lounge is often where others hear negative issues being discussed. It's the place to grumble and gossip. This is just as true in any other workplace. "Don't go into the break room with a lot of others," is the same advice for those who work on the as-

sembly line or in corporations. The atmosphere in these places easily turns into gripe-and-pessimism sessions. A few negative voices influence many others.

We want positive people and positive coworkers. We want to do what we can to ignite those positive feelings in the workplace.

People have come to me and shared their problems—the kind that I can't tell anyone else. Their concerns may be about sickness, marital issues, financial difficulties, or problems with the children. During the conversation, they often tell me about the individuals in our school who have been supportive.

"I know I did some negative things in a relationship," one teacher told me and added, "but she [another teacher] never judged me. She expressed concern. Although she urged me to get out of that relationship, she didn't condemn me or make me feel foolish. She didn't say I had been stupid, wrong, or weak—and I knew I had been all three. She constantly made me feel I could succeed if I left that relationship. Because of her encouragement, I finally found the courage to do just that."

I wish I could get everyone to focus on the opportunities to influence others in the workplace. Many times others come to us with their issues and they think they're a burden. Perhaps they are, but part of being who we are should mean we want to help lift some of the burden from our friends. Too often they don't realize we have our own issues. After I've heard really sad stories from others in the work environment, it makes me feel a little better to know that I'm not the only one with problems.

At times I've become so focused on my own problems and thought about them so much that I've made them bigger than they are. Just to hear others talk about their negative situations often brings me back to reality. As I leave the conversation, I sometimes say to myself, "And I thought I had problems."

I struggle every day with various issues—and it's a good reminder. I'm not the only person who seeks acceptance from

God and from other people. I'm like a lot of others who yearn for acceptance from my family at home or at work. Just to know that there are others who struggle with those same issues encourages me.

I'm one of those committed-but-flawed individuals, and acknowledging that reality also gives me an opportunity to help others. They know I'm dedicated but I'm not perfect. A generation ago, Henri Nouwen referred to the "wounded healer." That's how I feel. Because I've felt my own wounds, I can understand another's.

Along with this, I've also learned of something else quite important—the immortality of influence in the workplace. Throughout my career as a teacher and principal, older educators have often counseled me. As they talked, they told me stories about the mature teachers who had reached out to them. They let me know that they were passing on what they had received.

One man told me about an older teacher—barely five feet tall and weighing about ninety-eight pounds—who was the most respected teacher in the school. The man was in his first year of teaching and he simply couldn't control the children. (He confessed that he had been afraid of them.) The older teacher took him in hand and said, "You are the teacher. They are the pupils. You can control them." She showed him how and built up his confidence.

"That woman made me a teacher. Anything I do today is because of her advice."

That's how influence works—and it's like a virus that goes from one person to another (a good virus). People reach out and pull us up and encourage us. In our gratefulness, we pass on the same kind of help to others, and then they pass it on. Fifty years later, no one may remember the name of the original encourager and influencer, but they do know the immortal effects.

Here is another vivid example of immortal influence. A good

friend and mentor became the pastor of a small church in 1974. All the members had their favorite pews, and no one talked to anyone except after the service in the parking lot. When my friend entered the new church for his first Sunday morning service, he walked around before it began. He greeted people. He went out of his way to introduce himself to new members, as well as to older ones. Within months, the atmosphere in the church changed. Not everyone accepted his ways, but most of them did. Those who refused to open up to new people referred to the others as "the huggies" because they hugged each other.

My friend left that church in 1984 and since then the church has had two other pastors. The warm, hugging environment has prevailed. Do new members know where it started or who was the first hugger?

Probably not.

It doesn't matter—the influence has continued.

It's important for new employees, early in their careers, to meet those who reach out and interact and encourage them. A few years ago, I came to the realization that some people remain in their workplaces because of others who work with them. They might not particularly like their jobs and could do as well or better in another place, yet they stay. They stay because of the warm, supportive atmosphere. It is well known that in some companies it's rare for anyone to stay more than three years because the pressures are intense, and there is no support for those who work the hardest.

I've also had teachers say to me, "When I was recruited to teach, I heard many exciting things, and I thought it was just part of the sales pitch. But I joined the profession anyway. When I saw people actually doing those things, I knew it was more than mere words. I realized I had come to a place where people were committed—people who were like most of the other teachers in our society. So I had to be committed to do my best. Those examples inspired me."

Other educators did the same thing for me. People told me I would have to make sacrifices if I was going to have a positive effect on others. I didn't argue, but I'm not sure I believed them. Then I observed them as they made the sacrifices they spoke about. For example, they stayed in the inner city when it would have been easier and they would have made more money teaching in the affluent suburbs.

I know of a teacher, Eva Piper, from a Houston, Texas, suburb. Her husband, Don, was in the hospital for 104 days. He was in really bad shape after a car accident. She wanted to spend every day with him—especially the first month when physicians weren't sure he would survive. She ran out of sick days. Her coworkers—other teachers—donated their sick days by having the substitute come in their name.[13] They did that because they knew she needed their help at a critical time. I believe they also realized that one day they might be in a similar situation and need the same support. I think they also did it because Eva had been a source of inspiration and encouragement to many of them. That was an opportunity to repay her for her loving influence.

I have always known I could make whatever sacrifices were required to help others, because dedicated teachers showed me the way. More than once, I thought, "That's why I'm here. That's why I've chosen to do the things I've done—others made sacrifices for me. I must continue the cycle of support."

It doesn't matter whether we work at McDonald's or Donald Trump's Castle; all of us are influenced by others—and we influence others. There is one important thing we can do: We can choose those who impact us.

---

13. This account appears in Don Piper with Cecil Murphey, *90 Minutes in Heaven* (Fleming H. Revell, 2004).

We can't always choose those we impact, because we never know what we do or say that touches others. As pointed out in an earlier chapter, we influence and are influenced by the way people dress, the way others talk, the way they carry themselves, the way we treat families, and the way we act with coworkers. They also see how we treat ourselves—through what we eat and our exercise (or lack of it).

Every day, people in our work situations learn from us. Each day, we need to remind ourselves: *Today I will influence people. I am going to help shape their lives.*

I point out one warning: That influential shaping can be negative or positive. Every person I meet can influence me and can teach me lessons, negative or positive. They either teach me the right thing or they push me toward the negative.

Our responsibility is to push away from negative influences and be open and teachable to those who can make us better people. We can choose which things we're going to walk away from and which ones we allow to stick to us because they're positive.

As I considered the magnitude of influence in the workplace, I thought about the birth of our younger daughter, Nashetah. She was born February 29, 2004, although my wife's due date was June 2. Nashetah (a Native American name for *second-born warrior*) Kanene (Swahili for *important little one*) was born three months premature. At birth, she weighed one pound, thirteen ounces.

I vividly remember the day she was born because my wife had been hospitalized for nearly a month beforehand, and she had been on strict bed rest the entire time. She wasn't allowed to get up and couldn't even shower. She had to do everything from a supine position.

I had been scheduled to speak in Southern Maryland on Sunday morning, February 29, 2004, to an organization called BIG—Blacks in Government. All of their members are government employees, civilian and military. I was participating in one of their Black History Month events. I had to cancel my participation because my wife was ready to have the baby any minute.

I was at home with my older daughter, Macawi, because she had been sick. I had called Shawnna early in the morning to get instructions from a real mom on how to deal with our daughter's vomiting. After assisting me, Shawnna hung up the phone so she could get some rest. Minutes later, I received a call that she had gone into labor at Lankenau Hospital. Lankenau is an excellent health-care facility in an outlying suburb of Philadelphia that is well respected for its neonatal care division.

Macawi and I rushed to the hospital, and by the time we arrived, Shawnna had delivered our daughter at twenty-six-and-a-half weeks.

When we were able to talk, she said something that encouraged me, "When the baby came out, her eyes were wide open and she looked at me. When she looked at me—even if she couldn't actually see me—I felt as if her eyes were saying, 'I am here and I'm not going anywhere.' She let me know that although the odds were against her surviving and being healthy, she's going to make it."

Both of us had tears in our eyes.

The staff immediately rushed the baby to Neonatal Intensive Care, and right after that, the doctor came into the room and talked to us about how babies who were born before twenty-eight weeks had a rare chance to survive and to be healthy. If they were successful in keeping them alive, many times, the infants developed several potentially serious health problems.

Shawnna said, "She's going to beat the odds."

We understood what the doctor was doing—he was trying to be realistic and point out all the negative possibilities.

I simply asked him one question, "Are there any babies born this early who survive and are healthy?"

"Yes, it does happen at times, but it's rare."

"Well, Doctor, I'm going to pray that it happens one more time."

That's exactly what Shawnna and I did. We prayed then, and we prayed every day. The more we prayed, the more we were convinced God would answer our prayers.

Here's where the workplace influence became important. The doctor had given us all the negative information, and he did raise some doubts in my mind—that's negative thinking at work. Shawnna, however, wasn't discouraged for a second.

Shortly after the doctor left, a nurse walked into the room. "I've seen several babies as tiny as yours," she said, "and they are vigorous and healthy today. Don't let the statistics discourage you."

One after another, as well as I can remember, *every* nurse who worked in that department told us encouraging stories about babies who had survived. They also made it clear, without actually saying the words, that they were dedicated to keeping those babies alive and healthy.

Many times I walked inside the door of the Neonatal Intensive Care Unit and watched those nurses interact with each other. It was more than a few cheerful ones who buoyed the others. Every nurse I ever saw working with our daughter cared for her as if Nashetah were her own child. They helped each other and jumped in when one of them needed help. Sometimes they stayed beyond their shift because an infant wasn't doing well.

The influence they had on each other in that hospital was contagious. It also amazed me to see how they affected parents like us. Without hearing many words, we were encouraged by their professional conduct and the compassion they showed.

I said to myself, "It's such a blessing to have people who are dedicated to their work and who understand not only the influence they have on one another but also the impact they have on those who come into their workplace. It's important for people to walk out of a hospital and feel that their children or their family members are receiving the best care possible." I felt that way every time I visited.

Despite all the encouragement, it was difficult for me to go to the hospital every day and see my child connected to a number of machines. The nurses seemed to sense my pain. Through a combination of training and experience, they quickly detected when parents lost faith. And they knew how to respond.

Before I said a word, one of the nurses came up to me, touched my shoulder, and said, "Nashetah is getting stronger every day."

Those were exactly the words I needed to hear. After that, each day on the way to the hospital, I would say, "One more day and she's still alive. One more day and she's getting stronger."

The nurses told us that she probably wouldn't come home until close to her original due date. That would be June 2.

Shawnna and I continued to pray and so did many others who knew of the situation. One day when I visited the hospital, one of the nurses waved and then came over to me. "Things are looking better. Nashetah's now breathing on her own and she doesn't need the additional oxygen."

I felt so elated, I couldn't speak. As I walked away, I whispered, "Thank you, Lord. Thank you."

Every day when I visited, at least one nurse would give me positive information. Even when there was no significant change, somehow they helped me to feel that our daughter was going to be all right. They e-mailed us every day to give us updates, something they certainly didn't have to do.

After a few weeks, they started to ask me questions about education and wanted suggestions about where they should send their children to school. They asked about colleges and scholarships. I wanted to help them in any way that I could because they were helping my child.

During one of our visits with Nashetah, a nurse called out,

"I saw you on television." I had recently appeared on *The O'Reilly Factor*. Bill O'Reilly interviewed me about my previous book, *I Choose to Stay*, and we also talked about parenting and education.

We talked and the nurse asked about the book, which she hadn't heard of before. The next day I brought her a copy. The following day, other nurses laughingly told me they were upset because they didn't get a copy. The day after that, I brought in copies for several nurses in the unit. It felt like such a privilege for me to do that. They had done and were continuing to do so much for us, it seemed like such a small gift to show our deep appreciation.

Nashetah came home from the hospital on May 23, 2004, and we were thankful to God and to the staff for the loving care they had given our child. Even more, we were grateful that she was healthy, although she did have a few respiratory problems. The doctor said her health would improve as she became older. We had to take Nashetah to see an ophthalmologist to make sure her vision was all right. After a few visits he said she was fine with no problems whatsoever.

All of this was such a blessing. God was certainly involved in that situation. Even now, I often thank God for those nurses. They were caring and compassionate, and they gave us hope. After the nurses began to talk regularly to us, I rarely had a doubt about Nashetah being healthy. I knew that their faith helped me believe. Their positive influence helped me to feel encouraged.

I believe they also influenced each other at work and that allowed them to give the ultimate in health care to their patients.

That's just one example of how we affect others through the way we treat one another in the workplace. We are most productive when we positively influence each other. Those nurses gave us such a high level of care and support because they supported one another. They also gave Shawnna and me a new respect for nurses, especially for those in neonatal care, because the babies are so tiny. Whenever we saw a family take a child home, we knew there was a chance for us. We were happy for those families, and everyone said the same thing—thanking those nurses for all that they do.

From that personal experience, I realized the importance of influence in the workplace. Nashetah's nurses gave her a better chance at life because they improved each other's lives. I will be forever thankful to the nurses in the Neonatal Intensive Care Unit at Lankenau Hospital for giving all their patients great loving care and for caring about each other.

As I've already pointed out in this chapter, each of us has the ability to impact others. We can also learn to listen without interrupting. Sometimes that's the way we can have the most influence: We listen without offering advice or telling others how to solve their problems. As we actively listen—that is, when we try to grasp not only their words but also the emotions that go along with them—we feel their heart and their pain.

Our own pain begins to ease because we see others who struggle. Some of them are able to overcome problems because of our influence. That happens when we establish a relationship and it gives us the opportunity to lift them up when they feel low.

I've been able to deal with my own daily struggles because I have helped others while understanding that they were people on whom I can lean.

Many times I have looked for ways to ease my own pain, when the blessing was in helping someone else. By helping them, I helped myself. On many occasions, I've realized that in helping someone else, I was being blessed.

We meet people whom we would never have come into contact with if we hadn't taken our present jobs. What would it be like if we saw that our primary purpose in a job was not only to do the best work we're capable of *but also* to positively influence others? Instead of our work being our source of income, it becomes a place of service.

In the summer of 2005, I returned to Walt Disney World for the first time since my trip with the chess students in 1996. I wasn't on a quest to find the benefactor who had blessed fifteen students from the inner city of Philadelphia with admission to the park. This time, I was there on business. I attended a week-long conference at Disney's Contemporary Resort, hosted by Nova Southeastern University—the largest independent university in Florida. Although their main campus is in Fort Lauderdale, they have education centers or campuses in cities around the country as well as several international campuses. I am currently completing my doctorate in educational leadership at their education center in Bucks County, near Philadelphia.

On the first day of the conference, I had been asked to give a speech to open the session. I never imagined I would be blessed with the opportunity to meet so many students of all races from various parts of the country and the world. Many of the students were teachers, administrators, counselors, and social workers—all of them serving God by serving His children.

Later, as I ate alone in the restaurant, a female employee asked me if everything was going okay. I nodded, because I was thinking about a situation back in Philadelphia and I wasn't too much interested in talking. She seemed satisfied that I had acknowledged her.

To change my mood, I picked up the Orlando newspaper and began to read. I overheard her say to a much younger employee, "This is how we treat every customer in this restaurant."

The young woman was a new employee who was visiting from London.

I said to myself, "This is workplace influence in action." I had to talk with that wonderful woman who tried so hard to make people feel comfortable.

A few minutes later, I introduced myself. She told me her name was Betty Keaton Walker. She had been an employee at Walt Disney World for over thirty-one years and was a faithful member of the St. Mark A.M.E. Church in Orlando. She was proud to tell me she had learned to serve others from her church pastor, who was currently in Africa on a mission.

Betty's father, Wheeler, had been an employee at the same resort for more than thirty years. He had retired long ago and was now eighty years old. They had influenced and supported each other.

As soon as I left her, Betty moved to another table and talked to someone else. She did it effortlessly, and it was obvious it wasn't a job requirement—it was her gift to the Disney organization.

I smiled as I reflected on that scene in the restaurant. Her influence in the workplace was neither something I had just imagined nor a dying practice. Perhaps she was our long-lost benefactor who, ten years earlier, had seen to it that a group of kids from Philadelphia enjoyed their stay at Disney World. If not Betty, it surely must have been someone with the same kind of heart for helping others. I'll probably never know.

That attitude attracted me to the profession of teaching, because I observed people reaching out to help. It's not just in education but also in nursing, social work, counseling—all of what we call the "helping professions." *It's the spirit of service.* It's the spirit of making someone else's day a little brighter. It's truly a blessing to have that ability.

The sad part is that there are also individuals who have the gift to encourage and impact others, but they don't use that ability. To be able to make life a little easier or happier for someone else is truly a blessing in itself.

10

The Influence of Respect

All children need to learn respect from their parents or primary caregivers, and they need to learn it early in life. Parents teach respect by setting limits, honoring their word, and creating expectations for their children. Respect is also taught through sharing quality time, showing patience with children as they grow, imparting wisdom for living, and expressing love. Before children can comprehend words, they can understand the way their parents model behavior through signals such as eye contact, voice tone, and touching. When those signals are firm, kind, and considerate, children learn to understand how emotionally healthy human beings treat each other.

Parents and guardians, by actively attending to their children, also communicate to them life's important values. When adults require their children to reciprocate that attention, they sensitize their offspring to the value of the people who care for them, thus teaching them to be courteous.

The lessons learned early in the home generally carry over to the larger community. There are, of course, phases of development in which forms of behavior are more successfully displayed, and there may be situations of illness or stress that affect responses. Moreover, children may express fear or discomfort when they have to function in a different environment, such as staying with a babysitter, going to school for the first time, or eating in a restaurant. Those experiences may temporarily alter learned patterns of behavior. However, the home is the first community where children actively observe and imitate the give-and-take of human interactions. Investing the time and effort required to show how people should be treated yields positive results. That means children learn to respect themselves as well as others. They can't respect others if they don't respect themselves. The principle is obvious: If we don't appreciate ourselves, we can't appreciate others. They go together.

Respect, love, compassion, appreciation—regardless of the words we use—all mean mutual concern. The younger children are when they learn about love and respect, the easier it is for them to grasp. Parents, teachers, police officers, firefighters, and neighbors are their role models. If we demonstrate respect, we pattern the right kind of behavior.

As adults, we need to respect one another for our benefit, but also for the sake of the children. Respect doesn't mean we always agree. Respect is an attitude, not an agreement.

For example, I once attended a political meeting where a father who was more than sixty years old stood up and made a statement. Immediately thereafter, his son arose and said, "I respect my father enough to disagree with him." He then made his argument. He didn't say a disparaging word about his dad or minimize his point. Nor did he condescend to or patronize him. At the end of the meeting, the two men hugged each other, although neither man had changed his opinion.

That's a wonderful example of how respect works. We live in a diverse society, and as a result, our opinions vary. Just because people don't agree doesn't mean a discussion has to shrink to name-calling or mean-spiritedness. People of different faiths and political persuasions ought to respect the right of people to practice and promote what they believe. We may encounter a culture whose practices are strange to us. After seeking to understand those traditions, we should extend to them the same consideration we would like to receive.

I admire cultures that are different from mine and I learn from them. If we close our hearts to the values and customs of others, we may never be able to impact those individuals or embrace them as fellow human beings. That's how prejudice works—insisting that we are the only ones who are correct.

One of the ugliest words in the English language is *prejudice*. While prejudice generally means to look at the behavior of a part and ascribe that aspect to the whole, prejudice also makes us use our own culture as the only standard for correct living. Consequently, we look at unfamiliar behavior and assign a lesser value to it in comparison with ours. One of the reasons we have such a vast number of ethnic problems in the world is because we don't respect the beliefs and attitudes of others. We don't have to agree with them, but that doesn't mean we're wrong or they're wrong. It means we see things differently. Even if we are entirely convinced that they are wrong about one thing or even several, we must respect their freedom to believe as they do. If we respected others more, wouldn't we have fewer wars and less violence?

When I talk about respect, my use of the word implies understanding. As St. Francis of Assisi prayed, "We need to understand more than we need to be understood." If we understand others, we open the door for them to understand us. If we insist that we know what's right and others don't, not only do we misunderstand them, but it shows we don't respect them or their opinions.

The thirteenth-century mystic-poet Rumi wrote:

You were born with potential.
You were born with goodness and trust.
You were born with greatness . . .

Respect means understanding the points that Rumi makes. This mantra should be silently sung upon meeting each person. If we did that, we would change our actions.

My inner-city involvement made me realize long ago that I had to learn to accept where the children came from before I could teach them well. If I respect their background and understand some of the obstacles in their lives, it means I value them and accept them as they are. My job, I feel, is to help them move on and not remain cemented to any situation. But I must go to them emotionally before I can truly help in any tangible way.

I must admit that sharing a similar background in the inner city is advantageous in working with children. That doesn't limit me. In fact, I think it enables me to appreciate and enjoy working with children from all cultures and communities.

Children in schools use the word *dissing*. This term was directly derived from the word *disrespect*. When they ask someone, "Why are you trying to diss me?" what they really mean is, "Why do you disrespect me?" By disrespect, they mean they feel disregarded, disillusioned, or disenfranchised by the other. Even among themselves, they become sensitive to being dissed. They also use other terms such as *bussing* or *busting*, which mean publicly insulting someone. In a classroom, that type of behavior can become a never-ending tit-for-tat exchange, and yielding for the sake of peace can be perceived as a lack of self-respect.

The matter of dissing is more than an issue in school. For example, several violent incidents have become big media topics that involved various musicians and performers who felt they had been dissed by another artist. The issue of respect looms large in every community.

Culturally speaking, we African-Americans have many examples of positive entertainers. There are those who are mindful of the roles they take, and what they bring to that character or situation. We have singers and musicians who inspire and amuse us with their presentations. However, we can sometimes take humor to the edge by talking about physical characteristics in a way that can make some individuals feel self-conscious, sad, and ugly. Such so-called humor includes topics such as hair, skin tone, facial features, weight, and any body parts.

Although we want to be able to laugh at ourselves and not take everything too seriously, we should carefully examine the messages of *self-hatred* that we communicate in our humor. That happens when we joke in such a way that we put ourselves down. If we constantly comment on how stupid, inept, or weak we are, we're not only showing self-disrespect but teaching others to do the same. We don't want to hold on to the old stereotypes that once divided us as a people. Our children imitate what they see on television. If they see disrespect, they become disrespectful. When those kinds of attitudes and behaviors are played out in a classroom, tender hearts can be badly wounded, creating emotional scars that last a lifetime.

We need to be aware that our children often feel that the exposure to disrespect through television and music sanctions such forms of behavior. Although entertainers have to make a living, they should be mindful of the far-reaching effects of their performances. It is said that small minds talk about people; average minds talk about events; and great minds talk about ideas. Respect, therefore, is a lofty concept that requires us to think and not just act.

Rap or hip-hop songs are catchy with their rhythm and rhyme. Children repeat their lyrics all the time. Some words are humorous, some communicate about everyday life, and there are now many Christian rap songs on the market. However, some messages show absolute disrespect to females. It hurts me to watch young ladies dance to songs that actually put them down. I've chided teachers who don't take the responsibility for prescreening songs before they are played at parties or school celebrations.

Most adults in the home don't even realize some of the words and situations that many songs of that genre contain. With a television in every room, headphones, and computers, children who live in the same household may be exposed to an entirely separate life filled with the wrong influences. We have much work to do in this area because just as individuals must respect themselves, any race or group must display self-respect in order to extend it to others, and—equally important—to receive it from others.

We also have to become respectful and mindful that every person has significance. There are no throwaway people. A saying from a generation ago is still true: "God does not make junk." We can learn not to look for the negative in others, but focus on the positive, and build from there. The essence of Dr. Martin Luther King, Jr.'s famous "I Have a Dream" speech is that we respectfully walk together as human beings and discard shallow, external judgments.

Although I write about love in the next chapter, I want to make this point: We can't truly love people—in a healthy sense— if we don't respect them. I hear many, many stories about women in obvious situations of abuse. After receiving a healthy dose of support and advice, they sometimes respond and try to justify the bad situation with, "But he loves me," as if that makes up for every bit of bad behavior.

"That's not love. It's not respect," I tell them. "Those who care about you would never treat you that way. They wouldn't beat you, scream at you, or sexually molest you."

The greatest challenge in solving domestic violence cases, the experts tell us, is to get women to admit to themselves that they are in abusive relationships. It is a matter of respect for themselves. If they respect themselves, they will not allow others to disrespect them and live in those situations.

Experts also tell us that we teach people how to treat us. When our self-image is fractured, we may have a take-what-we-can-get attitude. When we feel good about ourselves, we send out signals that we expect to be treated accordingly. The challenge is for us to raise the level of self-realization of individuals so that they will accept only that which is healthy. Healthy attitudes can help adults break the cycles of disrespect and abuse that prevail with the women in our communities.

In 2003, almost 12,000 women contacted New York City's domestic violence hotline. They searched for a place to escape from abusive partners. The city has room for only 2,000 such women.

In Philadelphia, police receive 90,000 domestic violence reports each year, but there is only *one* shelter for battered women in the entire city. The shelter houses roughly twenty women and their children.

Respect also extends to our own property, as well as the property of others. Most people want to live in a nice neighborhood, but that takes a great deal of work and personal effort. Some communities are successful at maintaining order and beauty. Other communities are terribly blighted. The way a home and the surrounding area looks speaks loudly about the residents. When I visit various cities and see graffiti and trash, or watch people destroy property, it tells me they lack respect for themselves and for the property of others.

People indiscriminately discard their refuse wherever and whenever they want. I'm convinced that they don't realize to what extent they contribute to the demise of their own community. Just a small amount of effort on the part of everyone involved could reverse the bad conditions many people live in. The most modest home can be neatly maintained. We must learn to take care of our environment, and honor the property of others. Care and honor are both derived from the overall influence of respect.

Here is the point I want to make: Culture begins in the home. Indeed, parents are our children's first role models and teachers of respect. We are the primary role models and influences in the lives of our young. We need to be aware and learn more about our world and culture and pass that on to the children. We should always try to be the best at what we do, expose ourselves to as much culture as possible, and read as much as we can so we can pass that information on to our young people. Our actions communicate a respect for their education and future. That, in turn, will make us worthy of their respect.

The men in our communities need to respect and reach out to help young males. Many of our boys are notorious for not wanting to read. Too many young men come into our schools with their lives focused on video games and sports. They respect the image of highly paid athletes and entertainers. They're attracted to a kind of ideal—an imaginary ideal of the men who have it all because they have fame and money. They aren't able to see beyond the glitter and the glamour of the sports stars.

Men who are concerned about our legacy must learn to understand that men can respect and relate to other men. We also can become good fathers to our sons and our daughters. We must be more visible and available to our young men who struggle to identify with healthy masculine images.

I often think about Walter, one of my former students at Reynolds. He represents many of the young men at our school. That young man has struggled with anger all through his life. Because of his anger, he's been inconsistent with his school performance. At times, he's been an honor roll student, an athlete, and an excellent chess player. However, his anger has held him back.

He would simply shut down and not communicate with his teachers. Several times Walter stopped playing chess. He refused to come to practice or to the matches. That's when I learned about his anger issues. His teachers told me he needed support.

The thing that bothered me the most was the way he treated women and the girls in his class and his lack of respect for them. He was being raised by a hardworking and caring single mom but I suspected that, unconsciously, he sought a positive male role model to show him how to respect females properly. For example, Walter often raised his voice at his female classmates as well as his teachers. He appeared uninterested in what his teachers thought about his behavior.

"If you continue to disrespect the females in your life," I told him, "I can't continue to mentor you and allow you to play ball in our gym."

At first he didn't understand what I meant. He indulged in the only form of behavior he knew and didn't realize it was disrespectful. He agreed to work on changing—and he did.

Like me and like many other young men, Walter had never experienced much in the way of male affection or affirmation. He couldn't remember when a male had ever shown him special attention. After I realized that, I encouraged him to join Rodney Murray and a group of others who had begun lifting weights regularly. Walter had always been a basketball player but working out would be a new outlet for him. With some reluctance, he started to work out with Rodney and the others.

Within weeks, I saw a change. Because of the influence of Rodney and the other males in the group, Walter began to learn a better way to relate to females. It was totally new to him.

I realized as never before that our relationship with other men affects the way we relate to females. That almost sounds contradictory, but I truly believe that we treat women the way we do because of the male influences in our lives. (I assume the same may be true with girls and women.) The more positively men communicate with one another, the greater the potential for healthy relationships with and respect for females. Other men can show and teach us how to respect the women in our lives.

Many women complain that men don't communicate, won't open up, and can't talk about their emotions. Their lack of response leads to frustration, arguments, and breakups. Women feel that men withdraw within themselves because it's easier than engaging in an in-depth conversation with their mate. They're right, and a major reason is that many men don't know how. They've never learned how to open up emotionally with females.

When we communicate with other men—and they open up to us and express emotions and share their feelings—we learn to follow their example.

When I first began to work with Walter, I told him, "It's going to be impossible for me to work with you if you continue to be disrespectful to the two most important women in your life: your mother and your teacher. Your mother gave you the most important gift, which is life. Your teacher is giving you the second most important gift, and that's education. You disrespect both of them by projecting your anger onto others and not listening. Your mother tells you to come home at a certain time and you defy her. If you disobey her, you are not showing her respect."

He hung his head and I continued to lecture him about respect.

"If you respect your mother and your teacher, you will listen to what they say. You may think they are wrong about some of their decisions, but they want the best for you. They care about you, and if you refuse to listen, you are showing disrespect for them."

He admitted that I was correct. I repeated again that the only way I could continue to work with him was if he worked hard at being respectful.

"I will, Mr. EL," he said.

I knew he meant it.

Slowly, I began to see improvements in the way Walter treated his female teacher. He opened up more by saying what was bothering him. Sometimes he reverted to his old ways, but that happened less and less frequently.

I also saw something else. The more his relationship with me improved, the more he respected his mother and his teacher. He even gave his teacher a beautiful birthday card, and he admitted that she had helped him and she respected him. I'd like to think part of his change was because he realized that respect was as important to give as well as to receive.

Before I started to work with Walter, he had friction with everyone, even his friends. He'd get involved in arguments, yell at his friends, and call them names. The perception was that Walter had no respect for his friends or for himself. That gradually changed as well. I often talked to him about how he treated some of his friends and that he wasn't being fair.

The happy ending to this story is that Walter continued to change. After he graduated from Reynolds, he went on to Bartram High School for Human Services, a magnet high school in Philadelphia. One of my best friends, Rob Powlen, is a teacher there. He has continued to influence Walter's life. This is an excellent example of another positive male role model showing him respect and love. Walter has enrolled in a program for students who are interested in becoming teachers.

I'm proud of Walter.

11

The Influence of Love, Caring, and Friendship

My mother became sick in 2002, and she was hospitalized in the ICU of the cardiology unit at Temple University Hospital in Philadelphia. Many of the other patients on that wing were waiting for heart transplants. My mother was on that wing because that was the only space available. She wasn't waiting for a transplant; she was dying and she knew it. We also knew it. Her doctors were merely trying to keep her alive long enough to spend more time with her family.

The doctors knew that my mom's children and grandchildren were important to her.

I visited Mom every day. She had always been a powerful influence in my life. I knew I would lose her soon, and I wanted to absorb as much of her influence as I could before she passed on. Sometimes we talked about important issues, but mostly it was small talk. Often it was about events that had occurred during my younger years.

One day I mentioned to a friend, Kevin Compton, that I was on my way to Temple University Hospital to see my mother. Kevin and I had been friends since high school and we still play basketball together. We've played together in various leagues since then.

"Why don't you visit Alfie while you're there?"

"He's in the hospital?" I said. "I didn't know that."

"Yes, and he's not doing too well," Kevin said. He gave me Alfie's room number. It had been so long, I didn't remember Alfie's last name, but I've never forgotten Alfie the man.

Many of us grew up in single-parent homes. Our fathers never came around, or they spent little time with us. Alfie became the first father figure in my life—and not just for me, but for quite a few young men in our community. He was our basketball coach in the Zion Baptist Church Basketball League, but he was much more than a coach. He came around, picked us up in his van, and took us to every basketball game. He wouldn't chance one of us getting hurt on the streets of North Philadelphia. After the games, he took us out to eat or we'd sit and talk. He always insisted that we allow him to pick us up and drop us off at home.

That is the kind of thing fathers do. He was a warm, caring man. His family owned a variety store in the community, and he shared his blessings with as many young men as possible. We all looked up to Alfie. I never remember spending one penny when I was in his company. Many of the young men who spent time under his mentorship and coaching have gone on to graduate from college and return to the community to continue Alfie's influence. We didn't have many real men like that in our neighborhood.

After I graduated from high school in 1982 and went on to college, I lost track of him. Twenty years later, I walked into Alfie's hospital room. It was a great shock to see him in the hospital with a serious heart condition. He was hooked up to oxygen and heart monitors. He could get up and walk around, but he had to drag the metal stand behind him. He walked so slowly and painfully, I didn't want to look. Alfie had been a symbol of strength to us as young men and he had always been athletic and in good shape.

As I stared at him, memories flooded my mind. Many times over the years, I had said there had never been any male role models, but I had forgotten. Alfie was one of the first men who taught us about loving and caring for other males.

After we greeted each other, I told him how I had to come to see him, and that my mom was also in the same hospital.

He thanked me for visiting him and then he said, "I've read all the articles in the papers about you." He had saved many of the clippings and copied some of my television appearances on videotape. Before I could say anything more, he referred to the things I had done since I had graduated from college. "That chess program has got to be the best thing ever for the community," he said. "And what success you've had with those children."

As I listened to Alfie, I felt bad. He treated me the way I would have expected a father to act. Even though I hadn't contacted him in twenty years, he had not forgotten me. I didn't know Alfie's age, but I figured he must have been around fifty.

After that first visit, whenever I went to see my mom, I made sure I stopped by his room.

"I'm glad you came by," he said one day when I walked into his room. "I want to call my nephew, Dave. He lives in New York now." He paused and dialed, and the first words to his nephew were: "You won't believe who's sitting in my room! It's Salome!"

I had played basketball with Dave on the same team that Alfie coached. Dave was now a successful businessman in New York.

After a few words, Alfie gave me the phone and I said hello and we talked a minute or two before he said words that I'll never forget: "My uncle really loves you. You were always special to him."

That was a highly emotional moment for me. Just to hear those words touched me. I didn't know what to say, but I knew how deeply appreciative I was to hear from his nephew of Alfie's love for me.

After the phone call, I talked to Alfie a few minutes before I said, "I'm going to go back and see my mom."

I got up but I wasn't ready to leave. There was something I had to do first.

I stood next to his hospital bed and stared into the tired, pain-filled face. I took his hand. "I've probably never said this to you before, Alfie, but I love you. I want you to know I appreciate everything you've ever done for me."

"I love you like a son," he said. "You were someone special. I've always felt I influenced your life—"

"You have. More than you know."

"Seeing you now lets me know that I've made a difference. Keep up the good work. Every time I read about you or hear what you've done, it shows me that my life hasn't been in vain."

Yes, I wanted to cry, but I held back the tears.

No man had ever talked to me like that before. I didn't trust my voice to say much more. My life—my achievements—had meant that much to him. I had had no idea.

That was a powerful experience. I had said, "I love you," and it was almost like saying those words to my own father. Alfie had done more for me than most dads have done for their own children.

Although my dad didn't die until 1996, he left my mom to raise eight children as a single parent. My father came by occasionally to spend time with our family, but he never did anything fatherly with me. He never taught me values, played with me, or explained anything about what it means to be a young man. Like most of my friends, I relied on other males in the community and schools for information and sometimes what I learned was inaccurate.

"Here's something I want you to remember," Alfie said. "You've got to understand, young man, you're not going to be around forever and you're not always going to have your health. You need to take advantage of every opportunity you have to help someone else. Do what you can to make a difference in your community because nothing is promised to you. Tomorrow isn't promised to anyone."

I nodded. He was right, but it was difficult for me to accept those words.

He talked about how happy he was that he was able to do the things that he had done and grateful for the opportunity to influence young people.

Alfie wasn't a smoker; he was an athlete and he ate well, but his body had reached the age where it began to rebel. Because he had been athletic, it gave him another shot at life.

Being with him brought home for me the fact that I won't be healthy forever. I began to thank God that I had decided to become more serious about my own health.

I often felt depressed after my visits to Mom. She was in good spirits but the doctor had already made it clear that she wouldn't be around much longer. We were all trying to prepare ourselves for her death.

After my visit with Mom, I usually walked down the hall to Alfie's room. Even though he wasn't waiting for a heart transplant, the doctors didn't want to take any chances so they had put him in the same wing. Every time I visited, he was upbeat and positive even though I knew there were times he must have been in severe pain.

"Oh, I'm going to be home soon," he said. "I'm going to beat this."

He showed me that there's hope and that we can overcome the battles of life. Although physically he wasn't the same person, mentally and spiritually he was the same Alfie. I could still remember him saying during basketball games, "We're going to win this game even though we're down twenty points with two minutes left." Sometimes we pulled off a miracle—and much of that was because he made us feel we could win.

On the rare occasion when we lost a big game, he would say, "The best team doesn't always win." He always found ways to make it a little easier to deal with a loss.

Other times he said things such as, "Remember, you have to do well in school. The other things like playing sports are secondary. This is basketball, but it's only a game. It's something for you to do to keep you busy and to have fun. You're a winner because you're doing well in school and aspiring to be someone who is going to change the community and have an influence on others."

I was proud of Alfie and glad that I had a chance to see him and talk about all the good things he was able to do. That he was proud of me for doing so well gave me fresh inspiration. He gave me that long-needed fatherly approval.

Alfie had believed in me when I was a boy. He had loved me and encouraged me then. He continued to love and encourage me.

His condition improved and he was eventually released. I promised myself it would not be another twenty years before I visited with him.

Once I reconnected with Alfie, I thought of other males in my life—men who helped change me, men who loved me, and those whom I loved.

I had a male teacher at Simon Gratz High School named Michael Robinson, who taught Spanish. He was one of their few black male teachers, and the only black male foreign language teacher I've ever met. He also coached track.

That's not what I remember most about him. Whenever he'd see me on the street or in school, he'd hug me and say, "Man, I love you. Keep doing what you're doing." I wasn't the only one he reached out to—he was a man who truly cared about many of us kids.

Not long ago, I visited my old high school and discovered that he was still teaching.

When Mr. Robinson saw me, his face lit up, and he grabbed and hugged me. "I love you, Salome," were his first words.

He was the same loving, caring, and encouraging man he had been two decades earlier. I felt so blessed to have him in my life. He has been a great role model and example.

Over the years, I've received cards and letters from him. "Congratulations on your award," he would write. Whenever he learned of any of my successes, he contacted me and cheered me on.

The third father figure in my life is my barber, Claude, who has been cutting my hair since I was ten years old. Not only mine, but all my friends'. Before I left his shop, he would always say, "I love you." Sometimes he would say, "I love you like a son."

Claude has been a great example to me and a father figure to many kids in our community who had no father.

It has meant a lot to me for a few caring men to reach out to try to fill the void I felt from not having an active father in my life. Those men taught me that I could openly care about other men and be supportive of their achievements. Too often, we males compete with each other. We're afraid to show our tender side because we don't want other men to think of us as weak or feminine. When males become friendly, too many of us have gone on the defensive and asked ourselves, "What does he want?" Yes, there are predators out there, but there are also sincere, honest, caring men who serve as role models.

Men could do well to learn from women, who easily show affection for one another. They seem able to say, "I love you," without a lot of effort. I want to do that with other men because I want to cheer them on and to help them become successful. I want to be able to say, "I love you and I want you to be successful because when you're successful, it's an example and a model for other men."

By contrast, I know many women who have good friends— the kind to whom they can open up and talk. Sometimes they maintain relationships throughout their lives.

I'll give you an example. I walked into a local restaurant several years ago to pick up dinner for my family. I saw three young women I had known since they were schoolmates and they had been good friends back then. I remembered them as the three young girls who walked together to the corner store. Twenty years later, they were still doing the together thing and enjoying each other's company. That night they sat together, talked, and giggled often. I loved hearing their voices carry across the restaurant.

On an impulse, I walked over to their table and asked if I could sit down. When they said they didn't mind, I asked, "What is it about women that you can do this and interact so easily?"

They laughed at my question. They had been friends as far back as they could remember. They told me they have dinner together about once a month, and they talk on the phone almost every day. "The others are a big part of my life every day," one of them said.

"We check up on each other. If we don't have contact every day or so, we know something's wrong."

The third nodded.

"I wish men could do that." I told them about the fellows I had grown up with. We were close friends then; nowadays we rarely called each other. I thought about the men that I consider my best friends today. *Maybe* we talk once every two or three months. Occasionally we call, and most years we send Christmas cards.

That kind of ongoing relationship is something many of us men haven't explored. And we're poorer for it. We don't know the warmth, the understanding, and the encouragement that comes from opening up to one another.

If we men can learn to change, we'll begin to see a much different society and community. We'll have stronger and more confident men who respect and protect our women more because they have stronger and more definitive relationships with their brothers or with their fathers.

Most people learn to express love from examples they have witnessed. If that model is unhealthy, evil, or destructive, they will tend to emulate what they have seen. When we encounter negative individuals, it helps if we realize that they may be that way because it's the behavior they learned and they're only imitating those actions.

As strong, healthy, loving men, we need to learn to express how we feel and to admit that it's all right to care deeply about other men.

Like many other young boys, I never heard my father say, "I love you, son." I'm not alone. Countless young men have grown into manhood without ever hearing an important male in their lives say those words. Every day I tell my two daughters that I love them. If I had a son, I would say the same words to him.

Last night, I said to my older daughter, Macawi, "I love you; you're beautiful, you're smart, you're intelligent." Every night I say those words to Macawi and also to my younger daughter, Nashetah.

When my daughters grow up—and I hope this is true for all girls—they won't have to search for unhealthy love. I don't want them to seek the kind of love that mistreats and abuses them. I don't want my girls to look at that kind of relationship and think it's normal. They know abuse is abnormal, and they know that because they have received a healthy dose of love from their parents and from everyone who has an influence on them. That's the power of healthy love and influence.

When we show our children healthy love, we're giving them the ability to sense when love is *not* healthy. We all know predators are able to "zone in" on those young people who don't recognize healthy love. Some of those predators may truly believe the love they offer is healthy. The predators themselves may not recognize that it's unhealthy because they've never experienced true, compassionate love. They were neglected or abused as children, and they're prepared to offer the same kind of treatment as adults.

We need to encourage our young people to reach out to those who provide a positive impact. There are too many negative individuals, ready to influence them.

I'd like to see young people turn around and truly love others so that we could banish the power of negativity in our world. They can start behaving that way by refusing to participate in negative discussions or activities. When any of us become part of gripe sessions or pass on mean-spirited gossip, we're not loving those people. Grumbling, complaining, gossiping, and dissing are ways we hurt others. We not only hurt them, but also make ourselves unhappy. We fill our minds with negativity. By contrast, we become a positive influence on those around us when we love and support our friends.

All of us know loving people in our lives; we also know the negative types. We can choose those we want to influence us.

My older daughter is now five years old. I often hold her and talk to her about how strong she is and why she is loved. I believe that as I acknowledge her strength and she receives my love, she will believe it because it's true. Because I'm her parent and an authority figure in her life, she listens. I have the power to influence her now for the rest of her life. If I give her the correct messages about my love, about herself, and her relationship with others, she's less likely to become the victim of an abusive relationship.

I often tell her, "I love you because you are my daughter." I praise her for all the good and noble things I see in her. I'm not a fluent Spanish speaker, but I'm learning, and as I learn, I teach her words and phrases. I want my children to respect other cultures and languages. If she truly learns to love others, her words will express that, no matter what language she uses.

When Macawi travels with me, I want her to be able to converse with Spanish-speaking people. I also realize that she can influence them when they see that they matter because we are attempting to master their language. I want her to care enough to want to communicate with all people. Too often in our culture, we've implied, "You aren't good enough because your language and your customs don't meet our standards."

This influence, even though indirect, is powerful and life-changing.

One of the things I try to do with my students is to make sure each of those young people knows I love them. I've learned to say, "I love you."

Once in a while one of them will respond with, "I love you, too."

I don't hear it often enough.

Neither do the children.

Every child needs someone to be crazy about them. They need someone to say, "Take that hat off indoors," or "Pull those pants up," or "Put on a decent outfit," but they also need those same authority figures to say, "I love you."

Men need to understand that it's okay for us to love one another. Our children need to see that as men we're able to love other men, our wives, and our children. I've already mentioned how I felt about my father never saying to me, "I love you, son." I often talk about how we as young men rarely ever see men who hug one another, who talk to one another about their problems relating to health, family, and other areas of concern. The men in every community must understand that we need strong men in our lives. We don't need fragile men. By that, I mean men who are uncomfortable with loving other men and are too fragile to express affection. We need strong men who have the spirit of respect, of modesty, of deference, and who are able to say to another man, "In this situation you're more able to do this than I can. Let me support you. I love you enough to recognize your potential and your leadership and I'm willing to follow you."

Many men aren't able to love other men enough to follow them. When we visit some churches, especially black congregations, we see a building full of women. As men we've never learned to love one another, and love means being willing to learn from and to submit to the leadership of other males.

To be able to follow the leadership of a pastor, we have to respect and love that pastor. Too many of us never learned how to do that. By contrast, women out there understand and accept the concept of loving, respecting, and supporting their leaders, male or female.

There's a strong sense of responsibility that comes from being able to love another man—our brothers, cousins, uncles, friends, or coworkers. We need the support of one another and we need to be able to show others our concern for them.

For a long time I thought my situation with my father was simply related to the fact that he wasn't involved in my life and that's why he never really told me he loved me. But it's more than that.

Rex Crawley is a friend and a professor at Robert Morris University, near Pittsburgh. He's a member of Kappa Alpha Psi, the same fraternity to which I belong. We are both part of an organization called Brothers of the Academy. It's a group of strong black men who have received their doctorates or who are studying to receive them. The Brothers promote scholarship and support other men. They also encourage and nurture black men to become professors, because there are so few at the college level.

I spoke with Rex one day when I visited Pittsburgh and he told me he had been in a car accident recently. At the hospital, his father came in and kissed him on the top of his head. Later, Rex said, "That was the first time in my life that my father ever kissed me. I'm almost forty years old."

When he said that, I explained to him my situation and admitted, "All my life I felt that my father's inability to show me love was related to his lack of dedication as a father or to our financial situation." As we talked, I added, "I think this is something more systemic with men in general. We're not taught how to love one another."

When new students come into my school, we teachers can immediately sense the ones who receive love at home. They're confident and they're already talking about books they recognize or that have been read to them. Those are children who have been loved, and who feel good about themselves. Every child should feel like that.

If we could only come to embrace the concept of loving other people, we could then begin to understand the importance of our influence. It's our duty to teach our children to follow the principle of "Love thy neighbor." If we begin with the children, we can get more people to understand the power of loving one another.

12

The Influence of Faith

The first stanza of an old Christian song, "Faith of Our Fathers," written by Frederick W. Faber in the 1800s, includes these words:

Faith of our fathers! living still
In spite of dungeon, fire, and sword . . .

These words suggest a legacy or inheritance of a belief system—in this case, Christianity—that has withstood attempts to destroy its existence. By singing the subsequent words in the hymn, Christian disciples offer a pledge to be true to their religious heritage until death. Think of the implications if everyone, or even most Christians, kept that pledge. At one time in our country, the concept of loyalty to our faith was a tradition, but times have changed. For many, superficial knowledge of a particular religion doesn't guarantee that we will embrace it, even if our parents did. Living in a free society affords us an opportunity to believe what we will or to believe nothing. What has the greatest impact on us may be the way the followers of any religious group advertise their faith by their approach to life and their application of the tenets of that faith. They can have a significant impact only if they believe—if they have assurance—that they stand for the truth.

Africans who were brought to the United States were forced to practice Christianity. Despite that, many sincerely accepted the faith and used that faith as a means to survive one of the most evil periods of American history. Their testimony of faith against impossible odds has caused many to believe.

Likewise, the success of the Civil Rights Movement, led by the quiet strength of a Baptist minister, will forever echo in the annals of this nation's history. When we think of men and women of renown whose faith has directed or changed the course of their lives so that others knew they were operating out of their own religious convictions and principles, we must think of such luminaries as Dr. Martin Luther King, Jr., Malcolm X, Mahatma Gandhi, and Mother Teresa. Their faith influenced their lives; their lives have influenced our faith.

We don't have to limit this to the superstars of religion. Many of us may be able to mention people in our communities or in our homes whose lives impress us because they honor their faith enough to be directed by it. I've heard people say, "If there ever was a true Christian, it's—" and they mention an individual whose lifestyle has impacted them.

At the time I was born, my mother was studying Islam. Thus, I was born into a Muslim household. A Muslim is someone who is obedient to God. Our family held to the tenets of the faith, but our mother saw to it that we were never an exclusive faith. That is, she had a healthy respect for other faiths. Even though she had chosen to become a Muslim, she introduced all of us children to other faiths. When I was older, I explored Christianity myself. Eventually, I converted to Christianity. Largely because of the influence of my mother, I don't disrespect Muslims or those of any religious faith.

Regardless of our religion, if our belief system has changed and enriched our lives—and mine has—it becomes invaluable for us to share our faith with others.

Because it has worked for me; that is to say, given me hope, inspired me, comforted me, expanded the level of my consciousness, and provided me with a moral compass, it's significant enough for me to share with other people. If religious faith has changed my life and *positively* altered my course, what can faith do for others? Because of my belief in, and commitment to, the Christian faith, I am a better person, a better husband, and a better father. Christianity, I feel, has provided me with a solid basis for making the right choices for my family. Therefore, I am more focused, disciplined, and loving as the head of my household.

I have discovered a wonderful secret about this life: Part of the benefit and joy of experiencing anything that's important is to share it with others. In sharing, the value of my faith increases. For instance, if I discovered a diet plan or exercise routine that helped me, I'd rush out to tell my overweight, sedentary, and out-of-shape friends immediately. We often do that with diets, exercise routines, new vitamins, the latest videos or books. We don't always do that with our faith. We sometimes hesitate because we don't want to impose our faith, and we want to respect others' beliefs; however, many misdirected or faith-less individuals around us need to hear. We might be able to bring them exactly the message they need to change their ways. If our new diets work or if they find pleasure out of reading the books we suggest, why don't we also offer our faith?

Any faith should provide its followers with a platform for noble thoughts and actions. Basic to all good religions are benefits and rewards for right choices. Conversely, religions warn against consequences for bad choices. This doesn't make us robots or blind believers, but joins us with a community of people who ascribe to a similar philosophy or theology about life.

My faith makes me aware that the world is larger than my

immediate family. My relationship with God allows me to see that the world is filled with others of faith, but also with people who have no belief in God. If my belief in a sovereign power is real—that is, if I embrace it by submitting myself to its principles for living—I can influence others to seek this same powerful force so that they can lead better lives.

We need to let others know what the Lord has done for us. I don't believe we should knock on every door and loudly shout to people, although some may feel that there may be situations when this type of evangelism is necessary; however, we need to live consistent lives. A life that is disciplined and balanced draws the attention of others. Something about quiet control and inner peace causes observers to wonder about our source of strength. We have abundant opportunities to be witnesses about the way our faith has sustained us.

Earlier, I wrote about our daughter Nashetah, who was born prematurely. After the doctor gave us a poor prognosis, which he honestly needed to do, we could have been devastated by that news. We were initially disappointed, but our faith in God supported us. Although I had my moments of doubt about our baby girl's health prospects, both Shawnna and I took refuge by crying out to the God of Heaven who loves us and cares about us.

We're thankful that Nashetah is not only alive but healthy. If she had been born with any major health problems or defects, as tough a pill as that would have been to swallow, our faith would have sustained us. We would have been able to say, "The Lord is with us, He never makes mistakes. With His help we can cope with any problem in life." I truly believe those words. I also want to say without equivocation that I am overjoyed and grateful about the testimony we have, and we give God full credit for answering our heartfelt prayers on behalf of our daughter. We have entrusted her future to Him.

I know of people who didn't receive the kind of answer they

sought in prayer. Not everything I have asked for has been granted to me. This is when faith truly manifests its sustaining power. We receive a "peace that transcends all understanding."[14]

Too often, we focus on our failures or others' imperfections. Perhaps we need to turn that around and pause to think about what *is* working. We can begin by being thankful for the spiritual influences in our lives, or we can focus on the fact that we have influenced and helped others. Our spiritual brothers and sisters are better off because they have interacted with us and vice versa. That doesn't make us holy or special, but it does mean that our faith is practical. Because we were helped in our times of need, we help others.

A verse from the Bible says this for me very nicely: ". . . He comforts us in all our troubles so that we can comfort others. When others are troubled, we will be able to give them the same comfort God has given us."[15]

What is more rewarding than to know that we've helped to change other lives for the better? When we interact with people who are hurt and encourage them, we are giving them a hand up and not just a handout.

One significant aspect of the teachings of the Christian faith is to be thankful. For example, in the Bible, Paul wrote, "No matter what happens, always be thankful, for this is God's will for you who belong to Christ Jesus."[16]

Giving thanks is emphasized in other religions as well. None of us gives thanks and praise perfectly, but I've learned that the more thankful we become, the easier we're able to deal with life's problems. This is probably because it takes a conscious effort to have a grateful heart about things we ordinarily take for granted such as the dawn of a new day, good health, a sound

14. Philippians 4:7, Today's New International Version.
15. 2 Corinthians 1:4, New Living Translation.
16. 1 Thessalonians 5:18, New Living Translation.

mind, the love of a spouse, and the joy of a child. When we deliberately consider our wonderful daily blessings, life's critical issues seem so minuscule. We can embrace and savor those moments of peace, those occasions of mirth. In doing that, we give the proper balance to the affairs of life.

Hardships will come. They come in disparate ways in everyone's life. The amazing thing is, we often grow more during those times of adversity. Through difficult experiences, we learn that we can endure. A well-developed level of patience is a by-product of suffering because we have to "wait on God" or "hold out until our change comes." Sometimes in solitude we have to retreat to quiet places or seek the face of God on a higher, more intense level. Our faith sustains us, grows stronger, and prepares us for the next hardship we will encounter.

In pleasant seasons, we sometimes reflect on those periods of sickness, unemployment, estrangement or divorce, or the death of a loved one. We recognize that our faith sustained us, and in the long run, we've thrived. In fact, it's not merely making it through the difficult times, but making it through the difficult times *and* knowing we're stronger as a result. There will always be obstacles and hardships. That makes faith powerful—it enables us to survive problems of any dimension, any magnitude, if we understand how it works and put it into practice. Faith is like a muscle; when it is properly exercised in the midst of challenges, it becomes stronger. That's a wonderful legacy to pass on to someone else.

It becomes of paramount importance to examine how our spirituality is being cultivated. People of a faith should study its core curriculum—Bible, Torah, or Koran, or any other holy book. We should understand *why* we believe as well as *what* we believe.

I find it interesting that many of us will read and study an academic subject and do vast amounts of research. Yet when it comes to our faith, we think we receive it by osmosis. When we "study to show ourselves approved,"[17] we have the proper basis for believing as we do, and we can more clearly communicate our beliefs to others or defend them.

In our trials, we should become what I call "more reflective learners." The words of an old gospel song go, "My soul looks back and wonders how I got over." We should not take our "getting over" for granted. Rather, we should carefully consider the "faith factor." Through faith, we should see a direct correlation between our struggles and our successes. If this is not clear to us, we need to examine ourselves and ask, "What am I doing to increase my level of spirituality?" "Am I becoming a proactive faith agent?" Whether I'm involved in a church, synagogue, or mosque, I need to participate—to be committed. It takes more than one formal worship service each week. In fact, faith is only as strong as its practical workings.

A serious examination of our faith makes us ask:

- Am I taking what I've learned from my faith into the community?
- Do I truly understand the basis for my faith?
- Do I daily seek to strengthen it by prayer and study?
- Do I put my faith into action?
- Is my involvement in my faith showing in the way I respond to others in need?
- When others fall down, am I there to help them up and to encourage them?
- Have I become better, stronger, and more enriched from reading and studying, whether it's the Bible, the Torah, or the Koran?

As I've grown slowly, yet steadily, in my faith, I've also realized how much older, more mature believers have influenced

17. See 2 Timothy 2:15.

me by the way they lived more than anything else. Their joy radiates from within, and the peace they exude affects people around them.

One thing I love about my church and churches in general is that they focus on the improvement of the surrounding community. Many parishioners travel to churches in other neighborhoods. The people who live in those same communities may not necessarily attend that, or any other, church. The only opportunity for interaction between the two groups may be in passing by and watching other people pass by as they enter the church building. Exchanging simple courtesies, though nice, merely scratches the surface of Christian witnessing. As a result, there may be outreach ministries, such as food pantries, Alcoholics Anonymous, Narcotics Anonymous, job referral services, homework assistance, and senior care—all of which bridge the gap between "us" and "them." Even if the church is not actively involved in community affairs, something about its presence and the way the members behave within the community influences others for good. The maintenance of the building and property may signal a reverence for the things of God, and can inspire neighbors to care for their own possessions.

When we believe (and we show that belief because we live our faith each day), we improve the quality of the lives of those around us. They may not have the same beliefs and they may not join our congregations, but they can help to improve the community.

For example, my coauthor, Cecil Murphey, was a pastor in the Atlanta area. His church had an arrangement with the county human resources director, and that organization screened people who expressed various needs. When they were able to determine that individuals or families truly needed help, they sent them to his church. Members budgeted money to help supply emergency needs for others. For all of the ten years Cec was the pastor of Riverdale Presbyterian Church, the congregation paid the utility bills, put new tires on the cars, purchased food, and created employment opportunities for members of the community.

"Not one of those people ever joined our church," Cec said. "And that was all right. In fact, I used to tell our members, 'We don't do this to gain members, we do this to help people in need.'"

That's how faith works. True faith shows itself by positively touching people—inside the building and outside in the community. We all have the same needs. If we're blessed enough to have all our needs met, we ought to look at those in need and say, "There but for the grace of God go I," and remember that we are "blessed to be a blessing" to others.

Faith in action doesn't predict the outcome and then decide whether to help. True faith moves us by our compassion to meet needs. We must understand that not everyone will rise up and walk into a church. Members of churches and religious institutions must engage in the task of changing and improving lives outside their own institutional walls, even if they receive no direct benefit.

Although as Christians we have received the "Great Commission" to tell everyone about our faith, whether they accept it or not, we should still reach out and care for needy people— all needy people.

Sometimes those people need a hot meal. Maybe they need someone just to listen or to hug them. Maybe they want to hear, "You are worthwhile. You are not useless." Perhaps they long for someone to say, "I don't understand what you're going through, but I'm here for you."

Our faith works both ways. As we nurture others, we are also nurtured. In fact, Jesus said it this way, "It is more blessed to give than to receive."[18]

18. Acts 20:35, New International Version.

* * *

I have had a number of important religious influences in my life. Of course, my mother was first and by far the most important influence, because she lived the kind of life she talked about. She was attentive to me, but she also opened up her home to others. She endeavored to be a blessing to her family and her community. She gave abundantly to me, not just her limited material things, but she also freely shared her time and attention. She taught me how to treat people by her example. Beyond her, the person who had the most effect on my religious beliefs—and this goes back to my childhood—was my pastor, Rev. Herbert McClain, at Bethel Presbyterian Church. He took time with me and encouraged me to play basketball and participate in any of the sports at the church; he also taught us boys to pause and pray before we played. From him we learned to pray that we would behave well and be good sports and do our best, regardless of the outcome.

After the games, whether we won or lost, we prayed and asked God to always help us do our best in everything and not to hold any resentment toward other players. That was a powerful message for young boys to receive.

Rev. McClain urged us to attend church and the midweek Bible study. Because he cared for us and lived a godly life himself, we wanted to please him and we eagerly attended. Instead of a duty, we felt it was a great privilege to glean knowledge and wisdom from him. We studied, and as we did that, he explained the practical meaning of the Bible and that strengthened our faith.

He often talked to us about the way the neighborhood was changing. "It will be up to each one of you to improve our community," he said more than once. "We shouldn't turn to the government or someone else. We—every one of us—can make a difference as we join together through the church in various activities."

I was only a kid when Rev. McClain came into my life, but his faith and his influence have continued through all these years. Even while I was a college student, Rev. McClain wrote me regularly and sometimes phoned me. Because he knew I was one of eight children, and my mother struggled to support all of us, a few times he asked if I needed money. He never seemed to ask for anything in return. That made him even more special. That also made his faith more special and real to me.

Another spiritual influence in my life is Sean Wise, the pastor of Calvary Baptist Church, where Shawnna and I are members. I love him not only because he's personable and bright, but also because he talks about what the church can and should do. He constantly says, "We need to take the church to the community. Stop waiting for the community to come into the church."

He's the impetus behind innovative programs and activities. Because of him, our church started a ministry to prisoners. Other churches also do that, but we didn't stop there. Through his guidance, we've extended that outreach to support children who have incarcerated parents. After listening to the prisoners, he realized the effects of their absence on the lives of their offspring. In another project, we're involved in a mentoring program for young people. We do these things because we know that our faith influences those around us.

Several times Pastor Wise has come to me and said, "You're someone who has been blessed with the ability to reach children and to influence people who can go on to influence others. You have to use that power and avail yourself of that opportunity. I plan to use you to be able to get that message out." His words have both humbled me and given me a strong desire to live up to his assessment of my gifts and abilities. His faith has been contagious and I'm a better, more faithful Christian today because of his belief in me.

Isn't that how faith works? The more we give it away—pass it on—the more everyone benefits.

My pastor has done something else: He's opened up to me and made me realize how far he has come in his spiritual journey. Before he became a Christian, he was a young man with many serious problems, but his turning to God pulled him through. Now he uses his story—his own experience—as part of the message to point out that faith can change people. For example, Pastor Wise told me that, like many young teens who ran the streets, he used drugs and committed petty crimes. But once he became a believer, he decided, with God's help, to change his life. He had been out there with the violence, and the drugs. He knows all about the black nights and dark streets, but he has walked in the light and wants to shine a light for others to see the way to a better path. His personal story is powerful because struggling people sometimes look at believers and think either they have always been good people or that God has given something to those special Christians that He won't provide for them.

Throughout my adult life, I've taken students to church and often talked to them about getting involved and being in the church. One boy has been very special to me. His name is Stephen Young.

I met with Pastor Weathers at Miller Memorial Baptist Church, one of the churches that adopted Reynolds School. To adopt a school means to provide support in various areas. Sometimes the support is financial; oftentimes it means that the members of the church volunteer their time at the school for classroom support, serve as chaperones on trips and outings, and offer the use of their facility. The membership has dedicated a bulletin board in their church to our school. Miller Memorial, our faith-based partner, has actually posted a mission statement for Reynolds. I met with the pastor and we talked about ways his congregation could become more involved in the community and the school by collaborating with the community. While we were talking, he said, "By the way, do you know Stephen Young?"

"Yes, I do. He's one of our students. He's in third grade."

"I thought so." He told me that Stephen came to church every week, many times by himself. The pastor reached out to Stephen and took him under his wing. He demonstrated real care to that young man and caused him to want to be a part of his church. "We recently baptized Stephen and now he's bringing his younger brother to church with him."

That sounds like such a simple, obvious thing, and yet many children don't do that. Stephen is about eight years old, but he knows what God, the church, and the pastor have done for him. He's passing on his own faith influence—even at that young age.

While I spoke with the pastor, I reflected about children I had taken to church. For years, our chess players have visited many churches in Philadelphia with me. We receive so much support from congregations that we take time to visit and share our words of gratitude. Many of our students are members of their own churches, and some have visited our church. For example, one of my chess-playing students, Alphonso Rogers, came to visit Calvary Baptist Church one Sunday. I spotted him and stopped to talk with him. I had known Alphonso's family for years because his older sisters had been students at Vaux when I taught there.

"I'm proud of you for coming to church," I said, and we talked about the importance of involvement.

Several months later Alphonso rushed up to me and said, "Mr. EL, you weren't in church Sunday. I kept looking for you."

"I'm sorry to have missed the service, but I was out of town."

"I wanted you to know something. Something special." He grinned and waited for me to ask.

"Okay, so tell me," I said. "What was so special?"

"I joined the church Sunday."

I hugged him and we both smiled. I had remembered his visits with us, and I hoped they would be meaningful for him, but I had no idea that our congregation would have any lasting effect. He said I had influenced him to join the church. He added that his family had started to come with him and they had also joined.

No one was more surprised than I was. I had had no idea that my inviting students to church would make such a difference.

We never know how we affect others, do we?

More than our words, our faith encourages us and our way of life inspires other people. I firmly believe in the power of nonverbal communication. Living out our faith is the ultimate in nonverbal communication. By our dedication and commitment to living sacrificially—if it's real—we inspire others. Too often, we discount the significance of how our actions impact those around us.

As people of faith, we can become world changers. If we believe that, we will do whatever we can to enlist others in the war against injustice and poverty. They will join us if they realize we're sincere, and we enable them to catch our vision to make our homes, churches, and communities better.

Haven't we all seen people in our community, young and old, who seem to have no purpose and no hope? Their sad faces seem to say, "Today is terrible and tomorrow won't be any better." They've been beaten down and can't seem to do anything to shake their negative feelings.

They are exactly the people we need to reach. I don't understand how anyone is not moved with compassion at the sight of downhearted people. To some, they have become invisible, and they're not easy to be around. I suppose it's easier to ignore them. But we must do something—anything—to lift them up. Just to say a simple "Have a good day" is a start. Over the years when I've been able to engage some of them in conversation and talk about the positive things that our young people are doing, they often brighten up. Even if they don't say much, I often see hope in their eyes.

They may not have known that hope as a child, but interestingly, they can rejoice and live it through the children. In the inner city, we've observed that some of those downtrodden actually take the knowledge of the children's successes as a way to become engaged in conversation and then we can encourage them. We provide the children with opportunities; the children inspire them; they spur the children on. In doing this we create a faith ecosystem. We need their help to make permanent changes in our communities.

It's not the job of just one person; it's something all of us can do.

One day I visited a homeless shelter for teens. My first shock was that they were teens—homeless—with no place to live and no families to support them. Even in the inner city, I had never imagined there were teenagers who were in such desperate situations. Until then, I had assumed homeless people were older adults who lived on the streets, or perhaps were war veterans with serious problems. These young people lived independently in shelters with no other family members.

I went to that particular shelter because a man named Dan McVey had heard me speak at a conference on homeless children. A major focus of the conference was the invisible homeless children who live in our cities across America. That evening I had spoken about what we must do as adults to improve the lives of our young people.

Dan came to meet me at the end of the meeting and said, "I

appreciate your words, and I'd like you to spend thirty minutes with some young people if you can find the time." He explained that the young people were teens who had formerly been homeless and were now living in what he called Covenant House.

"What's that?" I asked.

"It's a shelter for homeless teenagers and young adults, and they're making their way back into the community."

After I told him I had never heard of such a place, I agreed to tour the facility, which is located in the Germantown section of Philadelphia.

I told him that I would bring a few copies of my book to give the young people to encourage and motivate them. As soon as I walked into the Covenant House building, which was well secured and brightly lit, one of the female employees welcomed me inside and asked, "Would you like something to eat?"

Later, I figured out that food was the first reason most people came to the door. I thanked her and said no. I explained I had come to speak to the residents.

She seemed to appear as if her job would not have been completed had I not eaten so I took her up on her offer of fried chicken and peach cobbler.

After I had finished eating, the woman wanted to make sure I had everything I needed. She impressed me because she made me feel as if I was a special guest and she wanted me to feel welcomed.

She explained that the students had planned a special program—one they created themselves—and I was their featured speaker. Some would sing, while others would play an instrument or recite poetry.

Just before the program began, several of the young people came up to me, introduced themselves, and thanked me for coming.

"Are you going to stay for the full program?" one of them asked.

"I'm not sure. I need to get back, but I'll stay as long as I can," I said. I had planned to come in for about thirty minutes, say a few words of encouragement, and return home to my family. After meeting those wonderful young people, I should have realized I would stay for the evening.

As I watched them sing and recite poetry, I wondered how they could focus on words and music. Perhaps like the slaves in the past, they took a horrible situation and made something beautiful out of it. They had no families they could call on for help. At some point, they would have to find a place to live.

At the end of the program, one of the students sang a gospel song. When she had finished, another teen came to me and said, "You ought to put her on the soundtrack of your movie." Some of the teens had read in the newspaper that the Walt Disney company purchased the movie rights to my first book.

I smiled but I also thought, "That's powerful for a young person to come to me about another peer when there's so much violence and hatred in the world." I told the young singer, "You give me your name and information on how to contact you, and I'll do whatever I can to help you."

The moment that moved me the most was when they recited a poem called "God, Why Did You Make Me Black?" I started to cry when I heard the students. The poem begins with questions to God about the negative implications of being black; it ends with God showing them all of the positive aspects of being black. (Many of my students at Reynolds have since memorized the poem.) Afterward, they spoke out of their pain and rejection but also with great hope for the future.

When I got up to talk, I didn't think they would receive much of what I would say because they were already dealing with so many other things every day—problems I had never had to face when I was their age. To my surprise, they were attentive and engaged.

Afterward, I stayed to answer questions. While I spoke, I kept staring at one young woman in the audience, who was maybe twenty years old. I couldn't remember her name but I was sure she had been a student at Vaux. When she stood and asked a question, I asked, "You went to Vaux, didn't you?"

She said, "Yes, Mr. EL, I did go to Vaux."

"I remember you."

She told me that there was also another former Vaux student who lived there. That shocked me. I hadn't considered that the children we teach might grow up and become homeless. The homeless were always nameless people and strangers. That experience forced me to think, "That homeless person I looked away from was once a child of promise in someone's home and classroom. Somehow that child's life became misdirected." I also realized that if the children we interact with are not properly nurtured and supported, they could very well end up in a similar situation.

That evening was an amazing experience for me. Despite the uncertainty of their lives, they didn't appear discouraged. Covenant House gave them hope and provided guidance and solid, practical help for them to live on their own. As I learned, they came in destitute and discouraged, but the workers there prayed with them, spoke to them about faith in Jesus Christ, helped them refocus their lives, and encouraged them to go out and survive in the world with jobs and with a heart to serve others.

As I got up to leave, every one of those teens smiled at me. It was nothing forced, but I sensed their genuine faith. Their smiles said, "Don't worry, Mr. EL, we're going to make it."

I believed them. Since then, I've heard from several of them. They have "graduated" from homeless status and now have good jobs and apartments. They are also helping others their own age, sharing their faith and influencing them in a positive way.

Covenant House is the largest privately funded childcare agency in the United States, providing shelter and service to homeless and runaway youth. It was incorporated in New York City in 1972 and has since expanded in the United States to Anchorage, Atlanta, Atlantic City, Detroit, Fort Lauderdale, Houston, Los Angeles, Newark, New Orleans, Oakland, Orlando, Philadelphia, St. Louis, Washington, D.C., and outside the United States, to Toronto, Vancouver, Guatemala, Honduras, Mexico, and Nicaragua.

In addition to food, shelter, clothing, and crisis care, Covenant House provides a variety of services to homeless youth, including health care, education, vocational preparation, drug abuse treatment and prevention programs, legal services, recreation, mother-child programs, transitional living programs, street outreach, and aftercare.

Covenant House provided residential and nonresidential services to over 76,000 youth in 2004. Over 14,500 young people came into Covenant House Crisis Shelters and Rights of Passage Programs. Another 27,000 received help in Community Service Centers or in aftercare and prevention services. Their outreach workers served an additional 35,000 youth on the street.

In 2004, Covenant House (1-800-999-9999; http://www.covenanthouse.org/about.html) received 51,000 crisis calls from youngsters all over the United States who needed immediate help and had nowhere else to turn.

Those young people at Covenant House were accustomed to people who came and went in their lives. It felt foolish and presumptuous to think that by being there an hour or two I could make a difference. Who was I to think I could impact them?

I was wrong. They wanted people to positively affect them. I also realized something else: In a matter of minutes, they had influenced me. Instead of being sullen or discouraged, they were alive, excited, and eager to move beyond living in Covenant House.

As I walked out the front door, I checked my watch. I had been there for more than two hours! I had planned to stay only thirty minutes.

That experience at Covenant House helped me to understand that we must use our faith, our energies, and our talents to invest in all our children. Our young people need to hear, learn, and understand about faith and commitment.

Just those two hours at Covenant House helped me to understand the importance of the influence of faith. I hadn't walked inside looking for a lesson in faith. I walked in simply to deliver a ten-minute speech and spend another twenty minutes, reflect on the experience, and go back to my life.

They challenged me. I saw their faith was alive and vital. They had come there, as one of them told me, because they had no place else to go. The vitality and vibrancy of their faith touched me. I saw that those children were tough—they had to be to have survived. Despite their hardships, not one of them complained or moaned about how bad life was.

I learned something powerful from those young people at Covenant House. They could have been bitter and pessimistic. They could have talked about indifference and cruelty. Instead, they radiated joy. They had a future and they were determined to make the most of it.

Too often when I speak to young people, I have to urge them not to focus on others' faults, but to look for the positives. I want them to have excellence as their mind-set and their goal. I didn't use those words at Covenant House because I sensed they had already grasped what I wanted to say.

Isn't it sad that so many young people have homes, food, even jobs, and yet they have no plan, no vision. They don't know where they're going. The Bible says, "Without a vision, the people perish."[19] I wish every discouraged young person could have the bright eyes and renewed life I saw in those young people. If they had them, they could change their world. Those young people may not have had that drive independent of their experience at Covenant House and that's when they learned a sense of value. In somewhat of a reversal, those who seemingly had nothing gave me so much.

During my down times when I examine my life and think about how tough I've had it, or begin to feel sorry for myself, I remember that evening. "Salome, you're not living at Covenant House and you're not homeless. You know where you're going to sleep tomorrow, next month, and next year. Those young people don't know about next week, but they thought enough to express love and appreciation. They said you encouraged them. Don't forget they encouraged *you*."

When I talk to myself that way, I feel better. It's too easy to forget how good my life really is.

One girl at Covenant House told me, "I started college and dropped out." She told me about the circumstances that pushed her to give up. "But after hearing you tonight, I'm going to go back to college. I'm going to go back and this time I'm going to finish."

"When you finish, you let me know," I said, "and I'll attend your graduation."

She had a look in her eyes that said, "I'm going to hold you to that. I'm going to invite you."

I'll definitely plan to be there.

---

19. Proverbs 29:18, King James Version.

*   *   *

Two verses from the Bible motivated me that evening and have continued to stay with me, especially when I try to talk to adults about how we influence others and to young people about how they influence others and can grow to become people of great influence to the world.

"And whoever welcomes a little child like this in my name, welcomes me."[20]

" . . . Let the little children come to me, and do not hinder them, for the kingdom of heaven belongs to such as these."[21]

Those two statements by Jesus make me aware that when we're close to our children and love them, we bring them closer to God. Those words remind me that we have a strong faith influence on them—and a powerful responsibility to bring those children to God and to teach them.

When I've mentioned those two verses, young people have sometimes asked, "Why does God put so many things in front of me? Why do I have so many trials and tribulations?"

"God won't give you a test that you can't pass," I tell them. That may sound glib, but I don't mean it that way. "God only tests his best students so they can learn and truly be the best." Sometimes I add, "God wants you to be an honor student in life and in service." We all know that an excellent life profoundly reflects faith.

20. Matthew 18:5, New International Version.
21. Matthew 19:14, New International Version.

13

Influence on Purpose

I'm actively involved with a group of young men in South Carolina who are enrolled in a scholarship teaching program titled Call Me MISTER. The program is named after the 1970 film that starred Sidney Poitier, *They Call Me Mister Tibbs*. Under the guidance and leadership of the director, Dr. Roy Jones, and field coordinator, Winston Holton, both from Clemson University, two hundred young black males study on nine different college campuses in the state of South Carolina. The program combines the strengths and resources of Clemson University with the unique instructional programs offered by nearby historically black colleges and two-year institutions. These young men have appeared on *The Oprah Winfrey Show*, they were featured in *USA Today*, and many magazines have told their stories.

All of the MISTERs receive four-year scholarships and are training to be teachers. Of the more than 20,000 elementary school teachers in the state of South Carolina, less than 1 percent are black men. There are more black men in prison in the state (about 14,000) than there are in college. When the first one hundred young men graduate, they will double the number of black men who are teaching in elementary schools in South Carolina. That's still far too few, but it's a positive beginning.

The first group graduated in 2004. I became involved with the young men as a mentor because some of them reached out to me after seeing me interviewed on C-SPAN. They were encouraged by my views on teaching and thought that I could benefit from meeting their director and other leaders. And they were correct.

Call Me MISTER

Many elementary schools face a dire shortage of African-American male teachers. Clemson University has developed an innovative educational program aimed at addressing this critical need through its Call Me MISTER program.

The program seeks to recruit, train, certify, and secure employment for two hundred black males as elementary teachers in South Carolina's public schools. The Call Me MISTER program provides:

- Tuition assistance to young men enrolled in elementary education at the three collaborating colleges.
- An academic support system to help assure their success.
- A cohort system for social and cultural support.

Call Me MISTER received national recognition upon its inception four years ago when the first wave of MISTER participants were featured on *The Oprah Winfrey Show* and were selected to be part of Oprah's Angel Network.

Ten MISTERs entered the workforce as elementary school teachers in the state of South Carolina in 2004.

One of the men in the program, Hayward Jean, contacted me by e-mail after watching Book TV and reading my book, *I Choose to Stay*. "I was touched to see a teacher who was dedicated and committed to staying in the inner city. It motivated me to continue in the program." He said that several of the men in the program needed encouragement and a few had begun to question their purpose.

In his e-mail he said, "We would love for you to visit and share your experiences as a black male teacher with us. We're in a very tough part of the program. We'll soon take our certification exams."

I was encouraged by Hayward's attempt to reach out to me but even more impressed by his servant attitude. This young man's purpose was to help others. I explained to him that my mother's family was from South Carolina and my wife's family lived in Augusta, Georgia. My visit to meet Hayward and his colleagues would give my wife and me an opportunity to see our families in the South. Hayward informed me that he and his twin brother, Howard, a MISTER Scholar at Claflin also, were raised near my wife's grandmother in Georgia. Their family lived in Aiken County.

In September 2003, I took my family and drove to Claflin University in Orangeburg, South Carolina. On the trip, I had questioned whether it was worth it to put my family on the road for the ten hours of driving. I already had a full schedule and didn't need to add any more to it. When I arrived in Orangeburg and met Hayward and others in the program, however, I stopped questioning myself.

The first thing Hayward did was to thank my wife for allowing me to disrupt our schedule and come to the college. That touched her and made her feel that she mattered and that they recognized her importance. He said he realized we had made a sacrifice to visit them. He hugged me, thanked me for coming, and said, "Everybody is looking forward to seeing you." Hayward told us about his role in his church and that he believed he was called to teach.

"I'm supposed to be here," I said, and as I heard myself say those words, I knew they were true.

I met most of the members of Call Me MISTER at Claflin. The program existed on various South Carolina campuses, so not all of the MISTERs could make it. I spoke to the Call Me MISTER students first and later I had the opportunity to address the entire campus community about the program and the importance of teaching. I emphasized that we needed similar programs to encourage and support students who wanted to serve. After the program, I had a chance to speak with the director, Dr. Jones, to thank and praise him for working with our young men. He was making a sacrifice to have a positive impact on the youth in his community.

I spoke that day about purpose—that we need to go forward with a strong sense of purpose to influence our young people. I praised the members of Call Me MISTER because they had discovered their purpose early in life and wanted to make a difference. As I had already learned, most of them came from humble beginnings and some from single-parent homes. They all agreed that the people who had had the most influence on them had been their teachers, and that influence had been a huge factor to motivate them to serve.

A few of them were young men who had graduated from high school and had originally decided against going to college. Sometimes it was the expense; sometimes it was that they weren't sure they could make it academically. Each man told a different story, of course, but all of them seemed to have that urgent sense of purpose to change the community and the world in which they lived. Many of them stressed that a former teacher had helped them to decide to apply to Call Me MISTER.

When I spoke to the men, I emphasized the importance of

knowing where they were going and of having a plan. "Don't just have a vision, because a vision without a plan is a hallucination."

I also said, "Some of you are struggling. You're not sure you should continue, but I urge you not to give up. You'll have the opportunity to teach in a classroom and you can help to improve the lives of your students. You can save many of those children who might be lost to the world. You won't reach them all, but you'll influence many. They'll become better people because of your presence in their lives."

As I spoke, my mind flashed to Willow Briggs, my former student. I didn't want them to experience similar tragic memories.

The first men in the program graduated in May 2004, and I've received e-mails and letters from several of them. In the South, most of the schools start in August and they had already started their teaching career by the time our school year started in September.

In writing to me, they said, in various ways, "Thanks for motivating and encouraging me. This is my purpose. This is what I should be doing and here is where I belong. The young children in my classroom now call me Mister."

I returned to South Carolina in July 2004. That time I went to speak to superintendents, central office administrators, and principals in Columbia. My purpose was to motivate them as they started the new school year with many challenges but also to celebrate their successes. I invited several members of Call Me MISTER to attend the event because I wanted to show them an example of purpose at work through the lives of people who were giving hope to children every day.

I wanted those school officials to see the results of their influence. Several of the young men in the program were graduates of the Columbia, South Carolina, school system, and many of the teachers and administrators in their home districts didn't know that those young men were in the program or that they were graduating. A few had already graduated. They seemed unaware that they wanted to become teachers and were available to be hired.

When I started to speak at their morning session, I said, "I know you came today to hear me, and you will. You are also going to have a chance to meet six dynamic young men who have found their life purpose. They found it because professionals like *you* sacrificed and influenced them and *you* gave them the tools they needed to be successful. Now they're graduating with honors." I named the programs they had majored in: Elementary and Secondary Education, Computer Science Education, English, and Math Education. "They're all men who want to give back to the community because of you."

After I introduced the six young men at the opening session, I spoke to the group of 300 educators. I told them about my life and the influence my teachers and principals had had on me. I also told them about my influence on other young people and that I found my purpose through working with children.

After I had finished, I answered some questions and invited the MISTER scholars to join me. I wanted those principals and teachers to hear from their former students. Their words would be more powerful than mine.

After several minutes, a school principal identified himself and turned and pointed to one of the young men. "I taught you in high school, but I had no idea you wanted to be an educator. I can't believe I didn't know what happened to you." He hugged the young man and said, "Here you are graduating and you're a teacher. It is because of students like you that I have realized I am doing something right. I've influenced you and I know I'm making a difference."

The principal and the young man went over to the side of the room and hugged each other. As they talked, we saw tears in their eyes. Many of us also had tears in our eyes.

That spontaneous event was exactly right. Those teachers needed to see a demonstration of how they had affected young people. They needed to see that their purpose was not only to educate, but to influence students to be successful and to become a strong part of the community. That one incident helped many of the principals and teachers realize how influential they really are.

After the presentation, I began to think about my visit to Orangeburg in 2003. Call Me MISTER scholars asked me to visit a local high school with them. I walked into Orangeburg Wilkinson High School in South Carolina with some of the same young men who were with me in Columbia. We were there to speak to the students about the importance of being serious in school and understanding their purpose early in life.

The students loved hearing from the soon-to-be teachers. They didn't want them to leave and begged the young men to stay longer. Afterward they sent e-mails and stayed in touch with us. The dedication and commitment of the MISTERs had overwhelmed them.

Hayward e-mailed me a year after our initial visit. "I hope you don't mind that, when I talk to people about you, I tell them you're my mentor and that you're someone who's made a difference and influenced my life."

I e-mailed back, "I'm honored to be your mentor."

I couldn't think of a more wonderful thing he could do, and I felt humbled to be known as his mentor.

Hayward now teaches in Aiken, South Carolina, and invited me to visit his classroom at any time. I will be honored to do that.

He's typical of many of the young men I've met in the Call Me MISTER program. Most of them have said, "I wasn't sure what I was prepared to do with my life, but once I enrolled in college and met other young men in this program who wanted to be educators, I knew that's where I wanted to go."

The Call Me MISTER scholars are under the leadership of strong men who understand the power of their influence. The young men dress and act like true professionals at all times. They understand that even as college students, "they are their brother's keeper."

They know their purpose. They want to influence others and they take that seriously.

Another organization that is building a movement of tremendous purpose is Teach For America. TFA is an organization that was started in 1989 by Wendy Kopp, although I was only vaguely aware of the program until 2003. That was the first full year we had the Teach For America program in Philadelphia.

The Philadelphia director of Teach For America, Stephanie Crement, called me and said, "We have one hundred teachers here and it's getting tough for some of them in Philadelphia. Some have started to question their purpose." It was almost Christmas and many of them were ready to go home for the holidays. Some of them weren't sure they wanted to return to teaching. They felt beaten down by the bureaucracy, difficult kids, and living in a tough city. After she explained their problems, she said, "We'd like you to speak to our group. Would you come and motivate us?"

It was January 2004 before we could work out our schedules but we did it. We chose January 15, the birthday of Dr. Martin Luther King, Jr. It was also the coldest day of the school year, and by the time we met that evening, the windchill factor was at least ten degrees below zero. We met in the auditorium of Sulzberger Middle School in West Philadelphia.

It was a wonderful experience to see that group of whites, blacks, Asians, Latinos, and Native Americans—all recent college graduates who had entered the teaching profession. I thought they would have a tough time getting the TFA members to attend because of the terrible weather. I told one of the coordinators, "I'll be happy if we get twenty of them here tonight."

I had come there to try to help motivate the teachers and to enable them to see they had a purpose in the inner city. To my surprise, almost every member showed up. We were overjoyed.

Once the program started, and as I waited for the introduction, I reflected on my own life. I realized that I had once been where they were. I hadn't been sure teaching was the right place for me. Like them, I had many questions and few answers.

Many of them had graduated from some of the best schools; others were individuals who could easily find jobs in corporations and command substantial salaries. They could do anything other than teach young people, yet they had chosen a life of service.

When I spoke, I told them I had grown up in the projects, and then I shared a few stories of my tough background in Philadelphia. "My teachers made the difference to me. They helped me to become who I am. Without people like them, I would not be as successful as I am today. I'm not the only one, because there are many of us—not as many as we'd like. Not that I'm a great person, but I'm here largely because of the dedication of caring teachers like you. Many have done greater things than I have, but I'm grateful because I've been able to change the direction of and challenge young people. Some of them are serving others today because I had the opportunity to motivate and encourage them.

"You're here. You are able to realize the immortality of your influence. Every time you reach someone and that person encourages someone else, you have multiplied yourself. You will impact people through several generations. I'm reaching young people because my teachers were able to reach me. They gave themselves to students like me. They have made the difference in my life."

I concluded by thanking them for giving their lives. Afterward, I waited around for anybody who wanted to talk. Many wanted to talk and take pictures. They were such a fun and light-spirited group. I could tell they were going to make it as teachers. Many of them later e-mailed me and I visited several of their schools.

Here is one e-mail, and the content is similar to what I received from others: "It's tough to teach in the inner city and for months I've complained about what I have to go through. As I listened to you speak, I realized it's nothing compared to the abuse that some of these young people deal with every day. I focused so much on my own hardships that I'd forgotten that I'm here to serve others. These children go through so much. I've learned my purpose. Thank you for helping me to understand and for sharing your message. Now that I've heard your story, I'm more dedicated."

Those e-mails and letters encouraged me—and all of us need as much encouragement as we can get. When I try to influence people, I try to do it through my own testimony, and I let them know I've made mistakes in my life. I've taken risks and sometimes I've fallen down. But each time I've gotten back up to make even more mistakes, but I'm still learning—from the wrong choices others made as well as through some of my own decisions. Each time trouble strikes, I respond a little better because I've become much stronger. And the Teach For America members will do the same.

During her senior year at Princeton University, Wendy Kopp developed the idea that became Teach For America. She was troubled by the educational inequities that faced children in low-income communities and was convinced that many in her generation were searching for a way to assume a significant responsibility that would make a real difference in the world.

Ms. Kopp developed a plan for the idea in her undergraduate senior thesis and received a grant from Mobil Corporation to get started. In the fall of 1989, a small team of talented recent graduates came together as the original Teach For America staff.

Teach For America is the national corps of outstanding recent college graduates of all academic majors. They commit two years to teach in urban and rural public schools and become lifelong leaders in the effort to expand educational opportunity. Their mission is to build the movement to eliminate educational inequity by enlisting some of our nation's most promising future leaders in the effort. Corps members ensure that more students growing up today in our nation's lowest-income communities have the educational opportunities they deserve. They seek to build a force of leaders with the insight and added credibility that comes from having taught in a low-income community. They work from inside education and from every other sector to effect the fundamental changes needed to ensure that all children have an equal chance in life.

Currently, 3,000 corps members are teaching in over 1,000 schools in 22 regions across the country. Their alumni, now numbering 9,000, are already starting schools, becoming principals and district administrators, winning accolades as teachers, and working to expand educational opportunity while pursuing careers in law, public policy, medicine, and business.

Every year, schools in the State System of Higher Education coordinate an Urban Seminar for student teachers in Pennsylvania. For two weeks, two hundred of them visit schools and community centers in Philadelphia because they want to get an urban experience. Although some of the students are African-American, Latino, and Asian, the majority of the participants are white. They were raised in communities with few minorities. For some, this is their first exposure to predominantly minority communities.

In 2004, the leaders of the Urban Seminar asked me to address the students at the end of the two-week program and talk to them about my experiences as a teacher in the Philadelphia public schools and also as a graduate of one of the state universities. (I graduated from East Stroudsburg University.)

For me, it was a great way to give back and to learn a great deal from aspiring teachers. I didn't think any of them were really paying attention to my words.

Several months after the Urban Seminar, I received a voice mail from a gentleman named Bill Machesky. "I'm the superintendent in the Uniontown School District." That is a school district in the western part of the state, right outside Pittsburgh. "My daughter attended the Urban Seminar where you spoke. I'd like you to call me back and to talk to you for a few minutes."

"What did I say that made her go home and tell her dad?" I asked myself. I wondered if I had said anything that frightened her about working in the public schools. Maybe I said something about my own experiences that offended her. I knew that most of what I said to the students was positive but I couldn't think of what I might have said to the young lady that would make a superintendent call me at home.

I called Dr. Machesky back. To my surprise, he immediately said that his daughter had enjoyed my lecture. That was a big relief for me. His daughter had read my book and brought it home and he read it. "I've made everyone in my house read it. My wife is a teacher and she read it. I have another daughter who's a teacher and she has also finished it. All of them loved your book."

I was delighted I had returned his call.

"I want you to know that I'm proud of you and the work that you're doing," he said. "I work in a school district where our students are often separated, based on economics. This much I know about working with young people: If we believe in them, they can be successful."

Of course, I agreed. He was talking my language.

"I'd like you to visit my school district and see if you can motivate not only the students but some of the adults that work with them. I want those teachers to believe in our young people and to know that I appreciate their hard work."

I told him that I would be delighted to do that. I visited his school district and spent some time at Lafayette Middle School. Those young people were so enjoyable. I expressed to Mr. Machesky how honored I felt to have the privilege of talking to those students. I also spoke to the teachers and encouraged them to stay committed to the young people and to education.

Every school district needs a Bill Machesky—someone who

can reach out to those from diverse backgrounds. He worked in a rural area, and he was white, older than I am, but he was open to influence, open to anyone who could make his district stronger. He influenced me in a powerful way.

One day I want to be in a position like his and feel comfortable calling someone and saying, "Please come out and help me."

I've formed a solid relationship with that man. I wanted to influence people and my words touched his daughter. My words touched her deeply enough that she told her father. That's how the concept of influence on purpose works. We try to reach others, and when we do, they, in turn, keep the motivation going.

Bill Machesky is someone who's had to fight the mind-set of various officials in the system. He wants help for the poor in the community. He's fighting hard and I have a lot of respect for him because this is a man who has a purpose in his life and knows what it is. He knows his job is to sacrifice himself for others.

Bill explained to me how he helps the young men who live in the community. He allows them to come freely into his home.

One time his daughter accepted a date to the prom from one of the African-American young men in the community and it was a nonissue for Bill. "I don't judge them based on who they are or what they look like. My attitude is based on their heart. Those young men who are friends with my daughter know that I want them to go to college. They've got to talk about going to college or I don't want them around. And they don't come into my house wearing their hats."

That is a real man. I cheered him on. He is sending the right message.

Meeting Bill Machesky reminds me that I'm not the only

one. There are thousands like him out there who have the same purpose, who are sending the same message, doing the same thing, and making the same sacrifices. All of us want to improve the lives of our young people and our communities.

That's purposeful influence at its highest level.

14

The Influence of Forgiveness

When we think about it, forgiveness is a complicated concept. Every hurtful and painful thing in our lives seems to demand retribution. We take the Old Testament idea of "an eye for an eye and a tooth for a tooth"[22] as our authority to pay back. (Instead of commanding such action, it is a limit to retribution. The command means, "If someone punches out your eye, don't do more than take an eye from that person.")

Jesus softened the command by saying, "You have heard that it was said, 'Eye for eye, and tooth for tooth.' But I tell you, do not resist an evil person. If anyone slaps you on the right cheek, turn to them the other cheek also."[23]

Repaying may seem like the thing to do at the moment. Anyone can get angry and repay violence with violence. That's the natural, immature response to life.

Life is filled with injustice and we can never right every wrong. We have laws designed to punish people who want to hurt other people, animals, property, or the environment. That

22. See Leviticus 24:20.
23. Matthew 5:38–39, Today's New International Version.

supposedly is a method to prevent or discourage unkind acts. It doesn't always work, and sometimes injustice and corruption seem to prevail.

It's easy to resort to what I call negative behavior, but we need to always remember that for every action we take, there will be consequences. If we become negative, we can't expect anything but negative results. We should try to maintain a reasonably orderly society, even if it doesn't always work out right.

Even though we should anticipate punishment for making poor choices and causing harm to others, we can reasonably expect to be rewarded for doing what is right. That doesn't always happen either.

We often say, "What goes around, comes around," meaning, "If I don't get you, something in the universe will," with the understanding being, "I hope I receive an invitation to the event."

Suppose we do something that hurts another person. We can expect the person to respond in kind. But what happens when that person steps outside conventional responses and says, "Even though you've wronged me, and I would be justified in harming you, I'm going to overlook your indiscretion."

That's freedom. I'm free even though I offended and the offended person is free.

That is a New Testament concept. Instead of demanding justice, we're directed to choose a more excellent way—not to merely overlook the matter, but to embrace and pray for the perpetrator. Even Jesus' disciples had a hard time with this one.

Understanding human nature, Peter once asked, "How many times should we forgive? Seven times?" And Jesus answered, "No, but seventy times seven."[24] He did not mean literally 490 times, but that we should forgive and forgive and keep on forgiving.

The need to forgive—to let go and move on—is a vital part

24. See Matthew 18:21–22, New Living Translation.

of our lives. People hurt us all the time; some deliberately, some without intent. We can hold grudges, let the anger seethe inside, do something to retaliate, or we can forgive. We have choices.

To be healthy and live the best life, we need to forgive—truly forgive. We also need to ask others to forgive us when we've offended them. True forgiveness happens when we are able to release our anger and resentment. People often use the phrase "forgive and forget." Forgetting may not be intellectually possible. We may never cognitively erase the wrongdoing, but we can release the passionate, negative sentiment connected with it. This means we do not deliberately bring up the incident in conversation to continually indict the offender; nor do we persist in conjuring it up in our minds to maintain a victim status. Even though people ought to be made aware when they have hurt us, the goal should be to settle the issue lovingly and quickly.

The best way I know to approach forgiveness is through understanding. Sometimes, people really don't know that they have hurt us. We can give them the benefit of the doubt. We may have attached a meaning to the remark or incident that the person had not intended. Playing the words out against our own background can change the intended meaning of a statement. It's easy to cast aspersions on other people by what we think we see, or the way we hear what they say. We may be right, but we may also be mistaken. Why risk it? We need to seek clarity before making decisions. If we can learn to look at life from the perspective of others, intentions will be better interpreted.

One of the first human relations lessons we teach children has to do with contrition. When very young people do something they shouldn't have, we may say, "You hurt Daddy," or we may pretend to cry. An exaggeration of emotions draws the child's attention to the situation. Through observation, children realize that something is wrong—something for which they are responsible. To hear a little child with a limited command of English, but an ample supply of sensitivity, say, "I sorry," melts the heart of the biggest cynic.

Children don't come with instruction manuals for parents. Many times we're not aware of a teaching opportunity in the small things our children do. Further, we often scold or punish children too readily to teach lessons they may not clearly understand. One or two explanations aren't usually enough for the young to successfully grasp the message. Ongoing good, living examples are the best teaching tools for forgiveness.

In the classroom, teachers may make a public example of a child's mistake: "Amir, apologize to John for knocking his pencil on the floor."

This rarely causes a child to seek true forgiveness. It may be worse to openly insist that a child apologize than to quietly call him over and talk about the incident. In the latter case, the child has been taught by example how to be sensitive to the feelings of others. At the time, that would seem to be the more important lesson. Sensitivity is a prerequisite for seeking and granting forgiveness. Because of our own upbringing, we may struggle ourselves with the very issues we want to teach our children.

On the opposite end of the spectrum, one of the most difficult lessons an adult may learn is to ask for forgiveness, especially from a child. There is something about condescending to a child in this manner that makes some adults want to change the rules. Sometimes adults may rationalize their behavior by saying things like, "You're too sensitive," or "You know I didn't mean that." Whether the offense was intended or not, we should make every effort to hear the hearts of our children. Children need to get a true sense that the adults in their lives are being honest and open. When adults apologize to children, those young people see strength, not weakness.

Two adults reconciling positively in the presence of other

adults and children can bring a wonderful sense of peace and trust to a family, school, or community.

Here's an example: One afternoon an angry mother stormed into the school because a teacher and I had disciplined her child.

"Why is this going on? Why are you treating my child like this? She's not doing anything she didn't do in her previous school. She never had trouble with her teachers over there."

She yelled, cursed, and told me I had no right to discipline her child. Anyone who walked by the office could hear her screaming at me.

I waited until she paused and then said softly, "Please calm down. Your children learn by watching you. I understand you're upset, but you don't want our children to start cursing and using profanity because then they'll get into more trouble."

"I'll cuss all I want!" The parent then let off a string of profanity.

"Ma'am, if you're going to disrespect our children, I'll have to ask you to leave my office and the school building. I can't allow the children to see your behavior and listen to you speak in such a disrespectful way."

She yelled again, and I told her a second time to leave.

"If you're going to treat me like that and force me to leave this school, I'll show you," she yelled. "When you come outside the school, I'm going to be waiting for you. I'm going to shoot you myself or I'll get someone else to do it."

"I would like you to understand something, ma'am. Every day I'm here and every day I go outside after school to protect my students. I want to make sure there aren't other people out there shooting and hurting them. I will be outside today around three P.M., as I am every day, to help my students go home safely. If you decide to shoot me, you will have to shoot me, *but* your threatening me is not going to stop me from going outside to watch over my students."

She kept yelling as she left the building. I looked out the window and saw her on her cell phone. I could tell she was yelling. I couldn't hear her words, but her wild gestures made her feelings clear.

My secretaries, who had heard what the mother said, were afraid for me and they wanted to call the police department. At times, there are city police officers in our neighborhood when our children enter and leave school, but not every day. I refused.

Within an hour, however, the word had spread throughout the school.

One of the school-based security officers came to my office and begged, "Don't go out after school today. That woman is crazy. You don't know what she's going to do."

"I understand and I appreciate your concern," I said, "but I can't hide inside the building. Besides, think about what might happen if I don't go outside. Instead of shooting me, that woman might shoot one of my students. I can't allow that to happen. I'm going to go out and do what I do every day."

"Then we need to call the police and have her arrested."

"No. That will only make it worse," I said.

I'm not sure where I got the courage to talk that way, because I didn't feel courageous. Was I scared? Yes, I was. I also felt sad for that woman. She was a single parent and I knew she had many burdens and heartaches. She had threatened to kill me, but she wasn't really angry with me.

Several teachers offered to go out and stand next to me, but I would not allow that to happen. I did come to my senses and dialed 911 before dismissal. My secretaries were relieved.

(The police showed up at the school about an hour after we called, and I explained to them that the parent had apologized and dedicated herself to getting help and supporting the school. We did not need another incarcerated parent.)

At 3:09 P.M., I walked out of the building with my students

the way I try to do every day. I went out against the final protests of my teachers and the security officers. I wanted to be out there when the students left school to be sure that they were safely walking home, getting on the correct bus, or climbing into their parents' cars. I had been threatened before, but this was the first time somebody had threatened to shoot me.

I don't believe she truly meant to hurt me, but I had lived in the inner city long enough to understand that anything was possible.

When I walked out of the school, I spotted the mother down the street. I turned my back on her and focused on the children. After they were all gone, I turned around and she stood about fifty feet away from me. Another woman was next to her and they were talking, but the upset parent kept her eyes focused on me.

After the students were safely on their way home from school, I started to walk toward her. To be honest, I was not sure she would not pull out her gun and shoot me before I reached her. But I had to speak with her. I couldn't go home with that issue unresolved. She didn't move and I stopped about three feet from her. "Ma'am, I came outside to support the students and not to show you up in any way. I will do whatever it takes to protect them and to make sure they get home safely. I hope you can respect me for that."

She said nothing but her eyes never left my face.

"I don't know what caused you to get upset like that, and I'm sorry, but I don't want you to think—"

"At my daughter's previous school, they banned me and told me I couldn't come back after I had a problem with the teachers and principal."

"I wouldn't do that."

"You wouldn't? After what I said and—?"

"No, ma'am, because by doing that it means I wouldn't allow you to be part of your child's educational life. I want you to be part of her education. She needs you to help her and encourage her. But that has to be done in a productive and positive manner. Your children need to know that they are important, but they also need to see you in a positive light. They learn almost everything from watching you."

For the first time, she dropped her gaze. She almost smiled. "Oh, well, I'm glad to hear that. You really mean that, don't you?"

"Yes, I do."

We stood on the street facing each other. I didn't look around but I knew my secretaries and teachers were at the windows watching. Later, some told me they were praying.

Finally she cleared her throat. "Please excuse me for the way I acted. I need to get some help with anger management. I—I shouldn't have done that. You were trying to help my daughter, but I—"

"I understand."

"After I left the school, I talked to two other parents," she said. "I told them I had had a big argument with you—and, well, I wanted them to support me, but they said, 'Mr. EL always tries to help our children.' They said you would be out here after school even after I threatened you and warned you not to show yourself. I didn't believe them—I was sure you'd be afraid. That's why I was standing here. I wanted to see for myself."

"I came out here because I want you to know that not only am I protecting your child but I'm out here also protecting all these children. Even when you told me my life was in danger, I couldn't let that stop me from making sure these children were safe. I'm willing to work with you on straightening out the problem, but I couldn't allow you to continue to disrespect me, to disrespect yourself, and to disrespect the school and the children and the community."

"I want to apologize to you. I'm sorry," she said. "I shouldn't have acted like that." Then she told me again about her previous school refusing to let her walk inside the building. I understood the school's action because the children are of the utmost importance. I believed the parent deserved some support and another chance.

"I would never tell you that. You are always welcome to come here. In fact, I want you to come to the school. You need to see what's going on with your child, so you can understand our mission and what we're doing."

"Really? I can come whenever I want?"

"You can. You need to understand that for many of our children, the school is the only safe place they have. Adults perpetrate the killing and drive-by shootings in the neighborhood. We need to protect our children, but instead we are causing them more harm. We have children enrolled in our school who come in the morning after hearing shots fired at night. They fear more gunfire in retaliation. Some of those kids won't even sit next to a window because they're afraid a stray bullet might come through and hit them."

I told her about a third-grade boy who had been murdered at a nearby elementary school. "The sad thing is almost everyone in the community knew who killed him, but they wouldn't turn the man in. The police found ninety-five shell casings from bullets in the school yard. One of the crossing guards was shot, but she recovered. We have to show our young people that we're not going to resort to violence, and we will do whatever we can to protect them."

By then she looked as if she understood my feelings. "I'm . . . I'm sorry."

"I won't prevent you from becoming part of our school." I took a step closer so she could look into my eyes. "I need you. I appreciate your apology and I understand you were angry and frustrated."

I knew she had only recently moved into the projects and she didn't know much about the school or that we maintained strong discipline.

She also admitted that at the time she felt so much hatred toward me, threatening to kill me was the only thing she could think of. But she also showed me that even when people make mistakes—serious mistakes—they can ask for forgiveness.

I told her I appreciated how hard it must have been for her to apologize. We developed a good relationship after that and she has since become involved in the school whenever she can.

I often think of how I risked my life to go out there because I didn't know if she would shoot me. I had to face the possibility that she would. Regardless, I made the right decision in facing her. The children must come first.

That incident on the street made me realize once again how important it is to understand before we ask to be understood. If I had insisted she was wrong and argued for what we were doing for the betterment of her child, she was so upset she might have pulled a gun and shot me right then. That didn't even occur to me until afterward. Right then, even in my fear, I knew she needed someone to reach out to her—and to understand. I am not suggesting that anyone should tempt fate. I am familiar with my school's community. Though that mother was irate, I wasn't a complete stranger. While I was entirely uncomfortable with her behavior, I sensed her frustration with her daughter, the school district, and also herself. I became the target of all that hostility. As ugly and threatening as her behavior was, I was able to look beyond her language and outbursts and see that she was one hurting mother. Because of my approach, as foolish as it may seem to some, and the support of others in the community, she was able to restructure and redirect her emotions.

That's what I mean by influencing through forgiveness.

We need to understand others, and in order to understand others, we need to understand their situation and sometimes their culture and environment. To understand someone often means we have to push past the insults and the angry words and realize that they're yelling and acting out of their own pain and frustration.

We need to learn to care—to love them—if we're going to teach and influence them. One of my teacher-mentors used to say that I couldn't really reach children whom I didn't love. The first time she said that, I didn't agree (although I didn't say so). Later, I realized she was correct. Love doesn't only mean feeling good about someone. Love also means caring and wanting the best for them. It also means we can acknowledge bad habits or offensive ways in ourselves or anyone else, but we can still love them and expect to be loved. If we determine to love people, that implies that we'll also do whatever we can to build bridges of understanding.

At times people experience some terrible problems and they strike out at others—and the object of those attacks often has nothing to do with their problem. We need to try to understand what they're going through. We may make decisions that impact their lives. Above all, however, we can't continue to hold their mistakes over them or continue to punish them. If we understand, we forgive.

One of the things that has always been attractive to me as an educator is that every day is an opportunity to start over again. Every day is a new day. We can erase failures and move on to better days and better grades. To have hostility and unforgiveness pile up every day places teachers and students under a heavy burden that can undermine the learning process.

One of the worst things I've heard one teacher say to another teacher is this: "Oh, you're going to have *that child* in your class this year? He was terrible in my class this past year. We couldn't do a thing with him. I feel sorry for you."

"We'll give him another chance." That's how I usually respond when they say such things to me.

One time a teacher from another school tried to give me a list of all the negative things one girl had done, and I stopped her. "You know, if I hear everything you want to tell me, I might remember and hold them against her when she comes to us. I'd like to give her a fresh start."

"Oh, uh, yes," she said and was embarrassed. "That's a good idea."

I believe in giving children another chance and letting them start fresh. A few times I've thought of mischievous and wrong things I did as a kid. What if someone had written those childish things down and passed them from teacher to teacher?

My coauthor used to teach school, and one day he received a letter in the mail from the former teacher of one of the children who would be coming into his sixth-grade class. The teacher said the boy had not been honest and he had stolen money, although they could never prove it. "Watch him carefully. He is a thief."

How should he have reacted? He did the right thing: He threw away the letter and didn't answer. "I didn't care about what he did last year; I do care about what he does this year. It would be awful to brand a child like that, wouldn't it?" he said to another teacher.

Sometimes those children with disciplinary problems end up as top students. Maybe they were bored or not challenged, or a dozen other things could have troubled them. Many times, the behaviors of children are only normal reactions to abnormal situations. Instead of punishing them or branding them as incorrigible, we might be able to help them overcome their past and lead exemplary lives.

We try to put them into a new school situation where they can start fresh. *They deserve that opportunity.* If we care, we must be willing to understand and forgive their mistakes or overlook actions that may not have been intended to be wrong.

Sometimes people will do things that are positive but we view them negatively because we're looking at them with a negative understanding. There may be certain things in a person's background that teach them to react differently. For example, we've had children enroll at our schools, who, in their socialization, have been taught they must never look directly into the eyes of adults. If they do, it's disrespectful and conveys that they consider themselves as equals.

Yet I've heard teachers try to talk to those children and they hang their heads—the way they were taught. The teacher, unaware of their culture, gets frustrated and says sternly. "Look me in the eye! Don't look away from me."

I understood the teacher, but the teacher didn't understand the child. The more we learn and accept others as they are, the better we are at loving and appreciating them. It also helps us realize how tough their battles are at home and away from school. Sometimes those we label as troublemakers are really resilient individuals. They've had to stand against so many hardships and problems that it may be hard for them not to rebel or defy authority. They need us to understand and to forgive them.

In middle-class America, many marriages these days end in divorce. By contrast, in the inner city we have an extremely high number of single mothers who are barely twenty years old and yet have two or three children. Some of them are bitter about life and angry at the person who hurt them. They aren't willing to forgive. Someone once told me, "If you don't forgive, you are carrying that person on your back every minute of every day."

None of us is perfect. We sin; we make mistakes. But we also need to realize that if we want to be forgiven, we need to forgive. I like the way Jesus said it: "For if you forgive others when they sin against you, your heavenly Father will also forgive you. But if you do not forgive others their sins, your Father will not forgive you."[25]

When we forgive—and it's obvious when we have forgiven—not only are the ones we forgive better off, but we're free from carrying a heavy burden. That also means we have an opportunity to be a positive influence on others.

Here's a true story from a pastor-friend: A church member named Dick pleaded with him for a loan. His mortgage was past due and he needed nine hundred dollars to hold on to this house. Dick had lost his job and was going to start a new one in two weeks. He promised to start repaying as soon as he got his first check.

Out of his own pocket and at a time when he could hardly afford it, the pastor loaned Dick the money. Four months went by and Dick not only didn't repay, but also stopped attending that church. Finally, the pastor wrote a letter to Dick that went something like this:

> Every day I've thought about you and the money you owe me. This letter is to inform you that your debt *in full* is due one month from today.
>
> If you do not pay the entire amount by that date, this is also to inform you that I will totally forgive your debt and you will owe me nothing.

Dick didn't pay the debt, didn't return to the church, and they never saw each other again. Dick never forgot that act of grace and love. He told that story to several people. Two families eventually came to the church Dick had left because a for-

25. Matthew 6:14–15, Today's New International Version.

given (and still ashamed) man told them about a pastor who lovingly forgave him.

One of the men told the pastor, "Anyone who could forgive a debt like that is a man who could probably forgive anything. That's why my family and my brother and his family came here. We figured this was a church that cared."

The influence of forgiveness travels exponentially.

15

The Influence of Leadership

People draw strength from leaders, especially in times of crisis. We need only to think of September 11, 2001, and the leadership of New York City Mayor Rudy Giuliani. Many called him a hero. By definition, he wasn't a hero, but he did exactly what a good leader does—he inspired and encouraged. New Yorkers and people around him felt stronger because of his stance.

My position as a school principal and administrator automatically casts me in a leadership role. In business matters and in social issues, people expect me to step out in front and guide. I try very hard to be an all-around leader. Things that seem simple and automatic require careful thought and vigilance. People may not realize that the position of a principal can be lonely. Many difficult decisions must be made annually, on a daily basis, or in the heat of the moment. That means I have to try to stay on the cutting edge of school district policies. I have to treat my staff with respect, I must value and affirm my students, I must be in touch with the community surrounding my school, my dress must be professional, and I must monitor my health.

Even during the transitional phases of life, especially as they confront individuals on my staff, I must help to set the tone for conversation and behavior. The position I take can have a positive or negative impact on the morale of my school. Teachers come from all cultures and regions; they are also socialized differently and have different philosophies of education. There are bound to be conflicts. Even though I am African-American, not all of my decisions favor African-Americans. I must use my position of leadership to be as objective and fair as possible.

Although I trust the teacher as the authority in the classroom, I must also listen to the children. Based on observations, I may determine that a teacher should be more assertive or more sensitive. I may speak with children in the teacher's presence to model a particular approach to dealing with a discipline problem. That's not an attempt to belittle or embarrass the teachers. It would merely be a visual way to offer a guideline. If it works well, that teacher may adopt my methods.

All of this means that there are many ways to lead. Some people lecture, some advise, some model through actions, and others lead by being good listeners. Moreover, some people accept leadership better when presented in one way than they do by another approach. Just as there are different styles of parenting and teaching, there are different styles of leading. Even though my most preferred style is to lead by example, I like to sometimes interject humor when I have to speak. It takes the edge off the communication, and people don't feel they're being preached to even when the issue is serious. With children, if they have told me something that is important to them, and I recall it to them at an opportune time, I've displayed for them an excellent leadership trait—the fact that I value those under my supervision and the details of their lives are important to me. Children don't mind following that kind of person. For that matter, neither do adults.

The opportunities for leadership aren't confined only to

those of a professional nature. Teachers come to work in the midst of life-altering circumstances and so do our children. While those serious things are going on outside the classroom, teachers must teach and the children must learn. I've learned that being transparent before my staff allows them to see how I balance my personal and professional issues.

For example, one of our teachers wanted to have a baby. It was not happening as quickly for her as she would have liked. Because I shared some of my family's challenges in a similar situation with her, she was encouraged to stay positive. I'm happy to report that she is now a mother.

I have a responsibility when we encounter death—the loss of employees, of parents, of students and former students. Our teachers have lost parents, siblings, and children in their families. On many of those occasions I've had to deliver the sad news to the staff, attend funerals, or console their students.

My leadership becomes extremely important when the media negatively portrays the school and I have to respond to the public as well as provide an explanation to the staff about the real issues. Some school buildings can have as many as four or five stories, but a principal's office is generally on the first floor. There is an obvious reason for that. For the most part, teachers are in their rooms, oblivious to some of the incidents that take place in the office. We try to minimize interruptions during instructional time. If anything has happened during the course of the day, teachers generally won't know about it until after school, if then. By that time, the story may have been embellished beyond any point of accuracy. The media would have to be dealt with in a very careful manner because, as we know, sensationalism sells papers.

Sometimes, I find myself having to provide answers for situations to which there are no easy solutions. The situations become so bad, quite honestly, I don't know what to do. I also hurt, and yet I have to help others as they struggle with their own pain. A few times when I've had to deliver the news of someone's death or a terrible accident, I've gone into my office, closed the door, sat at my desk, and let the tears fall.

I'm not ashamed of my tears—I used to be, but I've gotten past that. Publicly, however, I feel I have to project an image of strength in the midst of crisis. When people see me in public during those difficult times, they say, "I feel confident because you're always confident."

They need strength and encouragement during those times. Part of my role as leader is to project that strength. They don't realize there are times when I feel weak, when I weep and grieve, but it isn't always appropriate to show that side. It's not that I'm trying to hide, but leaders need to lead. I lead by showing my strength. I want everyone to know that even in the midst of the worst tragedies, we can still stand tall.

Sometimes I talk to the staff and deliver the bad news that our school didn't achieve the test scores we felt we should have. I won't distort the truth, but I will encourage them. "We still have a chance," I say, and I mean those words, because as long as those children are alive and we can teach them, we have the opportunity to help them improve.

Because of the teachers' dedication and commitment, many times our students have improved. They've worked hard and I believe that part of the reason is because I've encouraged them to believe they can do it. If I inspire the teachers, my influence moves on to the students. The teachers' relationship with their students is a reflection of the relationship I have developed with the teachers as their leader.

When I talk with the students, I sometimes say, "Maybe you failed today, but because you fail once, it does not make you a failure. What it should do is teach you to say, 'I need to try another way.' Let's continue and not give up."

All good leaders have that kind of influence. Their attitude, their words, and sometimes their pressure make people say, "I can do that. I can't quit now."

For that to happen, however, people need to trust their leaders. Those in positions of authority have to prove themselves, to show they care, to demonstrate that they know what they're doing. When people trust leaders, they'll follow them.

The difficulty for us leaders—and I think particularly of charismatic types who pull people toward them—is that personality alone isn't enough. As a matter of fact, the downside is people may be blinded by the charm and miss their whole vision as a leader. Yes, we want them to grasp the vision, but we want supporters to remain level-headed, and to see us as real people. Followers need to know that we have morals, ethical values, and a sincere belief system. If we lack those qualities, people may follow for a while, but not long. Eventually, we'll show who we truly are.

As leaders who want to influence others, we have to move in a direction that propels the organization forward. That's not always an easy task. Actually, it's seldom an easy job. Sometimes we have to make decisions that may not be in the best interest of some. Faithful leaders count the cost and put the greater good ahead of the desires or needs of a few, even when those few are good friends.

As proof of our leadership, we get results—perhaps not what we wanted or all that we wanted—but we motivate others to hold on, to expect good things, and to make changes. We encourage them to know they can improve and lead richer lives.

For those of us who want to influence others, one of the obstacles we face is that when we make decisions, some individuals may take it personally if they don't get what they wanted from us. I suppose that's understandable. My desire is that they would move into deciding issues by principle or moral values, so that when they don't get what they want, they won't feel that we've attacked or rejected them.

More than once, I've had to say to teachers, to students, to community leaders, and to parents, "This isn't personal. It's not a decision about you. It's about what is best for the children, the community, and the school."

Effective leaders have to learn that we can never please everyone, no matter how hard we try or how charismatic we are. We do the best we can. That's all God asks of us and that's all we can ask of ourselves. If we focus on doing our *best,* we will exert the right kind of influence.

As leaders, we also develop and foster leadership in others. Our goal isn't just to have many disciples, but to teach and enable others to reach the highest levels possible. True leaders beget other true leaders. This is true in every industry and profession, including education, ministry, medicine, law, and various levels in the corporate structure.

Our message and our influence impact others, so they may influence others to become servant leaders. That's what I mean by the term "the immortality of influence." If future leaders are guided positively, the potential power of their influence is limitless. My personal goal is to produce leaders who will have more influence on others than I will. It's like planting a seed. When done properly, the harvest yields more than one seed. We get fruit or vegetables that contain many seeds. That's the increase. Those seeds will also produce many more, and each time the harvest can be larger. It could be considered poor leadership if the vision dies when the leader is no longer on the scene. If there is life in the leader, someone must catch the vision.

Several years ago in Chicago, Dr. Lee Stith, the executive director of the National Council of Teachers of Mathematics (NCTM), told an audience about a young man who was planning to visit his daughter. He said to himself, "My daughter is growing up. She's dating and soon she'll graduate from college." He admitted a certain amount of anxiety over the young man who would soon come to his house to take his daughter out on a date.

A few evenings later, Dr. Stith answered a knock at the door. The young man who stood before him was one of his former students.

The surprised father greeted him and asked, "What are you here for?"

"I'm here to take your daughter out."

"You are going out with my daughter?"

"Yes, I am, sir."

Dr. Stith thought about that young man, who had been one of his students. The boy was intelligent and highly motivated, and he had challenged the boy to do even better. He appreciated the young man's forthright attitude. Subsequently, Dr. Stith was a major influence in seeing that the boy went to college.

If he hadn't tried to influence him, Dr. Stith wondered how the boy would have turned out. "What if I hadn't cared? What if I hadn't used my influence? I would never have forgiven myself," he said, "because that young man graduated from college, married my daughter, and will be the father of my grandchildren."

He went on to say he was proud to be the type of educator who cared about the influence he had on young people. "As a leader, I wanted to make sure that when my students went into the world, they would make a difference." He didn't anticipate that one of them would end up his son-in-law.

As leaders, we never know about the people who study under us or whom we influence. But if we give our best, some will become leaders and will challenge others—and perhaps even affect our own families.

*   *   *

Members of an organization need to see that their leaders are strong and able to endure tough battles so that the mission of the organization is accomplished, even during those times when everything around them seems to be chaotic or in a state of confusion.

Many young people talk to me and tell me, "I want to be a leader." I ask them to explain what they mean and they talk about things they want to do with their lives.

"That's good that you want to be a doctor," I told one eighth-grade student. "How are you going to make that happen? How will you get there?"

He shrugged. "Go to school, I guess."

He had no strategy. It was as if he expected doors to open for him and all he had to do was walk inside. He didn't realize that he had to work hard to discover the location of those doors.

Students come to me all the time and say they want to go to law school or medical school. They want to be businessmen and businesswomen, but they don't do well in school, don't turn in homework, and show no initiative. They don't obey their parents, don't go to church, and aren't involved in the community. What kind of strategy do they have in mind?

None. They want it to happen to them and not exert any effort. That's not how leadership happens. The things I've mentioned above are qualities that make young people mature and show that they're willing to pay the price to be leaders and to influence others.

If we're leaders, we lead. We step ahead of the crowd and they follow us. Followers need to know we're authentic, truthful, and honest. If we're leaders, we can't stand back and simply watch. We have to become part of their lives. I like to say it this way: To be leaders, we also have to know the failures and the successes of those below us. They learn about us when we share our stories. When they realize that we've failed—and failed many times yet we've started again—we not only give them hope, but provide them with an example.

People need to see that we're human. I can tell them that failing doesn't make anyone a failure. All of us can—and need to—learn from failures and mistakes. They teach us to get back up and try harder. We'll have setbacks (we all do), but we need to get back on that horse and ride it again. We continue to fight the right battles. Most of all, we fight for those who aren't able to fight for themselves.

For example, during the 2003–04 school year, a young third-grader named Faheem Thomas-Childs walked to school with his father. On the way to school, gunfire rang out. The children ran toward the school and most of them raced inside the school yard.

Faheem didn't make it inside. He was shot down as he rushed toward safety. Teachers found his body alongside the school crossing guard. She had also been shot, but she survived. After all the shooting, police counted more than ninety spent shell casings. All those bullets were aimed senselessly at children who were trying to get educated.

Every time I hear of those terrible tragedies, I'm convinced that the leadership in our country doesn't invest enough in our children. Violence must be at the forefront of what we want to eliminate. Someone has to speak for the children.

Faheem's death took place close to the time when Bill Cosby made some controversial statements and criticized inner-city children and their parents. I have often agreed with Mr. Cosby's philosophies, but that time he missed an opportunity to point out that even when our children try to do the right thing, they are still hurt by adults. The shooters were men—adults—and some were husbands and fathers themselves.

Faheem has now been dead more than two years, and the

police haven't found his murderer and probably never will. Many people in the community say they know who committed this heinous act, but everyone fears speaking up on behalf of this innocent child.

Our children neither choose their parents, nor choose to grow up in poverty. But if we teach them well, they can learn to choose their influences. As I've reflected on the many senseless murders and Mr. Cosby's statements, I wonder if his tirade wasn't a way of dealing with his own son's violent death. He had been another promising young man and future educator who lost his life to gun violence.

After so many of my students had been murdered, I thought of how innocent they were and that none of the senseless bloodshed had been their fault. As a community and as a larger society, we haven't taken responsibility for all children, regardless of their race, religion, culture, or background. We must realize and accept that we can make a profound influence on our young people.

Shively Willingham, the principal of Faheem's school, Pierce Elementary, is a true leader and a good friend. Although he has since retired, he was a teacher and principal in the inner city for more than forty years and had a tremendous influence on my own career. I know how deeply it hurt him to face the death of yet another student. He is a man of strength and compassion, who worked hard to make his students feel safe.

Many parents didn't want their children to go to school after Faheem's shooting. "Isn't that sad," Shively said to me, "that parents have to choose between keeping their children alive and getting them educated?"

Principal Willingham told the police, "This situation is unacceptable." He demanded better protection and pointed out, "If you had been in front of our school that day, Faheem might be alive."

He realized that members of the police force put their lives on the line every day to protect the community, just as all of us teachers do. He wasn't blaming the police; he wanted help. He wanted to save his children.

I understood his pain and frustration—and he's seen far more deaths than I have. I know there are other leaders, principals, teachers, counselors, social workers, and nurses who care—that's why they stay in dangerous places. *They care.*

As leaders, we need to be willing to use our influence to encourage others to use the gifts they possess so they, in turn, can influence others. That's how we increase our sphere of influence. We help people believe in themselves. Too often, they don't recognize their own abilities, and one common quality of true leaders is that they know how to help people see things in themselves that they may not recognize without help. Leaders sense those who can become champions. They sponsor them and catapult them forward.

Wise and skilled leaders provide tasks and opportunities so those under them can excel. They push others into situations where they may not know they're being set up to succeed. When leaders trust those under them, it's amazing how those individuals rise to the occasion.

I've observed this in school. When I've sensed someone has potential, I do whatever I can to get that person active. My pastor does the same thing. He's put people into leadership roles and they shine. They didn't know they could do the tasks until they had to do them. I've seen people who underestimated their own ability, but were motivated by leaders to say, "Yes, yes, I *can* do it."

And they did!

We lose so much because there are many fine individuals

with leadership qualities or amazing talents who never speak up or who seem to have no chance to say, "Let me make a difference," or "What can I do?" We need those people.

It's time for them to speak up, and maybe they need us to help them do just that. Part of my purpose is to be a voice for people who aren't heard or recognized. Many are them are young and live in the inner city. Unless there are others who had people pushing for them as I did, those children will never have their chance to be their best. Just like the young people in inner-city Philadelphia, children who live in Asia, Africa, South America, and other parts of the world have the same issues. They are ignored, abused, misused, and uneducated. They need people to speak for them and to fight for them. I've made that my mission and my ministry.

We tend to think that leaders have to be leading the parade down the street. That's certainly one kind of leader. There are other types. Not all leaders are the types who receive the accolades and the awards. Those who make the biggest sacrifices often do so behind the scenes.

I like to tell young people, "You don't have to be in front to be a leader." There are many who lead from behind, who lead from the flanks and from the sidelines.

Elaine Wright Colvin lives in the Seattle area but she works with writers all over the country. During the past twenty years, she has self-published one small book. That's not her strength: Her gift is to encourage other writers. When she spots talent, she works with the writers and pushes them until they publish their manuscripts. Most book buyers don't know who she is or realize she's been the motivator behind the scenes. Some of her protégés acknowledge her influence, but not all. Yet she still continues to lead them toward success.

Think about our presidents or top CEOs. Strong leaders surround themselves with strong and wise thinkers. Immediately I think of professional sports. When Larry Bird became head coach of the Indiana Pacers, he hired assistant coaches with twenty to thirty years' experience. Those people ran the team. Larry Bird had played basketball, excelled, and knew what it took to be a good ball player. He also knew he needed to rely on experienced coaches—people who could lead by teaching and working individually with players.

Maurice ("Mo") Cheeks, former coach of the Portland Trail Blazers and current coach of the Philadelphia Seventy-Sixers, is a good friend of mine. He encouraged me to become a teacher almost twenty years ago. Maurice himself was an NBA All-Star. When he landed the job as head coach in Portland, immediately he hired Jimmy Lynam, longtime NBA head coach, as his assistant. Many so-called sports experts were surprised Maurice wasn't afraid to say to Jimmy, "Help me." He wasn't worried about Jimmy receiving more respect because he was older and more experienced and had already been a head coach.

Mo sacrificed his own feelings for the team. He believed players would listen to Jimmy when he was not present because everyone knew Jimmy was a first-class leader. Jimmy was a coach who could lead from behind. He could also walk into the locker room and motivate those players. Because Jimmy gave his best, he helped Maurice become a better coach. He was also willing to teach Maurice the nuances of coaching at the highest level. Maurice had been an assistant coach for some years, but as many know, the position of leader is quite different and carries with it a different set of expectations.

Mo Cheeks recently decided to come home to Philadelphia to coach. He was an important factor on the championship team in 1983 with Julius Erving, Moses Malone, and Bobby Jones. Whom did Mo hire as an assistant upon his arrival in Philadelphia as coach? Jimmy Lynam. What a powerful influence he will have on those young men.

That's the attitude of truly good leaders. They don't think just of themselves, but of the team; and they bring in the best people to improve the organization.

I often look at those coaches when they receive their jobs, as well as newly appointed CEOs, and observe whom they hire. The smart ones hire people who are leaders themselves. Leaders are only as good as the people who make up their team, and they are attentive and encouraging to every member of the team.

16

Being Influenced

Some people won't allow themselves to be influenced. They have made up their minds about everything, aren't open to change, and resist anyone who tries to sway them. At one time, that might only have been said of adults who have lived lives full enough to develop strong philosophies and so have, as it were, become closed to new ideas. But nowadays, we see younger and younger children who don't appear to welcome the influences of adults. These types of individuals behave as if they know everything and don't need any help. However, they are being influenced whether they recognize it or not. We are hit on all sides by various images, sounds, and sights, and we react to them in some way.

At times, this influence is very clandestine. We find ourselves humming a tune or singing a song that just gets into our brain and won't leave. A fashion trend that at first seemed bizarre, soon looks hip. Diets pop up all over the place with strange food combinations. Conversations become riddled with phrases like, "Have you tried the new cabbage-and-grapefruit diet?" Advertisers have us pegged. They study us to the core. Song jingles, colors, and product placement in stores aren't random acts of influence. They realize that no one can go through life unaffected by the many stimuli.

The real issue is how we handle those influences. If we're teachable and the lesson we're learning has value, we grow and mature. I often hear my pastor say he wants us to have a teachable spirit. He means he wants us to be willing to learn, to share, and to be open to receive help from others. The Bible often refers to those resistant to growth as being stiff-necked or having hard hearts. Our teachers used to refer to us as having hard heads.

Many of us have learned to give to others, but we don't know how to receive. We may embrace the philosophy that it's better to give than to receive in a monetary or materialistic way, but when it comes to our ideas, thoughts, and opinions, we are the epitome of generosity. For some of us, giving makes us feel superior, and we act as if we don't have needs ourselves. Our attitudes about receiving make it difficult for others to reach out to us. Yet we all need others to help us and to influence us. Most of the time, there are people who want to help and encourage us, but we have to allow them to do that. It's sad, but many times those who know better watch the demise of individuals who just wouldn't listen to anyone.

When healthy influence comes and we accept it, we have to be positive about it. We are actually accepting two things—the information and the responsibility. We can't take that powerful impact and lock it up inside and keep it to ourselves. The responsibility is to allow that influence to touch others who are around us. As one friend says, "We need to share the prosperity."

Prosperity doesn't have only a financial reference. As a matter of fact, once we're "rich" by our ability to motivate or influence, we abound in that which will surpass time and money, because our influence changes thoughts and actions. We can be rich and foolish; we can be given time and remain old and foolish. But to have been changed for the better, and to be an agent for positive change, has to be one of the most affluent positions in life. Reverend Rick Warren, author of the *The Purpose-Driven Life*, has often commented that he studies the Bible to learn how to use his own affluence and influence in a positive way.

Once we have been motivated, and have acted on that motivation, we shouldn't be selfish and try to use our influence only on those we like or those we think are worthy. If we've had the right kind of influence, we gladly spread it out and hope that everyone will benefit just as we have. We do our best by sowing seeds the way they did it in ancient times. Jesus once told a parable that's often called "The Parable of the Sower."[26] A person went through the fields and indiscriminately cast out seed—the way they planted in biblical times. Some seed produced good crops and some didn't. The problem was not with the seed; the seed was the same no matter where it fell. The variable was the type of soil on which the seed fell. I like to think of people of influence as sowers. Our responsibility is to reach out to anyone and everyone with what we have even if they don't respond.

In my observation, those who indiscriminately encourage and motivate become the most influential and powerful. Perhaps it's because they don't try to manipulate or make themselves seem important. They give what they have and don't worry about how much power they have or can attain.

Each of us can become a vehicle for influence for others by passing on the things we have received. That is how we bring about significant change. It starts with one person. *Just one.* I believe in the power of one, but we also have to remember that each one has to teach one. If we're open, we receive, and we'll encounter others who want to be influenced by us.

26. See Mark 4:1-20.

In the early twentieth century, Frank Laubach wanted to teach the world to read. His motto was, "Each one teach one." He started teaching people in the Philippines in the 1930s, and continued with his message until he died in 1970 at the age of eighty-five. That was his mission, and because of his focused commitment, many world leaders referred to him as the apostle of literacy.

How do we choose the influences to which we respond? Young people are profoundly affected by peer pressure. We often think of that in a negative manner, but it can also work positively; however, almost immediately, our minds tend to turn to the defiant attitudes, the outlandish dressing, the risky behavior, or the rebellion against school. Adolescents can, and will, react favorably to strong, positive peer influences. If there are young people who have friends who achieve good grades in school and are otherwise doing well, those are the people they need to know better and to model their behavior after. These are individuals who can ultimately win over others and make them want to excel.

"If your friends give you ideas and tips on how to be a better student," I tell our children, "those are the people you want to listen to. They're trying to help you. They want you to learn and to achieve. If you follow their example, they're giving you the positive influence you need."

In the inner city, suburbs, or rural areas, it's not unusual for a teen to say to one of his friends, "Let's play with a gun," or "Let's go and use drugs or smoke cigarettes." They want to share, but they offer the negative influence because that's what they've been primarily exposed to in their situations.

We can choose what influences us. We can walk away or ignore negative voices. They don't have to impact our lives. If we want excellence, it's not a matter of chance; it's a matter of choice.

I often say to students, "I know you are young, but you're not too young to understand the difference between right and wrong. Surround yourselves with other positive young people, and collectively you can become a positive group that brings about change and makes a difference to everyone around you. That way you both receive and pass on the good influence."

My message isn't only for the children. Parents also need to teach their children how to recognize positive and negative messages. That isn't something they learn on their own. They certainly don't learn positive values from television or video games. Parents are their first teachers.

Studies conducted at Emory University in Atlanta have shown that kids who decided against drugs before they were actually exposed to them are the ones who typically don't get into drugs. However, those who didn't think about such issues until faced with them were more prone to get hooked. They faced the challenge and had no serious thoughts beforehand about drugs. When confronted for the first time, they often gave in. They allowed themselves to be changed and derailed by the wrong people.

This study reminds us that children are never too young to learn to make good decisions and to choose right over wrong. They quickly learn the difference between healthy and unhealthy or the difference between good and bad. I have always taught my students to understand that they can choose the behavior, but they can't choose the consequences of the behavior.

If parents teach them properly, children are more open to us as they grow older. We can continue to reinforce their values with wise and healthy choices. As we continue to influence them, we know they'll make mistakes—we all do—but we can also teach them about forgiveness and to learn from their mistakes. Even more important, we can show them how to learn from the mistakes of others.

Many of our students didn't fail in school as much as they fail in life. I failed to motivate them because I didn't continue to impress upon them the importance of making the right choices.

I often wonder about those failures in life. If only their parents and I had worked harder, we might have armed them with the ability to make decisions that stimulate them to do the right things. In our community, too many children have died and many others have lost their way. I've tried to learn from those lost battles. My failing doesn't make me a failure, but it has motivated me to try even harder to reach every child. I've learned that success can often be paralyzing, because we think we've won and we don't have to struggle as hard.

Despite the losses we've faced in the inner city, I've become stronger and wiser. I have become better at understanding and realizing positive ways to affect the children.

I want our young people to understand that when I tell them, "I want you to be out in front," it doesn't mean that I want them in front of everyone else showcasing themselves. I want them to become leaders in whatever capacity they have. I want them to challenge other young people. "Others will make decisions based on your decisions. If you hold to your commitments," I remind them, "you strengthen your friends to hold on to their values. You can select the influences you follow. One of the most important decisions you will make in your life is to allow in the right influences. You have the power, and you have the knowledge. I want you always to do the right thing."

*   *   *

This is a letter I received from a student named Brad Sullivan after I returned from a lecture at Nichols College, in Dudley, Massachusetts.

I was a student who attended your seminar, which was held at Nichols College in Dudley, Mass. I am proud to say that I went to see you but I'm ashamed at my reasons for going. Our college has a cultural program that says unless every student attends a certain number of cultural events in their time at Nichols College they will not graduate. Yesterday morning I awoke to a day of no work and two cultural events. As a graduating senior, I needed to jump on every opportunity I had to get a cultural event in because I want to graduate. I went to a film on the afternoon of the 21st. Then I found myself at my house between events wondering why I was going to another one that evening. I finally forced myself to get out of the house, into my truck, and drove to the college . . . I came into the door of Davis Hall and was offered a chance to win a book. And of course, being a foolish person and a lazy student, I thought, what would I do with that book anyway? Put it on my shelf and never read it or touch it again.

I denied myself the opportunity and joined the on-looking crowd ready to watch your upcoming performance. I sat down and my first thoughts were, Man, I hope this doesn't take too long. I was thinking that I had better things to do with my time and never thought about what I could learn from you.

Your speech moved me in a way that I had never been touched before. During your reading of the final chapter, I fought to hold back the tears the same way you fought to hold tears at the end of the graduation you attended of your first graduating college student. I fought and fought with myself to withhold the tears and the sadness I was feeling for your children and the happiness that I was feeling for them as well. Your students are lucky children and if I had had a million dollars in my pocket, I would have given every penny to you that night. I did not want to give you the money I wished I had because I felt bad for you. I wanted to give it to you that night because I was touched with the same pain you go through every day and that is the pain of poverty. I am an accounting major with a job already lined up after graduation. But after that moving speech I am not sure that I am going down the right road. I will keep in touch and hold the thought you left in my mind. That thought is that maybe some day I should pop into an inner-city school and say hi and show people that I care. I do care, and you're one of the greatest people I've ever seen. I would like to send you money or send you something but right now I don't have anything to send. The only thing that I can send at this time is my thanks. I am not thanking you for you helping me get another cultural event out of the way. I'm thanking you because you took your time to come out and see us and that time was worth more to me than any dollar amount imaginable.

Thank you so much. You've changed my life.

Enthusiastically,
Brad G. Sullivan

Like Brad, for us to be able to receive influence from others, we need an open heart and an open mind. We have to move forward in a relentless pursuit of knowledge as well as to have a desire to understand others. We need to learn to open ourselves and to say, "I want to be loved, to be affirmed, to be accepted, encouraged, and influenced by people like you."

I don't intend to present this as an example to build my own ego, but this demonstrates the power of influence—like the sower casting out the seeds. Brad comes from a different culture and community, but he allowed the story of my students' trials and tribulations to inspire him. He openly received the influence and I am grateful to him for that.

When I first graduated from college, I worked for a television station. During that time, I visited a school to speak about my job in the media. Some of my former teachers had invited me and encouraged me to talk to young people. I suspect those teachers had an ulterior motive. I've since wondered if they knew that once I was in the academic setting, surrounded by the voices of young people, I would get caught up and realize I needed to help children. Even though they told me the same things when I was younger, I never "heard" those teachers while I was still in school. My mother had also encouraged me to work with young people, but I guess I truly was hardheaded.

When I visited the high school, I thought I would talk about my job in television and tell them my goal was to become a television analyst for ABC news, ESPN, or HBO.

Afterward, a few students stood around and asked me questions. One of them said, "If you can come in and inspire us, how come you aren't a teacher?"

That was probably the first time in my life that someone had asked me a question to which I had no response. I had always been the guy who quickly dispensed answers to every question. That day, however, I didn't know what to say. Instead, I smiled and moved on to the next question.

A simple question influenced me. Those few words changed the direction of my life because—for the first time—I heard the message that others had tried to give me for a long time. The community desperately needs those they nurture to return and continue the influence. I had run from my destiny, but the children unknowingly helped me to free myself.

As I drove away from there, I tried to minimize what I had heard. I started rationalizing with myself, "I've got my own career in television and enjoy it." Later that night and for several days afterward, that thought of teaching children stayed inside my head. Eventually I was able to say to myself, "That was a calling."

In those days, I wouldn't have said God was calling me. I hadn't been open, but the children caught me when I was vulnerable, and I listened. That one child's question caught me off guard (and I had to have been off guard in those days to be influenced).

I couldn't get away from that question: "How come you aren't a teacher?" Yes, one simple question changed my career and the direction of my life. That's the immortality of influence.

Shortly after my visit to the school, I quit my television job and enrolled in graduate school. I earned a master's degree and received my teaching certificate. I returned to that same school to teach, and those same students, who were now older, came to me and said, "You know, Mr. EL, you were a fool to leave that TV job. We weren't serious."

Whether they were serious or not doesn't matter. It matters that one student had asked exactly the right question. That question became the influence that pushed me to make a major change in my life.

I never imagined a day would come after those students asked me to give my life to them that I would begin to lose children almost immediately. The loss of twenty children in ten years is difficult for the most battle-tested teacher. But losing those children also helps me to understand and appreciate when one child makes it. When Otis Bullock graduated from college—the first child I had taught that made it to graduation—I felt as if my life had been affirmed.

As other former students graduate, it helps me to understand that every time I motivate children, I prevent funerals. At each graduation I attend, I understand how significant it is to challenge the young.

I also know it works both ways. Those young people help me grow and I want to remain as open to them as I want them to be toward me. When we are open, our children can influence us. In the New Testament there is an account of children shouting praises to Jesus, and the teachers of the law—the rulers—rebuking them.

"Did you hear what these children are saying?" they asked him.

"Yes," replied Jesus, "have you never read, 'From the lips of children and infants you have ordained praise'?"[27]

In the spring of 2005, I spoke with a friend, Michelle Lockett, who was also an employee in the college of education at Drexel University. I first met Michelle when I was a young man involved in activities at Bright Hope Baptist Church in North Philadelphia. That church is the home of Reverend Bill Gray, former U.S. Congressman and president of the United Negro College Fund. On that day, we didn't talk about church, but we discussed the graduation from college of one of the church's young members. The young man had recently lost both his parents. Members of the church were going to travel to Florida to support him as he received his degree from Florida A&M University. Michelle, of course, was part of that group.

Michelle went on to tell me that her own daughter was a student at the same college. I asked about her older son and she proudly informed me that he was now a practicing pediatrician. Michelle had been a stay-at-home mom and an active member of the Philadelphia Home and School Association. I asked why she believed her children were influenced to go on to college and become successful when she didn't graduate from college.

What she told me did not surprise me. "I tried to influence my children by supporting the schools they attended and their pursuits outside of school." In the process, she realized that the

27. Matthew 21:16. New International Version.

hard work and dedication of her two children had actually influenced her. She began to question her own decisions. She had dropped out of college to raise a family. They influenced her to go back to college.

As I thanked her for sharing so much good news with me, she paused and said she had one more ounce of positive news to share. "I will receive my bachelor's degree from Drexel University at the end of the semester."

Michelle is an example of a woman who allowed the dedication of her children to influence her. She had all but forgotten her dreams, but her children influenced her to remember them. She had been open to the influence to receive the blessing.

I want the young to seize the power of interacting with others—young or old. They need to realize that the people with whom they associate can change their lives for good or for bad. Many young people don't understand how important it is to receive positive influences and to *choose* those influences. They can make choices, but of course, they can't choose the outcome. That makes it even more important for them to be careful about what they allow to divert their thinking. They have to make sure they surround themselves with like-minded people. They need to be around other young people who go to school, who attend church, and who are involved in the community.

Winners surround themselves with other winners. Losers feel most comfortable with other losers. Those who refuse to quit intimidate them. True winners also create other winners and leaders.

Frequently young people hang their heads after getting into trouble by following someone who led them astray. They usually start with something like, "I didn't know he would . . ."

"Yes, you may not have known that person was capable of doing something that bad," I say to them. "But you knew that person wasn't a good influence. So why not surround yourself with people who can encourage you positively? Good things will happen to you when you surround yourself with positive friends who want to go in the right direction."

An Asian proverb states that a lifetime of study cannot replace one day with an excellent teacher. True and excellent teachers use their influence to improve the lives of their students. When I reflect on that proverb, I hope my students will value the time we spent together.

17

The Influence of Giving Back

Howard Thurman was a minister, pastor, preacher, college professor, and the first black dean at a white university. He studied at Atlanta's Morehouse College and taught at Howard University, in Washington, D.C. In Thurman's autobiography, *With Head and Heart*, this is the end of the story, not the beginning.

When Howard Thurman was a junior high school student in Florida during the early part of the twentieth century, schooling stopped at the end of the seventh grade for black children. When Howard was in the seventh grade, his principal contacted the school district superintendent and said, "I have a student who can pass that eighth-grade test. I want him to take it." He made it clear that he wanted his student to enter high school.

"He can take the test," the man said with reluctance, "but I have to administer it myself."

The district superintendent oversaw the test and Howard Thurman passed. As a direct result, the state of Florida added the eighth grade to schools for blacks.

After the eighth grade, Thurman wanted to go on to high school but there were no high schools in his area. In fact, there were only three black high schools in the entire state of Florida. One of them was in Jacksonville. Relatives in that area agreed to allow him to stay with them. In exchange for room and board, he would do chores around the house.

Thurman packed all his things to go on to the school. He had a trunk and tied a rope around it because the trunk didn't have a lock. When he tried to buy a ticket at the train station, the clerk said, "You are not allowed to carry the trunk without a lock. You will have to ship it."

"But I don't have any more money," he protested.

The ticket agent shrugged and looked away.

Thurman went outside the station and sat down. He had always dreamed of getting an education. Just because he didn't have any more money, his dreams would never materialize. His heart was so broken he couldn't do anything except cry.

A large black man came up to him and asked, "Why are you crying?"

"I was going away to attend high school and prepare myself to be the first one in my family to go to college, but they won't allow me to carry my trunk on the train. They said I'd have to ship it. I don't have any money to ship the trunk."

"If you're trying to leave this town to educate yourself, the least I can do is help you."

The gentleman took Thurman inside the train station and he paid for the shipping of the trunk.

The boy turned around to thank the gentleman, but he had disappeared. Howard Thurman never saw him again. But that man and his one act of kindness changed Howard Thurman's life. Thurman became a man who changed thousands—perhaps millions—of lives over the next half century. He touched people of all races, faiths, and cultures.

That's the true definition of giving back. It's not giving just to those we know. We try to meet the needs of people we may never see again. Often, we are not aware of the results but we do it because it's the right thing for us to do. We do it because we remember what it was like to have help in our difficult times.

In my work with the America's Foundation for Chess (AF4C), headquartered in Seattle, we have designed a program called First Move, and its purpose is to teach chess to every second- and third-grade student in the nation.[28] The program is under the leadership of the president, Erik Anderson, and the executive director, Rourke O'Brien.

If this program succeeds, it will mean that every year 9 million children will learn the game of chess. We're not trying to make them into competitive players (unless, of course, they want to be), but they're going to learn the rules, etiquette, patience, problem-solving techniques, and critical thinking. This will help change the way we educate children in America.

Here's a true story that illustrates this point.

In early 2005, I was in Kansas City for a book signing and met a young woman who worked in a bookstore. She told me she had seen inner-city students playing chess. During the conversation she mentioned her nephew in high school, who had been a chess player before he developed a brain tumor. As they prepared him for surgery, a doctor responsible for brain mapping visited them. He told them he had completed his assessment and said, "I've never seen a young person's brain like this. It's difficult for me to chart the extent of the damage. It's almost as if there isn't any from the tumor." He then asked the family, "What does this young man do outside of school?"

"All he does is play chess."

The doctor replied that it appeared as if his chess activities helped his brain repair the damaged cells. He went on to say

---

28. For information, e-mail them at info@af4c.org or call 206-675-0490.

that if the federal government was aware of what he knew, every kindergarten student in the country would learn the game of chess.

The young woman told me her nephew had successfully undergone the surgery, and only two weeks later, he won his State High School Chess Championship.

That's only one story about the effects of chess. I've seen many poor but physically healthy children turn into brilliant students after they learned to play chess. That's the major reason I'm such a strong advocate of the game for our schools.

The terrible reality is that the United States is one of the few (if not the only) industrialized nations that doesn't include chess as part of its national curriculum. Our students struggle in international mathematics assessments against students from other countries, and we wonder why. Even students from small nations outperform students in the United States in mathematics and science, because we have failed to teach our children how to think critically. Our students deserve more.

Most experts agree that playing chess improves the critical thinking of young people. The overwhelming majority of educational research indicates that children who are not reading at grade level by the third grade almost never gain the ability to read as well as their peers. Children who think and analyze find reading much easier. The First Move program was designed so teachers could begin teaching our children to think critically and analytically at an early age.

The purpose of the program is to see that chess instruction becomes part of the school day. For an hour a day, at least one day a week, students are exposed to problem-solving and critical-thinking activities through the learning of chess. Students who play chess have higher SAT and ACT scores, higher college acceptance rates, and higher reading and math scores on state assessments. For students to become proficient chess players, they have to read many books, which makes them better readers and writers.

The AF4C seeks to minimize the cost of the program to all the schools by securing private funding to assist with expenses.

We already have a number of committed and dedicated influential people involved in the organization. Seattle Seahawks all-pro running back, Shaun Alexander, is a big supporter and has become involved in the program. He's also a good chess player. He's involved in the community and with Christian athletes who want to change the condition of our nation. We need more people like Shaun.

Other professional athletes are also involved in giving back to their communities. For example, Priest Holmes, a running back for the Kansas City Chiefs, is an excellent chess player and has become involved in the community. Hugh Douglas of the Philadelphia Eagles is another player who has committed himself to thinking about others. He helps support a bookmobile that the Philadelphia Eagles fill with books and send to schools along with several team members to give the books away and promote reading. The children are always excited to see the bookmobile arrive at their school.

Trey Thomas, an offensive lineman for the Philadelphia Eagles, is well aware of the importance of giving back. In conjunction with Wills Eye Hospital in Philadelphia, he paid for a vision van to travel around to inner-city schools and provide vision screening and glasses to students who need them. Trey did that because he grew up with a vision problem and didn't know it. His mission is to make sure that every child in Philadelphia who needs glasses gets them at no cost.

We need people like these professional athletes who give back and try to influence the young. They also want to influence adults by being models for them. Others see their example and the sacrifices they make, and that encourages them to get involved.

We give back and make a difference when we discover our purpose in life—a purpose larger than ourselves. Many of these big-name players have millions of dollars, but that's not the point. They want to give back not only because they are financially comfortable, but also because they realize there are others who don't have the means to pay for the things they need. They're also humble enough to admit that they had assistance in being able to reach their level of success, and that they have a responsibility to give back to those who supported them to get to where they are. They want to help others reach their level of success.

I know many professional athletes have benefited much from the community, and it troubles me when I see how few of them give back to those same communities. There are some who do give back, as I've already mentioned, but far too many others forget—not just athletes, but entertainers, entrepreneurs, and a great number of successful people who seemingly behave as if they alone are responsible for their success. They had help, and often a great deal of help, and I wish they remembered.

I would like to see professional organizations encourage their athletes and entertainers to be more committed to support the communities that nurtured them. They should be responsible for helping the same people who pay their salaries—the public. It's time to place a national assessment on any public figure (entertainers and athletes) who makes more than one million dollars per year. We could build schools for our children that resemble the great stadiums where the athletes live. We could do that if they were assessed just *one percent* from every contract they sign and the money was given back to the school district where they attended or the recreation department that provided the vehicle for their athletic improvement.

We know that close to 50 percent of the high school students in most major urban centers drop out before graduation. Most of those who do leave drop out in the ninth grade *or before*. In some inner-city schools, we lose half of our school population before the start of their ninth-grade year. That means we have to work harder and smarter to reach those at-risk children early.

We take the students to visit colleges while they are in elementary grades so that at an early age they can begin to envision a better future. I want to encourage colleges to give back to the community and invite those young people to their campuses. Those activities build good decision-making and critical-thinking skills. The exposure is important.

Our hope is that someday the First Move program will build those skills for children in every city in the country. We've already implemented the program in Seattle, San Diego, Tampa, Minneapolis, and Philadelphia and its surrounding school districts. We plan to move to additional cities soon on the East Coast such as Boston.

There is great danger in forgetting where we've come from. There are too many young people following us who have the same needs we once had. If we choose to leave them to fend for themselves, we rob ourselves of the opportunity to nurture the talents that will sustain future generations.

We have an obligation to use and to share our gifts. We can leave the community to improve ourselves, but at some point, we need to go back and improve that same community for those who are there after we're gone.

July 3, 2005, marked a significant milestone in the history of philanthropic events globally. Entertainers from around the world collaborated to perform in the Live 8 concerts. Organizers made an appeal to the eight leading industrialized nations to grant debt forgiveness to the impoverished countries of sub-Saharan Africa. On a local level, I was proud to be from Philadelphia, which was the only city in the United States to be selected as a concert site. We played host to such talents as Stevie Wonder, Destiny's Child, Will Smith, Alicia Keys, Kanye West, and the Dave Matthews Band—all united in the cause to end hunger. I use this illustration to show that the responsibility that those entertainers felt was in using their gifts to effect a political change that would ultimately make the lives of millions better. The world was their community and they felt obligated to improve it.

Our contributions don't have to be financial. We can give time. We can become mentors and reading coaches in schools. We can speak to children and youth and let them know we care. "I was once where you are," is a great way to start. We can encourage and motivate them.

We can thank the teachers who worked with us. This is important because many fine teachers across the country wonder if they really make a difference. We can do so much by saying, "Continue to fight. Continue to stay with those young people. I am who I am today because you influenced me."

18

Influence on Our Communities

In his book, *The Marriage Problem*, sociologist James Q. Wilson writes about marriage and families and refers to two nations in the United States. In many neighborhoods of our country, some children grow up in two-parent homes where both parents work, and jobs are available, their homes are safe, the community is safe, and it's free of crime. Children know they'll grow up and own their own home. They'll get married, have a family, and live in a safe environment. That's one nation.

The other nation consists of those young people who grow up in communities where most of the parents are unwed mothers and men don't have jobs. Because of this, the men are unsuccessful and aren't good fathers. In fact, most of the children grow up without fathers. The daughters grow up to raise children without fathers.

Instead of looking to churches and the schools for knowledge, love, and assurance, they gravitate toward gangs. The gang life is necessary for their survival. Those are the young people whom we, as responsible adults, have to steer back to the family, to the churches, and to our communities to receive love and education. It is imperative that these two worlds come together so that young people can all grow up in one and the same world.

In the second nation, the gang is the only place some young people can find acceptance. Instead of areas populated by gangs, we need to develop strong communities to surround and protect our children.

Occasionally a discouraged teacher will ask, "Why should I care about those young people? They don't live where I live. They don't work where I work. They don't play with my children. Why should I care?"

"Because *your* children are going to grow up in the world with *those* children," I answer. "Your children are going to go to college with those children or work with them. Those children may end up living in your neighborhood. They may end up renting or buying a house near you. Why not make sure they are quality individuals by educating them? I'd much rather meet one of those young people in the bank while they're depositing their check at the same time I'm depositing mine. I don't want them hanging around outside the bank and waiting to take my check and deposit it into their pocket."

We must find ways to bring the two nations together. The most effective method is to educate the children. We break the cycle of poverty by educating them and making them better parents for their children.

If we begin to teach young people, they become better, more responsible individuals and they join with us to change the community. We want to change the world, and we can do it only by changing one person at a time.

Many of our children are impressed by brand names and buy into the media and MTV. Many accept the implication that if they act a certain way, they will be successful in life. Our children need to understand that God doesn't recognize those brand names as important. He doesn't ask what they watch or who is the artist or group at the top of the charts. He looks at each child and asks, "How are you treating *yourself*? What are you giving back to the community?"

Brand names don't define us. What defines us is our giving back and treating others as we would like to be treated. Young people should know that what they give back becomes their legacy. That's what will define them as individuals and as a generation.

If each of us decided to influence others through our communities and connections, we would have a seamless transition and one of sustainability. We could continue to produce leaders and spread love and acceptance all around the world. If we don't share our dreams and intentions with our children, we cheat them. If they understand, they can also begin to influence others for good.

When we talk about giving back, we have to understand what we build with that influence when we give back. We can talk about building communities, or developing a more diverse and unified community, or providing a place where all children receive proper health care. A place where all children are free of violence.

Those dreams can't be realized unless we consciously move toward making them a reality. We do that by giving back to our communities, by remembering that people there gave us a leg up.

We must find a way to implement a uniform system of educating our children that also includes caring for our children. We can't allow a segment of our population not to receive prenatal care. We can't allow a generation to go through life unable to read and destined for prison or drug and alcohol abuse. We must find ways to help.

Recent data from the Children's Defense Fund noted that *every day* in America:

- Almost 200 children are arrested for committing violent crimes.
- Over 1,500 babies are born without health insurance.
- More than 2,000 babies are born into poverty.
- Almost 2,500 babies are born to mothers who are not high school graduates.
- Over 5,000 women and children are reported abused or neglected.

Violent behavior, apathy, and a deterioration of our communities directly result from these statistics. It's a monumental challenge to reverse these trends, but it's one we must undertake if we are to move toward developing communities where marriage and family are important, where the church and education are prominent, and where gang activity is not tolerated. Mental and physical abuse of women must no longer take place.

If we create those positive influences, we can impact our community and eventually the entire world.

My daughter, Macawi, attends the Bala House Montessori School. She's in the Pre-K program there. The school director, Diane Force, read in *I Choose to Stay* about the 100 Book Challenge program at Reynolds School.

When she talked to me, I told her we struggle to get enough books, because the students love to read so much. They become proficient, but they don't want to read the same books again and again.

Diane asked the parents and teachers at her school if they would collect as many books as they could and donate them to Reynolds. They joyfully agreed and made a large donation.

I thought it was so wonderful that the school and its students, most of who came from middle-class and affluent families, had done such a kind thing. I knew our children would receive the books gratefully, but I had no idea how excited they would be.

The story goes beyond mere excitement. Keyshonda Miles is an eighth-grader in our school. She had nearly always been recognized as one of the top students of every month. Her reward was to receive one of the first books donated by the Bala House families. Keyshonda held the gift book tightly and kept fingering the pages. She read the book every free moment she wasn't in class.

I relayed that story back to the folks at the Bala House. They were deeply touched and impressed that those children would appreciate and embrace those books like that.

That action sends a message to the larger community that there truly are people from two different communities, but they can communicate and share experiences through literacy. Just a few books sent by one group of caring schoolchildren, teachers, and parents to another group where many of the families struggle to make it from day to day have already made a difference in the lives of the children who received them.

Another organization that has sought to ease the pain of inner-city kids and their families is the Paradise Farm Camp in Downington, Pennsylvania. The camp invites young children and their parents to spend time away from the city every summer. They hold separate sessions for students as well as special sessions for single moms and their children.

The camp is sponsored by the Children's Country Week Association (CCWA), a private, nonprofit, nonsectarian charitable organization that provides summer camp experiences, environmental education, and other specialized services for children and families. The camp encompasses 600 acres of wooded countryside.

The one-week camp for single moms has been a tradition at

the site since 1913. While there, the moms get to meet new families, have fun with the kids, participate in sharing sessions with other moms, eat healthy foods, and relax in the outdoor setting. The children can swim, walk the grounds, or play games. This is an excellent opportunity for parents to spend quality time with their children. Mothers also get a little private time while the children engage in supervised activities.

I've visited the campsite and the children love it there. The CCWA has made a significant difference in the lives of the families in our community. The moms deserve a chance to relax and recover from "the most beautiful of all professions."

19

The Power of Unrecognized Influence

We influence others—even when we don't realize it. We know that in theory, but when we see the evidence years later, it helps us to know that we've done the right thing and that we've given ourselves to the right purposes.

I've spent much of my life trying to create the right influence; I don't always know if I've been successful. What if we lived every day with the awareness that we touch others? Every day we have the opportunity to impact others. That influence comes through our consistent lifestyle as much as through our words.

For example, my coauthor, Cec Murphey, was pastor of a suburban Atlanta church for a decade. Each year, the congregation hired a senior seminary student to work part-time, and that provided the students with invaluable experience. Of the students they hired over the years, Cec most remembers Richard Daws, a handsome, charismatic young man, as the one who was the ablest and who showed the most promise; he was also the most difficult to work with. Because he had gotten by for many years on his looks and charm, he rarely prepared, and he couldn't seem to follow instructions. Cec felt it was the one time he had failed to influence and help one of the students.

Eight years later, Dick wrote Cec a letter and thanked him for his leadership and guidance. "I wasn't open to you and you probably thought I never listened. I listened, but I didn't do anything about it." Dick went on to say that he had gone through a lot of difficulty during his first years out of seminary. "But I've learned a lot. And you know something? When I start to do something senseless or make wrong choices, I can hear your voice. I hear you say, 'Are you sure that's what you want to do?' You helped me in so many ways. I wish I had been more open then."

We never know the impact we make.

In the fall of 2004, I had the opportunity to speak to approximately five hundred freshman education students at Kutztown University in Pennsylvania. I brought five of my former students with me to the presentation: Demetrius Carroll, his cousin Earl Jenkins, Nathan Durant, Ralph Johnson, and Denise Pickard. All of them had come through Vaux Middle School as champion chess players, had graduated from high school with honors, and had gone on to Kutztown, where they were second- and third-year students.

I asked them to speak. Everyone there knew the stories of my former students because they had read *I Choose to Stay*. (It was required reading for all students before the session.) But they had not heard from the students themselves. The freshmen didn't know that they were students on the same campus with the chess players they had read about. Our former Vaux students had enrolled at Kutztown shortly before the book's release. I asked the five students to wait outside until I had introduced them. I wanted their attendance to bring about a big surprise for the Kutztown freshmen. Just before Denise walked in, I told them about her family's struggles and victories. Her mother was confined to a wheelchair, and loving though elderly grandparents had raised Denise. She had persisted, however, and before she graduated from Vaux, Denise had been ranked one of the top female scholastic chess players in the nation.

"This is the young lady that you were reading about, Denise Pickard, who has contended with and overcome so many of life's challenges. She is now a sophomore in this school."

When Denise walked into that auditorium, the room erupted with applause and the students gave her a standing ovation. When Denise finally had a chance to speak, she captivated the audience, myself included. She is petite and reserved and she amazed me at how articulate she was. When she stood behind the podium and in her modest way told us she had defeated Arnold Schwarzenegger in a game of chess when he visited our school, the students cheered wildly.

Demetrius, Earl, Nathan, and Ralph discussed their national championship victory in Knoxville, Tennessee, and the time they spent together at the High School for Engineering and Sciences in Philadelphia. Each of them also received a standing ovation. It was unbelievable.

It's interesting that 90 percent of the students at Kutztown are white, but there was no ethnic barrier there. They understood, supported, and encouraged the struggles of these students and applauded their success.

Immediately after the presentation, I held a question-and-answer session.

One student stood up and said, "I can already see the kind of influence that I'm going to have on my students as a teacher. I'm only a freshman, but I can see it now." That was nice, but then she smiled and said, "I can see the love that these students have for their teachers and the love that you have for them."

"That's my goal," I said. "I want teachers, principals, caregivers, and anyone who is thinking about improving our world to see that there is love in every person."

"I have a question for you," another student said. "I know you're influential—and you've already motivated me. Here's my question: Have you ever influenced any of *your* students to become teachers?"

Before I could respond, a young woman stood up in the audience.

"My name is Charisma Evans and I'm a graduate of Reynolds Elementary and Vaux Middle School. Mr. Thomas-EL was my teacher and assistant principal. I am a member of this freshman class, and I'm proud to say that I'm an education major. Have I answered the question for you?"

I was shocked. I stared for a few seconds before I rushed down to hug her. I hadn't seen her in the audience, so her presence was a complete surprise. She had grown up in a tough neighborhood in North Philadelphia, and the odds were against the kids there even to finish high school, but she had held on. Now there she stood, a poised young woman who knew where she wanted to go in her life.

The entire audience clapped and cheered. I hadn't seen Charisma in years. Although I remembered her, I hadn't even known she had entered college. Even as a sixth-grader, she had stood out as a girl who was smart and ambitious. I wasn't surprised she was in college; I was only surprised that she was there that day.

I felt so proud as I listened to her add, "I'm going to become a teacher. I've been influenced by many of my teachers from Reynolds Elementary and Vaux Middle School."

That was one of the proudest moments of my life. It was a moment when I witnessed the power of unrecognized influence. For nearly ten years, Charisma had planned to teach because of the impact of her teachers. I wasn't vain or foolish enough to think that she had come there solely because of my influence. Charisma had many splendid examples before her—dedicated teachers who cared and encouraged her.

That day the idea for this book was born. As I kept thinking about the incident, it occurred to me that we never realize how we influence others. We all know about influence and we've heard lectures and read about it; however, the day Charisma stood up, I understood. We, the dedicated teachers in two inner-city schools of Philadelphia, had changed that young woman's life forever.

"I'm proud to say that I'm an education major." Those words touched me deeply. That's when I knew I had made a difference in the lives of young people I would never know—and so have others. Immediately I thought of the people who had influenced me—and I wrote about some of them in earlier chapters.

I also have the power to affect the choices of others. So do the thousands upon thousands of other educators who work hard and struggle to get young people to understand the importance of their influence.

None of us realized the influence we had had on that young woman. After I returned to Philadelphia, I thanked the teachers I knew who had influenced her life. "This is one you know about. There are perhaps hundreds of others. But we can celebrate the life and the dedication of Charisma as one example that shows our commitment hasn't been in vain."

Charisma Evans had graduated from Bodine High School, one of Philadelphia's magnet schools. For some teachers, she may have been just another graduate; to others—and to me in retrospect—she was the product of years of faithful influence by committed teachers.

When I spoke to her teachers, none of them knew she aspired to be an educator. None of them seemed aware that they had affected Charisma's life so powerfully. That influence had been building for years unknown to the individuals who had planted the seeds.

"We never know, do we?" one teacher said with tears in her eyes. "On some days it seems as if we give so much of ourselves and no one cares or listens. Then we hear of one or two students who do something outstanding and we say, 'Yes, it is worth it.'"

And it is.

At the conclusion of the presentation, I offered to sign the books of any students who wanted to stay a little longer. I spoke for the five students as well and said they would also sign books.

I had expected perhaps twenty students to stay. Instead, about two hundred of them lined up and it took more than an hour to greet everyone. At the signing, many of the students bypassed me—which was fine. Instead they went to my five former students and to Charisma Evans. Those six were the stars of the day. They were living proof of the immortality of influence.

What did that experience at Kutztown University teach me? The lesson is simple: I call it the power of unrecognized influence.

We influence people and often we don't realize the effect we have on them. At work, for example, people observe how we carry ourselves or how we lead and they're challenged—negatively or positively. We may not realize the way we impact others because we don't make a conscious effort to do that. Yet we influence others by the way we lead, how we dress, or how we behave. After they have watched us, others may decide to dress more professionally because they see our example.

Because of our influence, some may decide to choose a particular career. I'm sure there are young people who decided that they wanted to be teachers or social workers or counselors because they've been influenced by teachers. They may never have said anything about their goals to their teachers. Because of us, our children can dare to dream of a future that may have seemed impossible. The right example and encouragement may have been the factors that made the dreams turn into reality.

My good friend Kevin Compton, a mentor and positive role model to many students, introduced me to Rasheeda Phillips, a graduate of the Philadelphia public schools. She is a young woman who fell into the trap of teenage pregnancy, but it wasn't just her, it was the story of her mother and her grandmother as well. The family, three strong and intelligent women, openly share their story for young girls to learn and understand what can be accomplished with hard work and dedication.

They are three generations of teenage mothers, but Rasheeda did not allow that trap to restrain her. The National Campaign to Prevent Teen Pregnancy says more than two-thirds of the girls who become pregnant before age eighteen drop out of school; six out of ten never get a diploma.

I don't intend to invoke a negative association to teen pregnancies or any other stressful situation, but there are people, young and old, who allow obstacles to trap them. Rasheeda did not. She knew that education was the secret to breaking the cycle in her family. She worked at various jobs to support her infant daughter while also attending Kensington High School, and then went on to further her education by graduating *summa cum laude* from Temple University in May 2005.

She had many positive influences throughout her journey. No one can battle life's many obstacles alone and without the influence of caring individuals. Rasheeda was supported by groups like Teen ELECT (Education Leading to Employment and Career Training), which is run by Communities in Schools and offers counseling, parenting courses, and support to teen parents. After the leaders there heard her story, they were inspired to support her in achieving her goals.

The bigger picture, however, is her young daughter, and the influence Rasheeda is having on her. I'm convinced her daughter is watching what her mother is doing, and even though she may not realize it, she is being influenced by her mother's drive and tenacity. In time, she will understand the benefits of hard work, good study habits, commitment to goals, and self-determination.

Rasheeda continues her positive influence and her personal growth because she is currently a student in Temple University's Law School. I'm sure every one of her former teachers is proud of her.

As I think of the teachers who influenced me, I never said to them, "I want to be like you." But I know I have always looked at those people and processed such thoughts. Those people have influenced me even though I didn't recognize to what extent. After I became a teacher, I saw that I was teaching exactly the way that they taught me by giving students the freedom to be creative. Many of my teachers tried to expose us to life beyond our studies and that influence of exposure is important. They took us to plays and various other events. When I started my career in education, I wanted to do that as well. I wanted to get students to venture outside their neighborhoods to see what life was like, and to receive education through venues outside of the classroom.

I also realize that I influence others, and I'm in a position to do that. More than once, friends have told me about going to a particular event and meeting one of my former students. They would say, "I heard him speak and he sounded just like you."

That makes me very proud. They didn't intentionally try to be like me—it just happened because I had motivated and influenced them. I've been encouraged to realize that years after students passed through my school, I heard of the effect I had on them. Most of us operate purely on doing our best and hope that we produce good results. We'd all like to believe that we make a difference.

Once in a while, former students come back and tell me how I was one of the forces that changed their lives. Regardless of whether I hear from them, I know this much: Many people are successful and each one of them had at least one significant teacher. I often think of the bumper sticker that says, IF YOU CAN READ THIS, THANK A TEACHER.

We can't always point specifically to actions that influenced us but we know we're stronger, better, wiser, and more knowledgeable because of their help. That influence is immortal. It lives not only in those we influence but also through them to the individuals they help to shape.

When a student comes back to Reynolds and says, "I finished high school," or "I graduated from college," or "I have been promoted at work," not only can I rejoice with them, but I'm also encouraged. Their testimonies show me that I haven't been laboring in vain.

I wasn't aware of the effect I had and could see it only in retrospect. Jesus urged his followers to let their lights shine. That's what we do and that's the best we can do. At times we don't know if anyone is aware of that light, but we keep trying to push away the darkness of ignorance or rebellion. Then once in a while—often enough to keep us encouraged—we hear a former student or another teacher or someone in our neighborhood say, "You have made a difference in my life."

* * *

After I'd been involved in middle schools for a few years, I decided to champion the cause of attracting more teachers to the inner city, especially men. I went to the central office building of our school district and nicely requested permission to meet some of the men who would be hired and processed in the near future. After several days, I received permission and I met with several potential male candidates. I wanted the men to know how much the children needed them. I wanted them to know how much other men in the district needed their support and the hope they offered our profession and society.

One of the men was Linwood Stevens. He was in his thirties, had been successful in business, but wanted to change careers and become a teacher. He wanted to teach at a school near where he and his family lived. I talked to him about Vaux, but it wasn't close to his home, so he politely said, "My family and I live in the Mount Airy section." Vaux would have been too far for him to commute.

We talked for several minutes, and I told him I admired the sacrifice and commitment he was making to become a teacher. "It's less money and more demand on your time and energy," I said. "Wherever you are, you're going to be helping someone's child and that's what's important."

"I'm really sorry I won't be able to come to Vaux, but it's too far."

"That's fine, and I understand. You'll be a great asset wherever you go." Just before I shook his hand and moved on, I said, "Let me give you my number. As a new teacher, no matter where you go, you're sure to have a few questions. Call me. I'll be happy to help in any way I can."

"You'd be willing to do that?"

"Yes, of course I would, because you're becoming a teacher. You're going to have a tremendous influence on a large number of people. If I can assist you, I can help those young people, too."

He thanked me, we parted, and I didn't think any more about our meeting that day. I talked to several other men, hoping I could get them to apply to Vaux. None of them seemed interested, and understandably, they wanted to teach in communities that were more affluent and I understood.

The one thing I admired about Linwood was that he had no problem about teaching in the inner city, only that it wasn't close to his home. He said he needed to be close enough so he could pick up his children from school every afternoon.

The next day I walked into the school office and I saw Linwood Stevens waiting for me. "What happened? Did you come to the wrong school?"

He said, "No, I chose to come to Vaux. This is where I want to be."

I could hardly believe it, and I just stared at him. It was one of those moments when I didn't know how to respond.

"After you left, I thought about the fact that you were a man who would give me his telephone number," he said, "and be willing to help me in my transition to a different school. Last night, I told my wife, 'I need to work at that school.' So I'm reporting for duty. My wife is going to help me out by picking up the kids so I can be here and help you."

His words brought tears to my eyes, but I didn't want him to come just because of that. "I didn't want to put any pressure on you. I wanted you to know I was supporting you."

"I understand that and I want you to know I appreciate what you're doing and I want to support you. And I'd like to be able to work under your leadership and to learn from you."

That moment in my office occurred almost ten years ago. Mr. Stevens still teaches at Vaux, and continues to be dedicated to the children and their families. He's tall—about six feet four—and he's a great athlete. He often goes to the gym at Vaux with his students, and they love to play ball with him. He also coaches the track team.

When I left Vaux to become the principal at Reynolds Elementary School in 1999, the presence of Mr. Stevens at Vaux made my departure a little easier. I strongly believed that in Linwood our students had a fine example of male influence as a teacher. There were several other men who were teachers at Vaux, and they also made a huge difference during the same time period.

Linwood Stevens and those other men are examples of the immortality of influence.

20

The Legacy of Influence

When we use the term *legacy*, we think of those rich, lasting inspirations that have altered the course of our lives for the better. We often think of people of great renown in all fields of achievement who, from afar, have seemed so much larger than life. We may see small pieces of the ordinary parts of their lives just as a starting point or reference. There may have even been a book we read or movie we viewed that told the profound story of their work and fight for humanity.

Heroes have been overrepresented in the fields of sports and entertainment. It may be because of overexposure or our own interest in those areas. There are certainly many positive people in those lines of work. But we must bring our focus closer to home—to those valiant men and women, young and old, whose lives we are privileged to see on a daily basis. We have to be more observant when it comes to those precious gems in our midst. They're not deliberately trying to be our idols and may even shun the spotlight. Their work speaks more for them than they ever would about themselves. So we have to look carefully. They are fathers, mothers, grandparents, teachers, pastors, students, relatives, and store owners who live lives of quiet inspiration.

For example, Otis Bullock was my first student to graduate from college. He earned his undergraduate degree in 2000 from West Chester University, which is less than an hour's drive west of Philadelphia. I felt privileged that he invited me to attend his graduation.

In May 2004, he graduated from Temple University Law School in Philadelphia. I also went to that graduation, and thoughts filled my mind of his previous college graduation. It had been such a journey for him and me. I had lost many of my students to violence and the streets, some of whom were his friends, and he would have wanted them to attend his graduation.

That was all behind him as he headed down the road of success. I attended his wedding in April 2004. His wife, Donna, had graduated from Temple University Law School a year ahead of him.

It was such a wonderful experience to go to the graduation and to see Otis inside Temple's indoor stadium, the Liacouris Center, with all the other graduates. Among them were not only American students, but also international students from Europe and Asia. I attended the graduation with three of Otis's former teachers, Florence Johnson, Octavia Lewis, and Ethelyn Young. All of those ladies were by Otis's side when he left Vaux to attend the High School for Engineering and Sciences, University City High School, and West Chester University. Ms. Johnson went on to become principal at University City and at Lamberton High School. Ms. Young is currently the principal at Overbrook High School, and Mrs. Lewis is my assistant principal at Reynolds Elementary School. Each woman was a tremendous influence on Otis and me.

The ceremony was special for all of us because the university allowed Otis's wife, Donna, to present him with his diploma.

After the graduation, I rushed down to the floor. "I have to see your diploma."

As I've mentioned earlier in this book, Otis was a young man who grew up in a large family, in a tough neighborhood, and the odds had been stacked against his making a success of his life. Through the influence of his teachers, parents, and people in the community, Otis not only made it through undergraduate school but also earned his law degree.

I grabbed the diploma and stared at it. "I want you to take this degree," I said, "and I want you to go back to the streets of North Philadelphia and show it to people everywhere. Let them see this as a symbol that they, too, can make it. Let them know they can do the same thing. Show it to young people, show it to old people, and let them know that there is hope and that they can see that hope through your example." I was so enthusiastic, I wanted the whole city to hear of his achievement.

Several weeks later, I watched the evening news and they broadcasted a story about the rebuilding of homes in North Philadelphia, which is a tough part of the city. The neighborhood was near Strawberry Mansion, where I began my teaching career. They had a ribbon-cutting ceremony and made a big event of it because they wanted to encourage people to come back into the community and make a difference.

Otis and his wife were some of the first people to purchase one of those homes. "They're investing in the community," I said. I didn't realize it then but they were beginning to build their own legacy of influence.

I had always been proud of Otis. I was even prouder then. He had listened to his teachers and mentors. If only we could get more young people to respond to the positive influences in their lives.

I talked to Otis and he told me that he planned to open a law practice in the community, where he'll be able to help people who are not able to receive good legal services. He wants to teach young people that they can grow up and leave a legacy of influence in the community.

Many of us in the community influenced Otis. He left the community to get educated and came right back so that he could make a difference. I'm especially proud of Otis because he didn't stop at an undergraduate degree but kept on and earned a professional degree. That's a great message for many young people.

Otis's story appears in my book *I Choose to Stay,* but it also appears in *Chicken Soup for the African American Soul.* The editors told me that they chose his story to be the last one in the compilation because they wanted the strongest story at the end. It is a wonderful, positive account of a man I admire. I'm proud that they selected his story. Out of more than three thousand entries, they chose only one hundred. I'm proud of Otis for so many things, but I'm proudest of him for choosing a life that will continue to influence people for such a long time.

I visited the Sue Cowan Williams Free Library in Little Rock, Arkansas, on July 31, 2004. Sue Cowan Williams was one of the first black teachers in Little Rock. That city is the home of the Little Rock Nine, the original students who wanted to integrate Central High School. It was the major chapter in the school desegregation movement.

I visited the library to talk with some educators and parents at the request of Patrick Oliver, an advocate for youth and literacy in Little Rock, and of Dr. Reginald Wilson from the state department of education.

One woman came up to me and said, "I'm homeless and live in a shelter, I don't have any money to buy a book, but I wanted to thank you for coming. I needed to hear your message."

"Where are you from?"

"I'm from New York, but I live in Little Rock."

"What's your name?"

"My name is Amena."

"That was my mother's name. My mother was from New York." Just to hear that name touched me and forced me to hold back a few tears.

"Why are you sad?"

"Because it's the first time I've ever met anyone who has my mom's name. For you to say you're homeless makes me sad." I handed her a book and thanked her for coming. My mother had come from the South and then moved to New York.

This Amena said she wasn't doing well but she had hope and said she wanted some inspiration, so she came to hear me. I thanked her.

I had to take a break for a minute because I felt that was my mother's way of saying thanks for allowing me to influence others.

After I went home, I told my wife, "I met a woman who has my mom's name and it touched me."

By then, my mother had been gone for almost two years and I'd never met anyone else who had her name. It was a touching moment for me but it also encouraged and motivated me to continue. Because there are times when I feel down, when I feel like I'm not making a difference, I'm not influencing people the way I'd like to, and then I meet somebody like that woman who used her last few coins to catch a bus to come and hear me speak.

As I've mentioned elsewhere, the legacy of my influence will be visible in the students I work with. I've already mentioned Otis Bullock. And there are many other students whom we know about. I met Demetrius Carroll when he was ten years old and an older sister and aunt were raising him. His father was incarcerated and his mother lived in South Carolina. He became one of my best chess players and went on to the High School for Engineering and Science, became an honor student, and enrolled at Kutztown University with a full four-year scholarship. In 2005, Demetrius was nominated for the national college dean's list, which is a rare honor—less than 5 percent of all college students are nominated for that award.

It's encouraging for me to recognize my influence on Demetrius. He has decided to major in speech communication, which was my major at East Stroudsburg University. He's moving forward and I know he'll do many positive things. When he works with young people, it's my hope and prayer that he'll know that he can make a difference in their lives.

I've already told you about Denise Pickard, who was raised by her elderly grandparents. Denise was an honor student, very quiet, and she also became one of the top fifty female chess players in her age division in the country. She was instrumental in bringing national acclaim to our school when Arnold Schwarzenegger visited us. He told us he had been a good chess player when he was young and living in Europe. He challenged Denise to a chess match and she checkmated him.

"You terminated the Terminator," he said and laughed. I think he was also greatly surprised that Denise was that good.

The important issue, however, is that Denise was influenced by her teachers to always be prepared. That's the legacy many of them leave behind.

Denise went on to high school, did well, and is now at the same college as Demetrius Carroll. I'm proud of Denise and I'm sure that she will continue the legacy of influence.

I recently visited Latoria Spann, the master of the intricate French Defense on our chess team. She is a new mom but still continues her studies in nursing school at Community College of Philadelphia. She will be a registered nurse (RN) when she finishes community college. When she finishes Temple University she will have a bachelor's in nursing (B.RN).

There's also Earl Jenkins, a cousin of Demetrius, who was another of our outstanding chess players. He went on to the same high school as Demetrius and is in the same college, where both of them are attending on scholarships. They are the legacy of many teachers who helped them along the way.

Nathan Durant attended elementary school with Demetrius and Earl and played on the chess team. He is also at Kutztown University on a scholarship, and he rooms with Demetrius and Earl. I'm proud of Nathan, a young man who was raised by a single mom.

I'm grateful to God that I've had a chance to be a father figure for those three young men and helped shape the life of some special young women.

In April 1996, I took them to Orlando, Florida, to compete in the National Junior High Chess Championship. And to think that a decade later, those same young people are preparing to graduate from college and go out and serve others. This is one of life's greatest rewards.

That's the power of influence. The legacy of influence.

Our students in Philadelphia and elsewhere are special and continue our legacies in a profound way. We have to offer them more opportunities to do so.

Students at Overbrook High School in Philadelphia were given an extraordinary opportunity to create their own legacies in April 2005, in the form of a trip to South Africa, courtesy of 1986 Overbrook graduate Will Smith. Smith, a successful actor, music artist, husband, and father, is well known for his commitment to his community and support of former South African President Nelson Mandela.

The Overbrook students spent several days with Smith, and they visited Mandela and the cities of Johannesburg and Soweto as well as Alexandria Township. Many of the students said they returned from the trip changed from the experience.

As poor as some of those students are, they talked of starting a book drive for the children in Africa. They also discussed raising money to help support an AIDS hospice they visited while in South Africa. My eyes filled with tears when I heard that.

My mentor and colleague, Ethelyn Young, the principal at Overbrook, told me, "We met Will in New York at an MTV event a month before the trip. Immediately after meeting the kids, he said he wanted them to go with him to South Africa. Can you imagine what it was like to get passports for eight inner-city kids who had never been outside Philadelphia?"

She did it and they had an unforgettable trip. God was with them. Will Smith's influence and his knowledge of South Africa touched the children.

Furthermore, the students relayed how impressed they were with the serious manner in which the African students approached school. "We have kids skipping school and selling drugs when children in Africa are fighting for their right to learn," said one of the lucky students who made it onto the plane. On their last night in South Africa, the students all put their money together and purchased a cake for Will Smith as a token of their appreciation. Will Smith has already built a legacy through those students from Overbrook that will undoubtedly transcend their generation.

There are many other former students who will continue my legacy. Thomas Allen is another. He was one of our best chess players. He's now in college near Pittsburgh, Pennsylvania. In May 1999, Thomas went to the National Junior High Chess

Championship in Columbus, Ohio, and finished as one of the top players. He had competed in the entire tournament and didn't lose a match.

Denise Pickard played in that same tournament and was the top female player in her division.

Anwar Smith, Anthony Harper, Ralph Johnson, Latoria Spann, Christina Spann, Alexis and Isaih Watson, Kenyetta Lucas, Danielle Jenkins, Kyle Tribble, Juadon Thomas, Julian Wright-Milledge, Nia Frazier, Raul Negron, Andre Wharwood, Tahir Stills, Isaiah Parks, Darryl Parks, Lamierra Fleet, Alphonso Rogers, Kindell Fields, and Baron Jackson were all great chess players. More important, they were good students who had wonderful and supportive parents.

It's encouraging for me to see parents who have had to overcome obstacles, and continue to make their children a priority. They are willing to do it so their children can have a better life. Those young people are my legacy. Whenever I get discouraged (and there are many, many opportunities in the inner city to get discouraged), I think of those who have continued on.

But no matter how many successes I see, there is always the one failure. I still think often of Willow Briggs.

I want to believe that one day there will be no more young people who end up like Willow—no more kids who are shot to death for simply standing on a street corner. I want to believe that those I influence will carry that positiveness forward throughout Philadelphia and to cities all over the world. My hope is that we'll change lives and have no more untimely deaths.

Each of us has only a limited time on this earth. Even if we live to be a hundred, it may still seem like a short life. William Shakespeare, in his play *Julius Caesar,* wrote, "The evil that men do lives after them; the good is oft interred within their bones . . ."

I dare to say that the positive influence we have on people will live after we have gone on, because we give to others and they, in turn, will give, and so it continues on. Influence is not made of flesh and bones, which wear out and dry up; influence is a powerful force that increases in its momentum as it is shared.

I know I can't reach everybody, but I'd like to believe that I can influence that one person who at the most critical moment will positively change a course of events. That will be my legacy—just to know that I've helped change lives for the better.

Just a Few of the Many Organizations of Influence

After School Activities Partnership	phillyasap.org
After School Alliance	afterschoolalliance.org
American Association of Retired Persons	aarp.org
American Cancer Society	cancer.org
American Family Coalition	americanfamilycoalition.org
American Federation of Teachers	aft.org
American Foundation for the Blind	afb.org
American Heart Association	americanheart.org
American Red Cross	redcross.org
America's Foundation for Chess	af4c.org
America's Promise	americaspromise.org
ASCD	ascd.org
Association of Black School Administrators	asba-pa.org
Big Brothers—Big Sisters of America	bigbrothersbigsisters.org
Bill and Melinda Gates Foundation	gatesfoundation.org
Black Women in Sport Foundation	blackwomeninsport.org
Blacks in Government	bignet.org
Boy Scouts of America	scouting.org
Boys and Girls Clubs of America	bgca.org
Brothers of the Academy	brothers of the academy.org
Call Me Mister	callmemister.clemson.edu
CARE	care.org
Center for Literacy	centerforliteracy.org
Center for Safe Schools	safeschools.info

Centers for Disease Control	cdc.gov
Chess Drum	chessdrum.net
Child Hope, Inc.	childhope.org.uk
Children's Defense Fund	childrensdefense.org
Colleges of Worcester Consortium	cowc.org
Communities in Schools	cisnet.org
Comprehensive Health Education Foundation	chef.org
Concerned Black Men	cbmnational.org
Covenant House	covenanthouse.org
Friends of the Children	friendsofthechildren.com
Girl Scouts of America	girlscouts.org
Habitat for Humanity	habitat.org
I Have a Dream Foundation	ihad.org
Kinship, Inc.	kinshipinc.org
Lutheran Services in America	lutheranservices.org
March of Dimes	marchofdimes.com
NAACP	naacp.org
NABSE	nabse.org
NAESP	naesp.org
NAMME	namme-hpe.org
NASA Office of Education	edu.larc.nasa.gov/pstc
NASSP	nassp.org
NBCDI	nbcdi.org
National Alliance for Hispanic Health	hispanichealth.org
National Center for Missing and Exploited Children	missingkids.com
National Dropout Prevention Center	dropoutprevention.org
National Education Association	nea.org
National Fatherhood Initiative	fatherhood.org
National Mentoring Partnership	mentoring.org

National Middle School Association	nmsa.org
National State School Boards Association	nsba.org
National Urban League	nul.org
Negro Educational Emergency Drive	needld.org
New Teacher Project	tntp.org
One Hundred Black Men of America	100blackmen.org
Oprah's Angel Network	oprahsangelnetwork.org
Paradise Farm Camps	paradisefarmcamps.org
Pennsylvania Head Start Association	paheadstart.org
Pennsylvania State Education Association	psea.org
Points of Light Foundation	pointsoflight.org
Police Athletic League	nationalpal.org
Principals Partnership	principalspartnership.com
Reading is Fundamental	rif.org
Save the Children	savethechildren.org
Shaun Alexander Foundation	shaunalexander.org
Sisters of the Academy	sistersoftheacademy.org
Teach for America	teachforamerica.org
Tom Joyner Foundation	tomjoyner.com
UNICEF	unicef.org
United States Chess Federation	uschess.org
United Negro College Fund	uncf.org
United Way of America	unitedway.org
Urban Education Fund	urbaneducationfund.org
YMCA USA	ymca.com
YWCA USA	ywca.org
Youth at Risk	essexcountyyouth.org